D. A. Kinsley

FAVOR THE BOLD

CUSTER: THE INDIAN FIGHTER

PROMONTORY PRESS

Library of Congress Catalog Card Number: 73-92083

ISBN 0-88394-030-2

Published by arrangement with Holt, Rinehart and Winston

Designer: Robert Aulicino

Printed in the United States of America

★ CONTENTS ★

Eight pages of black and white photographs
follow page 114.

★ PREFACE ★

COLONEL W. A. Graham, esteemed student of Custer, wrote that "but for the 'blaze of glory' that formed the setting for his dramatically tragic departure at the hands of yelling savages, he would probably be just another name of a long list of names in our histories of the Civil War, in which as 'The Boy General' he made an outstanding record as a leader of cavalry." But the Civil War hero and the demigod of the Wild West are brothers under the skin, and each is equally responsible for the transcendence of man into myth.

Those who brand Custer a "glory-hunter," in the worst sense of that word, unwittingly perpetuate the myth: a myth bred by notoriety and fed by controversy. Many would label Custer an exhibitionistic crackpot and suggest psychiatric treatment were he alive today. He escaped the age of scientized soul-searching, but nonetheless had to contend with the do-gooders of the "plush period."

"Pity the warrior who is content to crawl about in the beggardom of rules! What genius does must be the best of rules." Thus wrote Clausewitz, and thus acted Custer. The boy general won his spurs by breaking all the so-called rules. He was the great exception, and Destiny was his champion-apologist.

Much of Custer's character and personality is buried in the legend and controversy that enshroud him. The Chicago *Tribune,* in its 1876 obituary, appraised him as "a brave, brilliant soldier, handsome and dashing; but he was reckless, hasty and impulsive, preferring to make a dare-devil rush and take risks rather than to move slower and with more certainty; and it was his own mad-cap haste, rashness, and love of fame that cost him his own life."

Major Marcus A. Reno lamented that "so brilliant an officer as Custer" should have suffered from "great personal ambition," and Major General James H. Wilson commented: "The truth about Custer is that he was a pet soldier who had risen not above his merit, but higher than men of equal merit. He fought with Phil Sheridan, and through the patronage of Sheridan he rose; but while Sheridan liked his valor and his dash, he never trusted his judgment. . . . Custer was always aflame. He was like a thermometer. He had a touch of romance about him; and when the War broke out he used to go about dressed like one of Byron's pirates in the Archipelago, with waving shining locks and broad flapping sombrero. Rising to high command early in life, he lost the repose necessary to success in high command. . . . But we all liked Custer, and did not mind his little freaks any more than we would have minded temper in a woman. . . . Custer's glorious death and the valor of his men will become a legend in our history. . . . We all think, much as we lament Custer, that he sacrificed the 7th Cavalry to ambition and wounded vanity."

Colonel Samuel D. Sturgis, grieved at the loss of his son Jack (who died on Custer Hill), lashed out at the man and the myth: "What I especially deprecate is the manner in which some papers have sought to make a demigod out of Custer, and to erect a monument to Custer. . . . Custer was a brave man, but he was also a very selfish man. He was insanely ambitious for glory, and the phrase 'Custer's Luck' affords a good clue to his ruling passion."

Perhaps the most venomous of Custer's detractors was Captain Fred Benteen, who expressed himself thus: "I am not ready to subscribe to any effort of the public's opinion to convince me that Custer was a great man or great warrior. . . . I'm only too proud to say that I despised him." He added, however: "Cadets for ages to come will bow in humility at the Custer shrine at West Point;

and if it makes better soldiers & men of them, why the necessity of knocking the paste eye out of their idol?"

General McClellan regarded Custer as "a warm, unselfish & devoted friend"; as "one of the most brilliant ornaments of the Service & the Nation—a most able & gallant soldier, a pure & noble gentleman"; and felt that "his death was as he would have had it, with his face to the foe, encouraging his men to the last." Lawrence Barrett, the celebrated actor, also assures us that he "died as he would have wished to die," and Frederick Whittaker agrees that he "found the one thing needed to complete his character as an ideal hero of romance—a glorious and terrible death on the battle-field."

Therefore, although by virtue of virulent debate we are often led to believe it, tactics alone did not cause the disaster at the Little Bighorn. Perchance, tactics were merely a means to an end in the designs of individual destiny. Custer had reached the zenith of his glory in 1876. It was a suitable fate for a child of fortune: a fate that insured him immortality. As the tide of events would probably have turned had he been militarily successful, Custer could only have pined away like a caged animal; and it is hard to imagine the golden-haired hotspur as a pensioner, much less a featherbed politician. Besides, he was under a suicidal cloud: a cloud of "redemption or death."

In this century, the Custer Controversy was much inflamed by Van de Water's *Glory-Hunter,* a superb piece of debunkery, and by Errol Flynn's unexcelled portrayal in "They Died With Their Boots On," an equally superb piece of glamorization. Of course, Custer has always remained one of our greatest myths—a cliché oft repeated in jest—but periodically he is revived in earnest.

The recent official whitewash of Major Reno, a typical "anti-hero," has been part of the revitalized "discredit Custer" campaign —as were those puerile Indian-baby fables circulated so avidly by the late Mari Sandoz and others who, however, cannot produce "documentary evidence" to support them. And well-meaning Indian associations and others have vigorously protested the airing of WABC-TV's series suggestively titled "The Legend of Custer," and any projected movie spectacular not traditionally anti-Custer or pro-Indian, on the premise that "glamorizing Custer is like glamorizing Billy the Kid." So Custer continues to excite and obsess the popular imagination, and the great controversy rages on! But when all is said and done, it will remain the contention of this author that the tragedy of Custer is that he died at the hands of those he most admired. He died, in the best sense, a poetic death.

What Colonel Graham aptly called "the greatest battle ever waged between the red man and the white, between a receding and an advancing race," has caused more ink to be spilled than the Battle of Gettysburg; and so it is no wonder that the bibliography is monumental. However, only those works of major importance are listed at the end of this book.

Many thanks are again due to those individuals and institutions who kindly aided in this labor—among them the National Archives in Washington, D.C., which provided a copy of the original transcript of Custer's court-martial, and Mr. John W. Jackson, director of the Philadelphia Maritime Museum, an old acquaintance and fellow student of Custer, the Indians and the Civil War, and with whom the author refought the Battle of the Little Bighorn and came to G.A.C.'s defense in many a rare moment.

D. A. KINSLEY

Kansas City, Missouri
August, 1967

From Far Dakota's Canyons

(A Death-Sonnet for Custer)

From far Dakota's canyons,
Lands of the wild ravine, the dusky Sioux, the lonesome
    stretch, the silence,
Haply to-day a mournful wail, haply a trumpet-note for
    heroes.

The battle-bulletin,
The Indian ambuscade, the craft, the fatal environment,
The cavalry companies fighting to the last in sternest
    heroism,
In the midst of their little circle, with their slaughter'd
    horses for breast-works,
The fall of Custer and all his officers and men.

Continues yet the old, old legend of our race,
The loftiest of life upheld by death,
The ancient banner perfectly maintain'd,
O lesson opportune, O how I welcome thee!

As sitting in dark days,
Lone, sulky, through the time's thick murk looking in
    vain for light, for hope,
From unsuspected parts a fierce and momentary proof,
(The sun there at the centre though conceal'd,
Electric life forever at the centre,)
Breaks forth a lightning-flash.

Thou of the tawny flowing hair in battle,
I erewhile saw, with erect head, pressing ever in front,
    bearing a bright sword in thy hand,
Now ending well in death the splendid fever of thy deeds,
(I bring no dirge for it or thee, I bring a glad triumphal
    sonnet,)
Desperate and glorious, aye in defeat most desperate,
    most glorious,
After thy many battles in which never yielding up a gun
    or a color,
Leaving behind thee a memory sweet to soldiers,
Thou yieldest up thyself.

WALT WHITMAN

WASHINGTON: THE GRAND REVIEW

E SCORTED by Senator Zachariah Chandler and members of the Joint Committee on the Conduct of the War, Elizabeth Custer arrived at the Queen City of the South on board President Lincoln's personal gunboat, the *Baltimore,* in the evening of April 10, 1865.

Tuesday morning, April 11. George Armstrong Custer came bursting into the Executive Mansion at Richmond, bolted up the grand staircase, darted into President and Mrs. Jefferson Davis' private bedchamber. Quietly he approached the bed, leaned over, and planted a kiss on Libbie's cheek.

Libbie sat up. "Autie!" She flung her arms around his neck and hugged him. "Autie, what a delightful shock! I never expected . . ." And when he had dried her eyes she said, "Oh, Autie, when you heard of Lee's surrender, didn't you cry?"

He smiled. "With pleasure!"

They ran their fingers through each other's hair, gazing into each other's eyes. Autie broke the spell with a boyish grin. "By Jesus, I've been fighting four years to get into this place—and my little girl beat me to it!"

Saturday, April 15, 1865. President Abraham Lincoln was dead. "Now he belongs to the ages," Secretary of War Stanton remarked.

"Daughter! Daughter!" wrote Judge Bacon. "What is to become of us as a Nation & as Individuals? This is the most gloomy day in the History of the Continent. The thought that a man such as Andy Johnson—lunatic, drunkard—is to be at the Head of the Gov't at this, the most critical period of our National Existence, is *awful* beyond words. I may be one of those who will ask Gen'l Grant to take the Gov't in his own hands."

Meanwhile, Senator Chandler was saying to Secretary Stanton, "Don't you think Custer has done enough to have a full commission?"

"My God," Old Evil-Eye exclaimed, "what hasn't he done!"

The long march from Richmond to Washington delighted Autie and Libbie: "Libbie riding in a spring-waggon at the head of the column with me," Armstrong informed his father-in-law. "She endured the fatigue well, and enjoyed the novelty." In her own behalf Elizabeth added: "Father dear, remember how you used to try to frighten me out of marrying a soldier—'No better than gypsying in a covered-waggon on the Plains'? Well, I think it grand fun! Gen'l Sheridan says I make no trouble, and he is always willing I should come."

Yellow Tavern, Trevilian Station, Culpeper Courthouse, Brandy Station, Warrenton Junction, Catlett Station, Bull Run (Manassas Junction). These they passed, and many others. Familiar places, full of haunting memories: full of happiness and heartbreak, terror and valor, infamy and glory, hatred and love. Many a tale could be told of each, and was—by an eager knight to an attentive damsel.

> Farewell the tranquil mind; farewell content;
> Farewell the plumed troops, and the big wars,
> That makes ambition virtue. O, farewell.

Tuesday, May 23, 1865. 9 A.M. It was a sparkling-clear springtime morning, and the thunder of a thousand drums shivered the air, as a hundred thousand battle-scarred veterans of Mr. Lincoln's Army swung past the Capitol and swept straight up Pennsylvania Avenue.

←2→

From her seat in the Presidential reviewing stand, Elizabeth Custer watched with excitement and anticipation as the long broad ribbon of blue rolled slowly toward her from the glowing white dome on Capitol Hill.

Sabers drawn and trumpets sounding, Sheridan's ten thousand cavalry spearheaded the great parade; for they were the final cause of victory. Little Phil, on special duty in the Southwest, wasn't there to lead them; but he chose the next best man to take his place. And that man was the most glamorous hero of the Civil War. Merritt was Chief of the Cavalry Corps, but Sheridan had said, "You, Curly, will ride in my honor."

General Custer pranced up Pennsylvania Avenue on Don Juan, a magnificent, high-spirited, thoroughbred bay. Long golden curls, gleaming in the sunlight, danced on the star-studded collar of the boy general's dark-blue blouse. His bright-red necktie blazed like a crimson cascade, and his buckskin breeches were tucked into glossy-black jack boots flashing the same gold spurs worn by Santa Anna during the siege of the Alamo. White gauntlets and a broad-brimmed, star-emblazoned black turnup touched off the characteristic regalia of America's daredevil dandy.

Sabers glittered, guidons fluttered, and bands crashed from one end of Capitol Hill to the other. Thousands upon thousands of cheering, whistling, singing spectators were jam-packed along the tree-lined avenue. Mobs crammed the housetops and jammed the windows, and individuals half crazed with joy cluttered the trees.

"Here comes Custer!" they shrilled. "Hurrah for Old Curly!" People went wild, pressing halfway into the broad thoroughfare to lionize him.

Armstrong stared straight ahead, now and then cutting an eye at the roaring, tossing waves of his fans. Billows of soft-colored parasols, bobbing hats, and dazzling-white handkerchiefs made Don Juan snort and shake his head, pitching his rump from side to side in a kind of caracole. It was all Custer could do to keep the stallion under control and at the same time retain his own dignified composure.

The far-flung cavalcade, assembled by column of platoons, was now approaching the White House and the flag-festooned reviewing stand. Custer knew Libbie would be there watching, with General Grant and President Johnson and such government dignitaries as Secretary Stanton.

Arrayed in a white taffeta skirt, blue satin wrap, and black velvet riding cap garnished with a scarlet feather, Elizabeth Custer rose to her feet and waved the fringed linen towel that had helped make her husband the center of attraction at Appomattox. She had already sent her father the "surrender table," cautioning him to take good care of it and adding, "Don't give away even a splinter. They tell me I might sell it for a million dollars!" But she confessed to liking Sheridan's note of presentation more than the souvenir itself.

When General Custer was within two hundred yards of the reviewing stand, a shrieking flock of some three hundred white-clad schoolgirls began waving penny flags and bursting into song: "Hail to the Chief who in triumph advances!" It was the first big surprise of that stupendous day. It was also the most fateful. Suddenly, unexpectedly, Old Curly was pelted by a fragrant shower of wreaths and bouquets. Instead of dodging the floral missiles, he tried to catch a few of them; and that's when Don Juan took the bit in his teeth.

Before Custer could gather up the reins, the startled charger bolted forward like a bay-colored tornado. As horse and rider flew past the Presidential grandstand, Custer jerked up his sword to salute "Uncle Sam" and "King Andy." The impulsive attempt knocked off his hat, but before he could lose his balance as well, Custer dropped his blade and gag-checked his horse. Then, with his cinnamon-scented hair streaming in the sunshine, he wheeled around and dashed back to the head of the parade "by one of the most magnificent exhibitions of horsemanship."

"See him ride!" the crowd roared. "That's Custer!"

Meantime, Grant's eldest son and aide, Lieutenant Fred Dent Grant, who fairly idolized Old Curly, had darted out and picked up Custer's hat and sword. He ran down and handed them to the haggard-looking cavalier, whose ghostly face was now deeply flushed. Custer yanked the dusty turnup low over his eyes, then jogged on past the reviewing stand with head erect and saber at rest.

Disabled veterans of Antietam, Gettysburg, and the Wilderness staggered to their feet and hailed the boy general with cheer after cheer. Custer brightened when he heard them shout, "A tiger for Old Curly!"

He snatched off his hat in gallant salute and beamed at the multitudes screaming with delight. For a second he caught a glimpse of his "little girl," waving to him from the official grandstand almost directly behind white-bewhiskered Secretary Welles. He flicked his sword chivalrously, then flipped back his hat.

"Will those of us who saw that last grand review," wrote one eyewitness, "ever forget those two pictures—Custer conquering his runaway horse, and Custer at the head . . . of the most gallant cavalry division of the age, as with the hot flush of victory yet visible on their bronzed faces he led it through the Capital at a gallop march? It was but a momentary vision, but one that has fixed itself upon at least one memory in indelible lines."

This special reporter for the Detroit *Evening News* was joined in his "One Glimpse of Custer" enthusiasm by the New York *World* correspondent, who echoed the sentiments of a myriad on-lookers. General Custer's dash was "like the charge of a Sioux chieftain" and "attracted more attention, admiration & cheering to him than anything else could have done."

But there were those—perhaps disenchanted—who suspected that the Murat of the American Army had made a desperate play to the gallery. Major Henry E. Tremain, General Crook's A.D.C., was ambivalently impressed by "that notorious incident" which swept Custer "past the reviewing officer—the President of the United States—his Cabinet, the military, civil and diplomatic functionaries of this and many other countries, not in the stately and sedate manner of a warrior chief on his prancing charger, but shooting like the wind." He asked shrewdly, "Was this a disappointment, or was the sensation agreeable? Who among the

←5→

spectators or performers at this state occasion will forget 'how Custer's horse ran away with him'?"

> Farewell the neighing steed, and the shrill trump,
> The spirit-stirring drum, the ear-piercing fife,
> The royal banner, and all quality,
> Pride, pomp, and circumstance of glorious war.
> And o you mortal engines, whose rude throats
> The immortal Jove's dread clamours counterfeit,
> Farewell. Othello's occupation's gone!

TEXAS: THE AUGEAN TASK

Late afternoon, May 23, 1865. Shadows were fading in the outpost of advancing darkness. For an uncanny moment, Camp Arlington was hushed in tribute. Then: "Three cheers and a tiger for Old Curly!" Voices roared like cannon fire, and caps rocketed into the air like windrows of waterfowl. The end had truly come. This was farewell—forever. Libbie later wrote: "I began to realize, as I watched this sad parting, the truth of what Autie had been telling me—that no friendship was like that cemented by mutual danger on the battle-field."

He fought back the onslaughts of emotion which strove to unnerve him; and when he could fight no more, the tears streaked down his cheeks, his tightened lips trembled, and he quivered like one overcome with fright. When Libbie saw the suffering on her husband's face, and heard the ovation to him, she wept as well—in joy and in sorrow.

> I have touched the highest point of all my greatness;
> And from that full meridian of my glory,
> I haste now to my setting: I shall fall
> Like a bright exhalation in the evening,
> And no man see me more.

There seemed to be no honor too great for a grateful nation to bestow upon its beloved hero—a seat in Congress, a staff appointment in Washington, the governorship of Michigan, the Presidency of the United States.

Libbie was elated, but Autie was less enthusiastic. He respectfully refused to wear any laurels but those won in battle to save the Union. The "blushing honors" of public office were not his ambition, nor was he a "featherbed soldier." George Armstrong Custer was by nature and aspiration a knight-adventurer, a paladin somehow strayed from the age of chivalry, and as such he sought his destiny and glory.

Elizabeth was disappointed at first that her husband didn't accept one of the several political jobs so lavishly offered him as meal tickets to the White House. But she soon changed her attitude when Judge Daniel Stanton Bacon stepped in and admonished her thus: "My Child, put no obstacles in the way to the fulfillment of his Destiny. He chose his profession; he is a born Soldier; there he must abide."

More understanding now of Autie's spiritual happiness, the hunger of his soul that must be satisfied if he was to live at peace with himself, Libbie replied to her father appreciatively: "I am married to an independent, high-minded man. I have nothing more to ask for, as I believe the best of everything on earth has already been given to me. I am prouder far to be his wife than I would be to be Mrs. President or a Queen."

"Daughter," the Judge answered, "continue to do as you have always done. Follow Armstrong every where."

And so, when Custer followed Sheridan into the wild and wanton Southwest, Libbie went with him. She had roughed it before, and she would rough it again—all for her Autie.

Custer hastened to Texas at the beck and call of Little Phil, who desperately needed a man of mettle to help him clean out the hornet's nests of bounty jumpers, jayhawkers, mosstroopers, bushwhackers, and scalawag carpetbaggers, who were flagrantly riding roughshod over the lawless yucca country.

General Grant agreed with General Sheridan that General Custer was equal to the Augean task. "I mean to endorse Gen'l Custer in a high degree," Grant wrote to Mr. Stanton. Sheridan's sentiments were a matter of public record. "Custer," he had said openly, "you're the only man that never failed me."

Phil had been appointed Military Commander of the 5th Reconstruction District (Military Division of the Southwest and Gulf, comprising Louisiana and Texas, with headquarters at New Orleans) and his orders were explicit: to protect this hotbed of rebellion from the imperialistic ambitions of Louis Napoleon's puppet, Maximilian, who, in defiance of the Monroe Doctrine, had raped Mexico while Uncle Sam was embroiled in a schizophrenic disorder; and (in Grant's words) "to restore Texas & that part of Louisiana held by the enemy to the Union in the shortest practicable time, in a way most effectual for securing permanent peace." In this full-scale peace offensive, General Custer was appointed Chief of Cavalry, Military Department of Texas.

The long trip south—by train to Louisville, by steamer to New Orleans and Alexandria—was a refreshing *divertissement* to a warworn and anxiety-wasted couple, and Eliza's agreeable chatter enlivened the otherwise uneventful evenings: "Well, Miss Libbie, I set in to see the war—beginnin' and end. There was many niggers that cut into cities and huddled up thar, and laid around and saw hard times; but I didn't set down to wait and have 'em all free *me*. I helped to free myself!"

In early July of '65, Armstrong wrote to Father Bacon from "Aleck" (Alexandria, Louisiana), a Godforsaken pesthole crawling with vermin and varmints: "When the waggons are loaded, we will start for Texas. . . . This country is wholly unlike Virginia. It is more like notions formed from 'Uncle Tom's Cabin.' Slavery was not as mild as in States whose proximity to Free States made kindness desirable to prevent the enslaved from seeking freedom across the border. The knowledge that runaways would have to traverse hundreds of miles of slave or hostile country placed slaves at the mercy of their owners, in the Red River country, and every plantation had its Simon Legree & humble Uncle Tom. In the mansion where I now write is a young negro woman whose back bears the scars of 500 lashes given at one time, for going beyond the limits of her master's plantation. If the War has attained nothing else, it has placed America under a debt of gratitude for all time—for removal of this evil."

Having seen the inhuman horrors of Deep South slavery, Custer (influenced by the relatively civilized status of slaves in Maryland and Virginia) altered his old view that "It is the Union we are fighting for, not the abolition of slavery." Ignorance of politics and economics had blinded him to the fact that disunion was the direct result of a social-political states-rights controversy over slavery and North-South economic rivalry.

Advising the Judge to invest in rich soil which was now ("owing to the absence of slave-labor & current money") two thirds cheaper than before the war, Armstrong prophesied rampant squatterism and carpetbaggery: "Immigration from the Free States to the Southern & South-western country is likely to come soon. . . . A wealthy planter informed me that land bought at $150 per acre paid for itself in 2 yrs. . . . P.S.—Libbie bids me tell you my hair is cut short. She cut it for me. I find it more comfortable in this climate."

While at the Alexandria cavalry depot, organizing and provisioning the 2nd Volunteer Cavalry Division, Old Curly was challenged by forces that swore he would never reach Texas alive. The buckoes with whom he had to contend were rawhide, rough-riding veterans of the Western armies, seasoned to loose discipline and freebooting action. Exiled to "hell's kitchen" and dull routine, after four years of fighting and foraging, these men were tired and homesick. Besides, they wanted no part of a possible war with imperial Mexico. Smoldering dissatisfaction flared in outbursts of insubordination and desertion—to such an alarming extent that an all-out mutiny of Sheridan's occupation forces seemed imminent, until Custer nipped the evil in the bud.

He acted with the same dispatch that prompted him to cane a sneering restaurant proprietor who had refused to serve Eliza because she was a "dirty nigger." Deterrent examples were made of a troublemaking sergeant and a bounty-jumping private of the 3rd Michigan Cavalry. They were arrested, court-martialed, sentenced to be shot. The regiment reacted with a threat: "If they die, Custer dies."

Armstrong smiled at his frightened wife. "A barking dog rarely bites. I'll call their bluff."

"Oh, Autie, don't——!"

"Don't *what?* Don't execute my sworn duty as an officer? I have no choice. A question of who is in command here needs to be settled, once and for all. It's either me or them. God help this country if it's *them!* They'll cut loose and run riot from here to the Lakes."

The day of decision dawned, the prisoners paraded into the town square. It was to be a public spectacle, as it had been at Front Royal in the Shenandoah. Staff officers appealed to Custer not to be present, implored him to pack a revolver. He laughed. "I've weathered four years of war with only a scratch. Am I now to die like a dog in this Godforsaken hole?" He ordered them to appear unarmed, like himself. "Give 'em no cause to doubt our purpose, most of all our resolution. If we must die, it will be in cold blood. But never fear, gentlemen. I have faith in human nature."

And with this faith, he rode forth with his trembling staff to stare death out of countenance. The assembled troopers—fully armed! —followed his glare as he faced them down, man by man, slow-pacing along the lines while a firing squad prepared the culprits for execution. Though muscles tightened, expressions contorted, no one moved and none spoke a word. This was the test. Back at headquarters, a tearful wife buried her head in a pillow—awaiting the worst.

Custer's voice rattled: "If any man of you has a mind to take my life, let him do so now." No response. "Very well, Major"— he addressed the provost marshal—"carry out the execution."

"Ready!" the P.M. said; at which Custer spurred forward, grabbing the blindfolded sergeant's arm and pulling him aside. "Aim! *Fire!*" The marauding deserter dropped into his grave. The insubordinate mischiefmaker, spared at the last second by Custer's design, lived to swear eternal loyalty to Old Curly.

There was no more trouble with the 3rd Michigan. But there were forty-five hundred men in that division, and not all of them believed this story, nor were they impressed by examples. For this reason, Sheridan gave Custer a free hand to "Use such summary measures as you deem proper to overcome the mutinous disposition of the individuals in your Command." He used them, with success!

August found the 2nd Cavalry Division on a grueling 150-mile westward march—through reeking pine barrens, over dust-gagging flats and hog-wallow prairie—to Hempstead, Texas, their base camp on the Brenham & Galveston Railroad. There, in late summer and fall, General Custer began to plunderproof the Lone Star State by issuing the following general order to all volunteer occupation troops under his command:

"Numerous complaints having reached these Head-Quarters of depredations having been committed by persons belonging to this Command, all Officers & Soldiers are hereby urged to use every exertion to prevent the committal of acts of lawlessness which, if permitted to pass unpunished, will bring discredit upon the Command. Now that the War is virtually ended, the Rebellion put down, and peace about to be restored to our entire Country, let not the lustre of the past 4 years be dimmed by a single act of misconduct toward the persons or property of those with whom we may be brought in contact. . . . All Officers & Soldiers of this Command are earnestly reminded to treat the inhabitants of this Department with conciliation and kindness, and particularly is this injunction necessary when we are brought in contact with those who lately were in arms against us. You can well afford to be generous and magnanimous. It is expected, and it will be required, that those who were once our enemies, but are now to be treated as friends, will in return refrain from idle boasts which can only result in harm to themselves. If there still be any who, blind to the events of the past 4 years, continue to indulge in seditious harangues, all such disturbers of the peace will be arrested and brought to these Head-Quarters. Every Enlisted Man committing depredations on the persons or property of Citizens will have his head shaved and, in addition, will receive twenty-five (25) lashes in his back—well laid on."

The relentless and successful execution of these measures to restore law and order soon aroused a storm of self-righteous indignation and protest from a swarm of Reconstruction Radicals, carpetbaggers and scalawags, and uninformed (or misinformed) do-gooders. Custer was blacklisted for "wanton brutality," for "flogging and degrading men who had fought for their country, while favoring those who had turned traitor to it." He was even accused of violating the so-called Reconstruction Laws, which provided that "no cruel or unjust punishment shall be inflicted" on "disturbers of the public peace and criminals."

Custer answered these charges immediately, in a detailed report to District Adjutant General A. L. Lee: "Regarding the report that Gen'l Custer issued orders to flog any soldier who shall forage, altho' the troops under his command complain that they are not properly subsisted & have no money wherewith to purchase supplies; that they are in a rebellious district, surrounded by Rebels who have plenty, &c., &c., I respectfully submit: . . . Unauthorized foraging by soldiers not under legitimate organized control, or absent without leave, is highway robbery & housebreaking—often murder. Indiscriminate foraging was of daily occurrence when I assumed command late in June, 1865. Citizens were assailed, knocked down & robbed in open day. Houses were broken into & ransacked, women insulted & maltreated. Yet no steps were taken by Regimental Officers to check these outrages. My instructions from Maj.-Gen'l Sheridan were 'to treat the inhabitants of the country in a conciliatory manner, and to establish a rigid discipline among the troops, and to prevent outrages on private persons & property.' Since my order—head-shaving & lashes—discipline has been restored. Complaints of outrages have ceased. In my opinion, conditions were such that nothing less severe would have had any effect."

A New York *Times* correspondent reported in March of 1866: "Gen'l Custer, knowing that the trial for desertion was a farce, tried every humane way to save his army from going to pieces, but failed. He then tried a new way, and flogged several men & shaved their heads. This had the desired effect, but brought down the friends of these soldiers upon him, who charge him with being disloyal, inhuman, and everything that is bad. Now, I leave it to every one if Custer didn't do right."

Following Lincoln's assassination, with anarchy imminent, Judge Bacon had prophesied: "Oh! the worst of this calamity will not be confined to war. Our Land, even after peace is restored, will be filled with cut-throats & villains."

Not all those "cut-throats & villains" were a "lost generation" of Confederate veterans, discharged or reactivated Federals, and freed Negroes. Many were vengeful planters, deprived of free labor; political opportunists, waving the bloody shirt; prideful citizens, resenting Yankee intrusion on their "sacred soil." Addressing himself to the problem of "political banditti," Sheridan had wired Grant and Custer: "Texas has not yet suffered from the War, and will require some intimidation." Southern scalawags and spoilsmongers were rooted out only to be replaced by Northern carpetbaggers and five-percenters.

But Texans were soon reconciled to "foreign" occupation, so long as the "damnyankees" protected their lives and property from boodlers and freebooters both Northern and Southern. Libbie was then able to declare, perhaps with her usual "noble temptation to see too much in everything": "You would hardly believe in the short time we have been here what a favorite Autie has become. He could be elected to Congress! There seems no honor too high for them to bestow on him. The soldiers are now in an excellent state of discipline, and the planters live undisturbed. . . . Our own relatives (aside from the home ones) would not do so much for us as some of these Texans who were prominent & active Rebels. We shall never forget their kindness to us. No country in the world can equal the South for hospitality."

She added proudly, "Autie has fine opportunities every day for making a fortune in land, or cotton, or horses, or in buying Gov't claims; but he feels that so long as the Gov't needs his active services, he should not invest."

Although Armstrong kept a loaded revolver under his pillow at night, he penned to Judge and Mrs. Bacon from Camp Hempstead: "We are leading a quiet, contented, normal life. Horseback-riding is one of our chief pleasures. Libbie (I never saw her in better health) is now an expert horse-woman, so fearless she thinks nothing of mounting a girthless saddle on a strange horse. You should see her ride across these Texas prairies at such a gait that even some of the staff-officers are left behind!" And then to matters of moment: "I am in favor of elevating the negro to the extent of his capacity & intelligence, and of our doing everything in our power to advance the race morally & mentally as well as physically—also socially. But I am opposed to making this advance by correspondingly debasing any portion of the white race. . . . I regard the solution of the negro problem as involving difficulty & requiring greater statesmanship than any political matter that has arisen for years."

In order to gauge Southern sentiment toward the Negro—with a view to solving the explosive problems of social resentment and racial hostility, removing the state of martial law, and eventually evacuating all forces of occupation—Custer assigned his adjutant general (Captain Jacob L. Greene) the unenviable task of acting as intelligence agent for the Department of Texas. Greene reported in January, 1866: "Self-interest no longer demands consideration for the negro. As Freedman he is disliked, despised. Murders of negroes are frequent, and actual slavery exists in regions remote from the troops. A war of races, indiscriminate murder & destruction of property—every outrage would result were Gov't protection now withdrawn."

Thus was Custer faced not only with insubordination and desertion and marauding, but with sedition and corruption and intrigue. Equal to the task, he restored a semblance of civilized law and order to what had been a savage wilderness of terrorism and mob rule. King Chaos answered to King Custer, and bowed to a just *argumentum baculinum*.

←15→

Old Pop Custer, itching with wanderlust, came to the Lone Star State as forage agent for Old Curly's division of occupation. "Little to do & fine pay" was a splendid inducement, besides satisfying the pioneer spirit. With him came Nettie Humphrey— now Mrs. Jake Greene—a welcome companion for Libbie.

Agent Emanuel, Aide Tom, and General Aut rode to the hunt with raucous packs: the dog-loving knight's beloved squires. Afflicted with buck fever, Tom accidentally shot one of his brother's dogs—and was never allowed to forget it. "Oh, Tom's a good shot, a sure aim. He's sure to hit something!" And pertinent newspaper clippings were "carelessly" dropped on Tom's dresser. For example: "An editor went hunting the other day, for the first time in 22 years, and he was lucky enough to bring down an old farmer by a shot in the leg. The distance was 66 yards."

Libbie disliked hunting, and it pained her to see dead game, but she philosophically reconciled herself to the distasteful traits in Autie's character.

Dogs! They and horses were ever Libbie's rivals for Autie's exclusive attention. But the conflict thus aroused was harmless and humorous, and Libbie delighted in Eliza's good-natured wigging: "You keer more for those *pesky, sassy* old hounds than you does for Miss Libbie. Gin'l, I'd be 'shamed if I was you. What would your Mother Custer think of you now?"

Wintertime found the 2nd Cavalry Division again on the move, through mesquite barrens and over prairies the color of dry blood, trekking 125 miles westward to Austin, King City of Texas. There, the chase gave place to the race; and Armstrong was again in his element. "Now, Father," Elizabeth penned monitorily, "don't wrinkle up your brows when I tell you that we race horses. . . . Autie is considered the best judge of a horse here. The Texans supposed no one in the world could ride as well as themselves—and they do ride splendidly—but those who saw Armstrong keep his place in the saddle when 'Don Juan' ran away with him at the Grand Review in Washington concede that he *does* know how to ride, however mistaken his views on patriotism may be. We now have 3 running-horses & a fast pony, none of which has been beaten. . . . We are running out to the stables half our time."

Armstrong was having the time of his life, even while performing the unpleasant and unrewarding task of taming Texas. His uncommon energy and enterprise were inexhaustible, galvanic, almost superhuman. He met every challenge, every emergency, and triumphed.

The Honorable Alexander J. Hamilton, Provisional Governor of Texas, testified to General Custer's "wise and efficient conduct of an affair as much administrative as military." General Sheridan also praised him for successfully handling a tough job, recommending (with Mr. Bingham) that he be commissioned a full Major General in the Regular Army. But to no avail. The jackleg politicians and spoilsmongers stuck at nothing to comb Custer out of their hair; and they finally made a connection, publicly branding him a "Copperhead Democrat" while they privately characterized him as a "nigger-loving Radical."

The bureaucratic, self-interested "powers that be" quickly disposed of Custer when his period of enlistment was up. He was mustered out of the Volunteer Army on January 31, 1866 (without pension or praise) and "kicked downstairs" to his old Regular Army rank of Captain, 5th U.S. Cavalry. His "compo" of $8,000 a year was accordingly reduced to $2,000, and he was ordered to report to Washington pending further instructions. At twenty-six, Custer considered himself a busted man, stripped of all the dignity and honor he had ever rated as a warrior-patriot.

Sick at heart, he chased trains back East—alone. He couldn't afford to take his wife, so Elizabeth journeyed up to Monroe (on the last of their savings) to stay with her folks.

April found Armstrong on a fortune-hunting junket in New York City, still waiting for something to turn up at Washington concerning his future in Uncle Sam's Army. Social, political, and economic contacts came easy to him; for he was a big name, a *rara avis,* a commercial advantage. Society lionized him; the worlds of business and politics began to revolve around him, and he was offered executive positions and government posts. But Custer could not fancy himself a jack-in-office, a swivel-chair man, a featherbed civvy. He felt conspicuously uncomfortable in toppers and swallowtails, and longed for slouchers and buckskins. These were anxious, uncertain days of readjustment, of drifting and groping. These were days without blazing glory, made bearable only by retreat into shadowy glamour: the fool's paradise of would-bes and has-beens.

General Custer was wined and dined by such bigwigs as George Bancroft, William Cullen Bryant, and Charles O'Conor. But the solicitations of every celebrity in New York City made him none the richer, save in sophistication. He was obviously out of his element, yearning for the hard but simple life.

Friday, May 18, 1866. Judge Daniel Stanton Bacon died of heart disease. Armstrong rushed out to Monroe for the funeral. The whole town mourned its most venerable citizen, pioneer, and enterpriser. A hero's bright homecoming was overshadowed by gloom.

Elizabeth penciled in her diary: "I should be far more miserable but for Armstrong's care. He keeps me out-of-doors as much as he can. I do not wear deep mourning. He is opposed to it. . . . Armstrong is thinking of going to Mexico. The [Juárez] Gov't there offered him handsome inducements. I am opposed to it. I do not want him ever to go into battle again. But if he goes, I shall go with him."

★3★

MIDWEST:
SWING AROUND THE CIRCLE

B ENITO JUÁREZ and Porfirio
Díaz were determined to rid their homeland of Emperor Maximilian. They offered Custer a commission as Major General of *Caballeros,* adjutant general of the Mexican revolutionary forces, and a yearly pay of $16,000 in gold—on condition that Custer supply at least a thousand mounted mercenaries, the expense of which would be incurred by Juárez & Co.

Sheridan and Grant were highly "enthused." "If you conclude to go," Phil scrawled from New Orleans, "you would have my warmest support."

U. S. Grant, now General of the Army, sent a letter of recommendation to the Mexican ambassador in Washington, Don Matías Romero: "This will introduce to your acquaintance Gen'l Custer, who rendered such distinguished service as a Cavalry Officer during the War. There was no officer in that branch of the Service who had the confidence of Gen'l Sheridan to a greater degree than Gen'l C., and there is no officer in whose judgment I have greater faith than in Sheridan's. Please understand, then, that I mean by this to endorse Gen'l Custer in a high degree."

Captain G. A. Custer, 5th U.S. Cavalry, applied to the War Department for a year's leave of absence. Object: special duty in Mexico as military attaché (soldier of fortune) to the army of independence and deputy-defender of the Monroe Doctrine. Permission denied by Executive Order, despite Mr. Stanton's begging and abuse. With the nation's wounds sorely in need of binding,

President Johnson sought to pursue a foreign policy of noninterference. Besides, he dared not entrust such an unprecedented enterprise to a twenty-six-year-old prodigy, the reckless boy wonder of a gentleman's war.

Captain Custer was again kicking and cooling his heels, "awaiting orders." As of April 28, he was granted leave of absence "till further orders"—but was forbidden to leave the country under penalty of losing his commission.

In mid-March of '66, a bill had passed through Congress increasing the standing army by ten new Regular cavalry regiments, to be raised for special duty in the South and West. Stanton offered one of these virgin outfits to Custer—full colonelcy of the 9th Cavalry, a Negro regiment—but on July 6, Custer applied for appointment to a more influentially active post: that of Inspector General, U.S. Cavalry. Now, with all the political support he deemed necessary, Custer flattered himself that Fortune would again smile upon him; that the job would be his, merely for the asking. But certain bigwigs in Washington—many of them pretended friends—were reluctant, even afraid, to entrust such freehanded authority and executive responsibility to a potential, if not proven, "wild man." Kept in a subordinate (and therefore politically "safe") role, the ambitious maverick could do precious little damage to bureaucratic machinery, well greased with oil of palms.

The fates had frowned once more—despite the fact that Old Curly was bombarded with bribes to run for political office, as Congressman or even Governor of Michigan or Ohio. "But I'm no speechmaker," he protested. Besides, he was leery of politics. Perhaps he was aiming for the virtually unattainable: generalship of the Army. Would that satisfy him? Hardly. It was just another desk job. Meantime, he must wait—and hope.

July 28, 1866. Through the persuasion of General Grant, and the special favor of Secretary Stanton, George Armstrong Custer was commissioned Lieutenant Colonel of the newly raised 7th

U.S. Cavalry, destined to become the most glorious and notorious outfit in the American army.

Custer was now a top-rate Regular with a virgin regiment. His assignment: Fort Riley, Kansas, Lieutenant General William Tecumseh Sherman's Military Division of the Missouri. The Western Frontier! The Great Plains! Active duty! A brave new world to conquer! Libbie's prayers, and Custer's Luck, had prevailed.

Before heading out to the tall-grass country, General and Mrs. Custer joined President Andrew Johnson's National Union Party and accompanied him by special invitation on his sensational "Swing Around the Circle," a grand junket organized to sell King Andy's liberal Reconstruction Policy. As a glamorously popular figure, Custer was (hopefully) bound to improve Johnson's unenviable image; among radical Republicans and mossback Democrats, the President was considered a sottish Southern sympathizer who played kid-glove politics. Besides, "His Accidency" felt he owed the boy general this *beau geste,* since Custer had politely refused the pretentious offer of colonelcy of the 9th (all-Negro) Cavalry.

"Andy is as firm & upright as a tomb-stone," Armstrong had written in admiration. "I believe in acts, not words. Unlike some public characters, he does not swallow his own words." And so Custer served as Johnson's personal bodyguard and image-builder. He occupied the adjoining room in every hotel suite, with loaded revolvers at his bedside, because Mr. President had been threatened with assassination. And while Autie slept like a log, Libbie suffered many a restless night. With good reason! Flames of fury had been whipped by such winds as Chandler and Wade and Congressman Bingham, crackling and roaring that the former Confederate States of America must be treated as a conquered nation deprived of ante-bellum autonomy. In a self-righteous play for power, they demanded the so-called slave vote: the unqualified enfranchisement and naturalization of the Negro.

General Custer was one of four delegates at the National Union Convention in Philadelphia on August 14, 1866; he could not in good conscience endorse a pseudo-liberal program (or "aboli-

←21→

tionist plot") designed by rival forces to reopen the nation's wounds for partisan advantage by political, economic, and social subjugation of Dixie. He had seen the Deep South's dangerously precarious position, wavering on the brink of mobocracy; and he was certain that an absolute reign of terror, enforced by lynch law, would sweep the former slave states were whites virtually disenfranchised and blacks unconditionally licensed. As he had often written and said, "I am *opposed* to elevating the negro by correspondingly debasing the white-man. This, to me, is a travesty tantamount to National suicide." So he supported Johnson, who stood on a platform of Lincolnian sincerity and common sense. And he signed a manifesto that "We who fought and gave our blood to perpetuate this Union will not permit it to be severed by Chas. Sumner, Thad. Stevens, and other [Radical-Abolitionist] co-conspirators." For Custer, the political die was cast.

At Buffalo, wild cheers of "Speech! speech!" obliged Armstrong to respond blushfully, then forcefully, "I'm no speechmaker, but I fought four years to defend the Constitution and to save the Union. Now, come election, I only hope that you good people will vote for the Constitution as it is and the Union as it was. Thank you!"

Cleveland; Detroit. Jeering mobs greeted the Presidential party. "Hang him!" agitators hooted at King Andy. The Illinois *State Register* advised all "loyal citizens" to avoid Johnson "as they would any other convicted criminal." The Illinois *State Journal* accused "Gen. Custer and his associates" of consorting with "subjugated traitors": the old copperhead smear.

When the Presidential party rode the rails into Michigan, it was the first week in September, 1866. The lightning express had to be backed up the track from Detroit to Monroe for a whistle stop rally in the Custers' home town. Trumpet-tongued crowds of flag-waving "Wolverines" welcomed their boy hero and the cluster of government dignitaries.

Fiery old Secretary of State William H. Seward stepped out on the rear platform of the flag-festooned caboose, held up his hands for silence, then shouted to the expectant throng, "I find that

General Custer has a difference in the way he enters towns. When he enters an enemy town, he goes in straight forward and the enemy backs out. When he brings us into his own town, he backs us in!" The welcoming crowd rumbled with laughter. "I give you the two great cities of ancient and modern times—Nineveh and Monroe—both distinguished for light-horsemen before the Lord: Nimrod and Custer!"

Wild, whistling cheers and three rip-roaring tiger yells greeted the home-coming hero.

In St. Louis, extremist bands played "The Rogue's March." Grant got drunk, Seward got violent—as usual. And Johnson, in a fit of pot-valor, lost his dignity by shouting, "Stevens, Sumner, and [Wendell] Phillips liken themselves to Jesus Christ and call everybody else Judas. *Hah!* Well, if we must hang, thank God they shall be crucified!"

When the crowds grew uglier, drew too close for comfort, General Custer took the Chief Executive by the arm and urged him to beat a dignified retreat.

The Terre Haute lunatic fringe failed to derail the Presidential express; but a prearranged riot came off splendidly at Indianapolis, where pistol-packing rowdies cried, "Shoot the damned traitor!" and plugged some poor devil who happened to object.

General Grant, in one of his rarest rages, endeavored to silence the mob by appealing to their lost sense of honor: "For the credit of your city, hear us all speak!"

A heckler guffawed and answered, "For the sake of our city, go to hell!"

"God damn 'em!" Custer grated, itching to do what the permissive police seemed content to leave undone: read the riot act with bats and bullets. Libbie shuddered in horror, hearing the uproar and fearing the worst, hidden in a hotel with other terrified ladies of the grand but inglorious "Swing Around the Circle."

When billies swung and brawlers scattered, Armstrong commented sharply to Admiral David G. Farragut, "Wait till October [and the nominations of Congressional candidates], and more groans than these will be heard."

O tempora! O mores! In almost every city, at nearly every whistle stop, the campaigners were confronted with organized hostility incited by local bosses masquerading as respectable citizens. In vain, Secretary Seward introduced President Johnson as "an absolutely honest man" who "gave up fortune—everything—for the preservation of principles that patriots hold sacred." In the public mind, His Accidency was an unregenerate Rebel, an ass in lion's skin. The North wanted the South to pay dearly for its folly, for the bloodshed and sorrow of four dreadful years; and when King Andy refused to hang Jeff Davis & Co., pleading that passion and prejudice be laid aside for the common good, the Age of Hate came into its own.

At New Market (Scio), Ohio, Johnson was booed and Custer hurrahed by placard-bearing crowds at the railroad station. Custer turned to Johnson in apologetic embarrassment, saying, "This is my native town, but I'm ashamed of it."

"Down with King Andy!" agitators chanted. "A rope for His Accidency! Hang Sir Veto!"

Red-faced and wild-eyed, Custer leaned over the platform rail and shrilled, "I was born only a few miles from here, and I'm ashamed of you! Your insults to the President are an insult to me." He then swung aside. "Conductor, signal the engineer. We're leaving this damned place at once." He darted into the coach, rattling to Libbie, "By Jesus, I'll never visit this place again. We're not welcome."

Spotting another swarm of rabble-rousers at Steubenville, Custer advised Johnson to move on to Cadiz without stopping. As they rolled through the station, Armstrong poked his golden head out a window and accosted the mob in language that made Elizabeth shudder.

The reception at Cadiz was cool but polite, prompting Custer to remark, "As a Harrison County man, I'm glad for the President's sake to meet some respectable citizens of the district—having hitherto encountered some of the worst."

"Not worse than the Rebels!" someone retorted.

"Oh, worse by far!" said Custer. "For the Rebels have repented."

In private he said to Elizabeth, "I've had enough of this madness," and she agreed.

They sped to Monroe, for a final farewell before departure to St. Louis and the Great Plains. The Presidential Reconstruction Tour had been a smashing failure, and Custer was in no mood to remain and help pick up the pieces. Politics and politicians be damned! He had been used, injured in the public eye, for a noble purpose doomed to ignominy. Never more! It was army life for him, the elements he understood and loved.

"Nothing hurt Custer's political and military future like the movements of this summer," Whittaker concludes, "all of which were owing to his generous impulsive way of doing things. Honest to the backbone himself, he could not imagine that others could be less so; and he fell, bound hand and foot, into the midst of a den of hungry political wolves who would have picked his bones clean had he staid much longer. Like Juvenal refusing to go to Rome, he could reply when he was asked the cause of his non-success in politics, 'Nescio mentire' [I know not how to lie]. It tells the whole story."

KANSAS: THE GREAT PLAINS

O CTOBER 7, 1866. In Libbie's words, "exuberance of spirits" and "wild demonstrations of joy" attended the last moments of packing. Autie pranced about like an imp. The West would perchance prove the greatest, most glorious challenge of his life. Vast, majestic, untamed virgin lands peopled by free-spirited savages and noble beasts. The siren song of the wild had captured his fancy, intoxicated his senses.

With four horses, a pack of dogs, a small menagerie, and Aunt Eliza, General and Mrs. Custer set forth by train on their great adventure into the Garden of the West.

At St. Louis, en route to Fort Riley, the Custers struck up a lifelong friendship with Lawrence Barrett. Custer was something of a frustrated footlighter, and Barrett had served as an infantry captain in the Civil War, so both social lions had a lot in common. Whenever they met backstage, or in a hotel room, the great tragedian would hail the boy general with "Well, old fellow, hard at work making history, are you?" Each having a flair for the dramatic, even in private life, where they continued to act out their public roles, the two would then engage in some Shakespearean swordplay—to the indulgent amusement of Libbie.

Libbie again clipped Autie's hair rather short before they left St. Louis. He asked her to do it, because long curls would make the stifling heat of the Plains even less agreeable.

About 110 miles west of Kansas City, nestled in the fork of the Republican and Smoky Hill rivers, Fort Riley stood as a lone sentinel in the trackless, treeless expanse of rippling reddish-yellow buffalo grass: the Great Plains. It was November 3, but that quadrangular adobe outpost still baked beneath a blazing clear-blue sky heaped with pillars of cloud and steeped in a soft haze on the far horizon. It was a gorgeous spectacle of Nature's primitive simplicity. Now, as never before, Old Curly's reckless and restless spirit could wander free as the air over the Great Spirit's "happy hunting-grounds."

"Old Cump" Sherman (G.O.C., Military Division of the Missouri) was one of the first to welcome the Custers to their new home. He was a lean, slouchy "spitfire" with wrinkled red face, thatchy grizzled-red hair, a close-clipped rusty beard, and sharp beady eyes. He acted and spoke on the spur of the moment, chewing and puffing on one cigar after another.

"General Sherman," Custer said, "I want you to know my wife. She slept four months in a wagon and twice that in a tent."

"How d'you do, ma'am?" Sherman snapped, bobbing his head cordially. Seconds later he remarked, "Child, you'll find the air of the Plains is like champagne!"

He laughed at Old Curly's quip: "It's easier to command a whole division of cavalry than one woman!" Old Billy was a married man, too, and a trifle henpecked.

The first few weeks in a strange new land were full of wonder, excitement, and discovery. Libbie penciled in her diary: "Autie scarcely leaves the garrison behind him, where he is bound by chains of form & ceremony, when he becomes the wildest & most frolicsome of light-hearted boys. His horse & he are one."

Husband and wife would tease each other in dashes across the prairie; but Autie, flying far ahead of Libbie, was always the greatest wag. "Come on, Old Lady! Hurry up that old plug of yours! I have one orderly—don't want another!"

Once, when their mounts were galloping neck and neck, Armstrong gave Elizabeth the shock of her life by snatching her out of the saddle "with one powerful arm" and holding her poised for a moment in mid-air: a stunt made memorable by the genius of artist Frederic Remington. Sir Galahad never wearied of demonstrating his prowess and playfulness.

The dead winter months in a frontier fort were enlivened by the buffalo-hunting visits of such "great guns" as James Gordon Bennett and P. T. Barnum. When not "on the grind," training raw troopers or entertaining distinguished guests with hunting excursions, Custer was hard at work writing his war memoirs for *Galaxy Magazine*. With his wife sitting beside him in the study, reading or sewing, he would sometimes look up and say, "Aren't we happy, Libbie?"

⋆5⋆

SMOKY HILL:
THE HANCOCK EXPEDITION

WEDNESDAY, March 27, 1867. The 7th U.S. Cavalry, Colonel Andrew Jackson Smith and Lieutenant Colonel George Armstrong Custer commanding, rolled westward out of Fort Riley over a wind-swept prairie plateau and across the Republican River. The regimental band played "The Girl I Left Behind Me" till the long blue ribbon of horsemen had faded into the purple haze of the horizon.

There was breathless silence as the column left the garrison. No expedition was launched with shout and song when loving, tearful women were left behind. The barrack rooms and Officers' Row were as still as if death had set its seal upon the doors. There was no sound but the sobbing of wives and sweethearts.

The hours of those first wakeful nights seemed endless to Elizabeth.

"Miss Libbie, is you awake?" Eliza would whisper anxiously, sitting in a rocker by the bed.

"Oh, yes—and have been for ever so long."

"What's you doin', child?"

"Counting, saying over hymns, snatches of poetry, the Lord's Prayer backward—anything to try and put myself to sleep."

"Oh, in mercy's name, child, say some rhyme to me; for I's past all hope of sleep while I's so unhappy now the Gin'l's gone!"

Libbie recited to a humming and rocking Eliza:

"There's something in the parting hour
Will chill the warmest heart;
Yet kindred, comrades, lovers, friends
Are fated all to part.
But this I've seen, and many a pang
Has pressed it on my mind—
The one who goes is happier
Than those he leaves behind."

Major General Winfield Scott Hancock, "Thunderbolt of the Grand Army of the Potomac," was in the saddle, masterminding this full-scale spring campaign against hostile Indians—mostly "Dog-Soldiers" (*Hotâmitânyo*) or berserkers—who had been raiding construction crews of the Union and Kansas Pacific Railroads and making a deadly nuisance of themselves at white settlements along the Republican and Smoky Hill rivers.

Centers of attraction on the grand punitive expedition included special correspondent Henry M. Stanley of Bennett's New York *Herald,* artist-reporter T. R. Davis of *Harper's Weekly,* and chief scout James Butler ("Wild Bill") Hickok: a strapping, golden-haired, long-mustachioed gunslinger pranked out in a ten-gallon hat, buckskin pants, and a jazzy Zouave jacket of scarlet, black, and gold.

The biggest military force ever seen on the Plains—fourteen hundred horse and foot, light artillery, and pontoon train—had hit the glory trail at a cost to Eastern taxpayers of approximately $1,500,000. Colonel Andy ("Old Rawhide") Smith, on detached service with Hancock's headquarters, turned all eight companies of the 7th over to his indispensable and indefatigable "hell-driver."

"Old Eagle-Eye" Hancock—"Hancock the Superb" of the gilded era of glorious war—was Old Tecumseh's subordinate as C.O., Department of the Missouri (Military Division of the Missouri), and his much-publicized Kansas Expedition would be the last glory-grab of a fading soldier who had seen better days as "Thunderbolt of the G.A.P."

"Sherman the Crazy," as he was jocosely called early in the

Civil War, progressed by leaps and bounds to "Sherman the Terrible": a (to him) flattering title that still applied, but now to the Plains Indian in lieu of the Southern Secessionist. He had wired General Grant with characteristically practical decisiveness: "We must proceed with vindictive earnestness against the hostile Indians—even to their extermination—men, women & children. Nothing less will reach the root of the case." And to Hancock he declared: "By Hell, sir, we must take these wild Indians in hand and give 'em a devil of a thrashing!" And with good reason, echoed the Montana *Post*. "It is high time the sickly sentimentalism about humane treatment and conciliatory measures should be consigned to novel-writers, and if the Indians continue their barbarities, wipe them out."

The *Hotâmitânyo,* or Sioux-Cheyenne dog-warrior society, was so called because of its roving, predatory ferocity and foulness. It was (in Custer's words) "the most mischievous, blood-thirsty & barbarous band of Indians that infest the Plains." Like rabid curs, these perverse bucks preyed upon red man and white with equal violence and virulence. The fact that they were outcasts and outlaws, hated and feared by their own people, points up the most significant underlying tragedy of the Indian Wars: the difficult distinction rarely made between "hostiles" and "friendlies," between the vicious pariah dogs and the pedigreed hunters. All Indians apparently looked alike—or so the excuse was—and to make distinctions seemed relatively unimportant; there was no place for "savages" in the sun of "civilization." To the Army, goaded by settlers and guided by Indian agents, went the task of distinguishing—and extinguishing.

In his *Galaxy* memoirs, General Custer stated: "The clique generally known as the Indian Ring [pseudo-humanitarian bureaucrats of the Department of the Interior] were particularly malevolent and bitter in their denunciations of General Hancock for precipitating, as they expressed it, an Indian war. . . . It may be asked, what had the Indians done to make this incursion necessary. They had been guilty of numerous thefts and murders during the preceding summer and fall, for none of which had they been called to account. They had attacked the stations of the overland-mail route, killed the employees, burned the stations, and captured the stock. Citizens had been murdered in their homes on the frontier of Kansas; murders had been committed on the Arkansas route. The principal perpetrators of these acts were the Cheyennes and Sioux. The agent of the former [Colonel Edward W. Wynkoop, Fort Larned], if not a party to the murder on the Arkansas, knew who the guilty persons were, yet took no steps to bring the murderers to punishment. Such a course would have interfered with his trade and profits. It was not to punish for these sins of the past that the expedition was set on foot, but rather by its imposing appearance and its early presence in the Indian country to check or intimidate the Indians from a repetition of their late conduct."

Turning off the Smoky Hill Stage Road at Fort Harker, a log-and-mud stockade seventy-five miles southwest of Fort Riley, Hancock's column crossed Smoky Hill River and followed the snowswept Santa Fe Trail another seventy-five miles southwestward to Fort Larned on the Arkansas River. There, for the first time in his life, Custer came into close contact with someone other than the "noble savage" of James Fenimore Cooper.

He was quick to note that "each one was supplied with either a breech-loading rifle or revolver—sometimes with both—the latter obtained thro' the wise foresight & strong love of fair play which prevails in the Indian Dept., which (seeing that its wards are determined to fight) is equally determined that there shall be no advantage taken, but that the two sides shall be armed alike; proving, too, in this manner the wonderful liberality of our Gov't, which not only is able to furnish its soldiers with the latest improved style of breech-loaders to defend it & themselves, but is equally able & willing to give the same pattern of arms to their common foe. The only difference is that the soldier, if he loses his weapon, is charged double-price for it; while to avoid making any such charge against the Indian, his weapons are given him without conditions attached."

General Hancock had instructed Agent Wynkoop to call a peace council of all tribes then amassed in the snow-blown Arkansas-Smoky Hill river basin. When only a token handful of chiefs and braves showed themselves for the grand powwow, Old Eagle-Eye smelled a rat and ordered Custer out to hunt up the wild bands —reputedly encamped in the area of Pawnee Fork, about forty miles west of Larned.

Warm, thawing winds whisked the valley bare of its white mantle of winter. Custer and the 7th Cavalry dashed away in dead of night, April 15, followed at daybreak by Hancock's slow-moving infantry and artillery. A couple of hours' hard riding brought the hunters to their quarry, a large and apparently sleeping village.

Enacting simple strategy, Custer dismounted his troopers and surrounded the swarm of tepees—only to find them abandoned, lifeless, but for a few dogs and invalids.

Disappointment flared to indignation when Armstrong entered a chief's lodge and discovered, wrapped in a buffalo robe, "a little Indian girl—probably 10 yrs. old—not a full-blood, but a half-breed." At first an object of curiosity, she soon proved an object of pity; for "The Indians—an unusual thing for them to do toward their own blood—had wilfully deserted her. But this, alas! was the least of their injuries to her. After being shamefully abandoned by the entire village, a few of the young men of the tribe returned to the deserted lodge & upon the person of this little girl committed outrages the details of which are too sickening for me to describe."

At twenty minutes to three in the morning, Autie penciled to Libbie: "I do not anticipate war, or even difficulty, as the Indians are frightened to death & only ran away from fear."

As Custer himself styled it, a futile pursuit followed. The Indians seemed to vanish in that mysterious purple haze. Frustrated, infuriated, dispirited, he shut himself up in his tent to brood and sulk. He had at last met his match, an elusive challenge, and it maddened him to be outwitted. But heartening thoughts of Elizabeth soon imposed upon this boyish abandon, luring him back to his usual airiness and deterministic self-assurance. He then scribbled: "In years long-numbered with the past, when I was verging upon manhood, my every thought was ambitious—not to be wealthy, not to be learned, but to be great. I desired to link my name with acts & men, and in such a manner as to be a mark of honor—not only to the present, but to future generations. Now, my ambition has been turned into an entirely new channel. Where I was once eager to acquire worldly honors & distinctions, I am content to try & modestly wear what I have —and feel grateful for them when they come—but also my desire now is to make myself a man worthy of the blessings heaped upon me."

While Hancock marched south to Fort Dodge on the Arkansas, there to parley with the Kiowas and Arapahoes, Custer continued his northward pursuit of the marauding Sioux-Cheyenne dog-warriors across Smoky Hill River.

Scout Hickok, patrolling the Smoky Hill Stage Road west of Fort Hays, "obtained intelligence which confirmed our worst fears as to the extent of the Indian outbreak. Stage-stations at various points along the route had been attacked & burned, and the in-mates driven off or murdered. All travel across the Plains was suspended, and an Indian war with all its barbarities had been forced upon the people of the Frontier." At Lookout Station, fifteen miles west of Hays, Custer found smoldering ruins and three stationkeepers—"so mangled & burned as to be scarcely recognizable as human beings. The Indians had evidently tortured them before putting an end to their sufferings. They were scalped & horribly disfigured. Their bodies were badly burned, but whether before or after death could not be determined."

Custer immediately reported these atrocities to Hancock, who later notified Grant, in response to a trumped-up charge that he had precipitated hostilities by pursuing a punitive policy: "When I learned from Gen'l Custer (who investigated these matters on the spot) that . . . they [the hostile Indians] attacked & burned a mail-station on the Smoky Hill, killed the white-men at it, dis-embowelled & burned them, fired into another station, endeavored to gain admittance to a third, fired on my express-men both on the Smoky Hill & on their way to Larned, I concluded that this must be war, and therefore deemed it my duty to take the first opportunity which presented itself to resent these hostilities & outrages."

Custer pointedly remarks in his memoirs: "This . . . was the signal for an extensive pen-and-ink war, directed against him [Hancock] & his forces. This was to be expected. The pecuniary loss and deprivation of opportunities to speculate in Indian commodities, as practised by most Indian-agents, were too great to be submitted to without a murmur." Pointing a finger of guilt at Colonels Jesse W. Leavenworth and E. W. Wynkoop, Custer records that both these agents "admitted to Gen'l Hancock in conversation that Indians had been guilty of all the outrages charged against them; but each asserted the innocence of the particular tribes under his charge & endeavored to lay their crimes at the door of their neighbors." He concludes: "Here was positive evidence from the Agents themselves that the Indians against whom we were operating were guilty & deserving of severe punishment. The only conflicting portion of the testimony was as to which tribe was most guilty. Subsequent events proved, however, that all . . . had combined for a general war throughout the Plains & along our Frontier."

Wynkoop's Cheyennes, particularly the *Hotâmitânyo,* had already demonstrated their hostility; and Leavenworth's Kiowas, soon after the Fort Dodge powwow, were found to have butchered several white families on the Texas border. The "Box Massacre" was typical. This family of seven was assaulted in their wagon by Chief Satanta and his "braves," whose salutatory volley killed the father and one of the children. These two were scalped and otherwise mutilated. The youngest child, a babe of a few months, was snatched from its mother's arms and dashed against a tree. The four survivors were later sold to the highest bidders, for use as vehicles of lust.

On May 1, 1867, Armstrong wrote to Elizabeth from Fort Hays, one hundred twenty-five miles southwest of Fort Riley:

"Nothing heard of Indians for days. 'All quiet on the Smoky Hill. . . .' Tell Eliza I am in search of an Indian husband for her —one who won't bother her to sew buttons on his shirts & pants. Nor would his washing be heavy! And one dish at a meal would satisfy him."

He wrote the following day: "When we surrounded the Indian camp [at Pawnee Fork], I mentioned having found a little half-breed girl, almost insensible, covered with blood. When able to talk she said, 'Those Indian men did me bad.' God knows how many times they had violated her. Woe to them if I overtake them! . . . I wrote a very strong letter recently (to Gen'l Sherman) *against* an Indian war, depicting as strongly as I could the serious results that would follow—putting a stop to trains on the Overland Route, interfering with the work on the U. Pacific RR., &c.—all of which would be a National calamity. I regard the recent outrages as the work of small groups of irresponsible young bucks, eager for war. The Indian stampede, I said, I consider caused by fear of our forces. I ended my letter with the hope that my opinion would be received as intended; that should a war be waged, none would be more determined than I to make it a war of extermination. But I consider we are not yet justified in declaring such a war. . . . How I wish you were here! You would enjoy a buffalo-hunt. There is nothing so nearly resembling a cavalry charge as a buffalo chase. You would be carried away with excitement!"

While scouting for hostiles beyond a flying detachment, Armstrong himself was carried away with excitement, a bad case of "buffalo fever" that nearly cost him his life.

Scanning the misty-green ocean of grassland with his field glass, Custer spotted a huge bison grazing alone about a mile ahead. A nearby arroyo would enable him to approach the animal unseen till almost within pistol range.

Calling his half-dozen staghounds to follow him, Custer nudged his thoroughbred steed forward at a jog trot into the gully. They sprang up on the range several hundred yards from the buffalo, who jerked up his short-horned and shaggy-maned head, stared for a few seconds, then swung around and went lumbering away as fast as his beefy legs could carry him.

Custer whipped out his revolver, clapped heels to his horse, and gave chase after the bull, the lean white staghounds barking at its hoofs. Moments later, Custer was galloping neck and neck with the biggest bison he had ever seen.

Any number of times he could have pressed the muzzle of his six-shooter against the shaggy body of the huge humped beast, close by whose side he yelled in delight, but each time he withdrew the weapon, as if to prolong the excitement.

Mile after mile they sped over the prairie, till a drooping tongue and husky breathing made clear the buffalo's struggle. Determined to end the chase and bring down his game, Custer pressed the muzzle of his revolver against the animal's shoulder. In that split second the bison swerved to gore the horse, which veered aside to avoid the attack. Custer raised his pistol hand to keep control of the reins. As he did so, his finger accidentally yanked the trigger.

A bullet penetrated the horse's brain. Running at full speed, the charger fell dead in a flying tumble. Catapulted out of the stirrups, Custer vaulted into the air and sprawled on the plain. Leaping to his feet, he stood like a statue. The buffalo stared at him, and he stared at the buffalo. Then, with a defiant snort, the brute lurched aside and loped away. Custer's never-forgotten sensation of "staring down a buffalo," was immortalized by Remington.

"What a fine fix we're in!" Custer said to his staghounds, who were sniffing at the carcass and whining ominously.

Alone and lost, in the heart of hostile country, with a dead horse and buzzards circling high overhead, he looked all around, wondering which way to go. The dogs kept peering in one particular direction, anxious to leave this deathly spot. They yapped and howled at his heels. He decided to oblige them.

With one parting glance at his dead steed, and clutching a Colt in each hand, Armstrong set out on an uncertain journey. As long as the buzzard-clustered carcass was visible, he kept gazing back at it as his guiding point, thus holding a steady course as he limped along across the shimmering flats, under a boiling sun. When he lost sight of the carcass, he had to direct his steps by means of weed tufts or buffalo skulls. He constantly scanned the horizon, each moment expecting to find himself pounced upon by Indians.

Custer had slogged three or four miles when far ahead he saw a slowly rising column of dust being kicked up by one of three things: white men, red men, or the humpbacks of the Plains. He crawled into a gully, calling his dogs to huddle around him, keep still, and hold their tongues. The cause of his anxiety was still several miles away; but whoever or whatever it was, it was certainly approaching.

Custer leveled his field glass on the edge of the arroyo. Through an almost blinding glare and clouds of dust, he could barely make out the forms of mounted men. *Indians!*

Never during the War had Old Curly peeled an eye at a masked battery or an oncoming column with half the apprehension he now suffered, watching till his eyes burned. Then—*hallelujah!* He spotted a cavalry guidon fluttering above the onrushing riders, who were veiled in drifts of dust. Never had the display of stars and stripes been more gloriously welcome than now!

Custer scrambled over the top and waved his hat. The dogs were surely in for a splendid meal that carefree evening!

★6★

FORT HAYS:
GROWING PAINS OF THE 7th

ARMY life at Fort Hays, a
desolate hell of sandblast wind and blistering heat, was described
by Autie to Libbie in glowing terms of a resort of unlimited sport.
The harsh, rugged realities of nature in the raw thrilled him and
filled him with a sense of power: a reckless romance that blinded
him to eyesores, deadened him to heartaches. He took to this
wild, wanton land, and he made himself a part of it, body and
soul.

But others could not adapt, and would not—with good reason.
As one old soldier expressed it: "In a life of monotony, away
from home, what was there for a man to do—but desert or get
drunk?" *Forty miles a day on beans and hay!*

Ravening ghouls of the desert drove raw recruits to desperation, madness. Wayworn horses, broken down by extreme heat
and cold, dropped dead because there was no feed at Hays. It had
all been bartered or sold to the Indians, by black marketeers
masquerading as government agents. And so had the fresh army
rations, leaving Hancock's troops to sicken or starve on Civil
War surplus: moldy bacon, maggoty hardtack, wormy beans.

According to Custer, "desertions from the ranks became so
frequent & extensive as to cause no little anxiety." Citing "the
insufficiency & inferior quality of the rations furnished the men,"
who were made "the victims of fraud" by profiteers in the Quartermaster's Department at Fort Leavenworth, Custer elaborated:

"Unbroken packages of provisions shipped from the main depôt

←39→

of supplies [Fort Leavenworth] . . . were, when opened, discovered to contain huge stones for which the Gov't had paid so much per pound according to contract price. Boxes of bread were shipped & issued to the soldiers of my Command, the contents of which had been baked in 1861—yet this was in 1867! . . . Bad provisions were a fruitful cause of bad health. Inactivity led to restlessness & dissatisfaction. Scurvy made its appearance, and cholera attacked neighboring stations. For all these evils, desertion became the most popular antidote. To such an extent was this the case, that in one year one regiment lost by desertion alone more than half of its effective force."

Custer was here referring to the 7th Iowa Volunteer Cavalry, then garrisoned with the 7th U.S. Regular Cavalry at Fort Hays. His methods of putting down mutiny, insubordination, drunkenness, and desertion were no more popular in Kansas than in Louisiana and Texas; for they were the methods of a man who would shake other men into discipline with an exemplary vengeance.

Mutineers were shaved bald, stripped naked, paraded through camp in the broiling noonday sun—to the degrading rhythms of "*The Rogue's March.*" Insubordinates were dumped into the hoosegow: a hole in the ground, fifteen feet deep by thirty feet square, boarded over and labeled *Guard-House.* Drunkards were treated to a ducking-stool douse in the river. And deserters were horsewhipped and "skinned" by the regimental barber. To prevent desertion and drunkenness, a cordon of sentries was strung around the 7th bivouac, with orders to shoot prowlers and that "No enlisted man shall be permitted to visit the Post ["a perfect sink of iniquity," says Whittaker] without a written order signed by the Adjutant." To prevent insubordination and mutiny, the following admonition was issued: "Insurgents and deserters shall be hanged or shot without benefit of trial."

For "outrageous and relentless brutalization" of the 7th Iowa, it was proposed in the legislature of that state that Colonel Custer "should be brought to trial and subjected to condign punishment." The proposition never materialized, but its cautionary repercussions served to change Custer's methods from retaliatory to re-habilitative. As he informed Libbie: "I have notified the Companies that on the 4th [of May] we will have a foot-race—distance, 300 yds.—the Co. producing the winner to be excused from guard & fatigue duty for one week, the winner from same duties for 20 days. I hear much excitement about it. I want to give the men exercise, innocent amusement, something to do. It is also proposed that the officers of the 7th Cav. match those of the Post-master's Division, the party that kills the smallest number of buffalo to pay for a champagne-supper for the entire group."

Shipping the moldy bacon and maggoty bread back to Leavenworth, with a note advising the Commissary Department to investigate its crooked contractors, Custer organized hunting parties and scoured the country in quest of fresh meat: bison, elk, antelope, and other big game. These hunts also served a functional and monotony-breaking purpose, as Armstrong noted to Libbie: "I know of no better drill for perfecting men in the use of fire-arms on horseback, and thoro'ly accustoming them to the saddle, than buffalo-hunting over a moderately rough country. No amount of riding under the best of drill-masters will give that confidence & security in the saddle which will result from a few spirited charges into a buffalo-herd."

May 4, '67: "I have just returned from Gen'l Hancock's tent. He leaves at 6 for Ft. Leavenworth. Col. Smith will go with him as far as Ft. Harker, perhaps to Riley. If so, you could come back with him. . . . Should he go no farther than Harker, I will start for you on his return here. So look for Col. S. or me within 7 days, and commence packing. . . . We have a most beautiful camp. You will be delighted with the country. . . . Oh, we will be so, *so* happy!"

May 6: "You remember how eager I was to have you for my little wife? Well, I was not as impatient then as now! I almost feel tempted to desert & fly to you!! I would come if the cars were running, this far. [The railhead was then at Fort Harker.] We will probably go on another scout shortly, and I don't want to lose a day with you."

←41→

May 7: "Your Boy went buffalo-hunting! Seven officers in our party. Maj. Cooper was sent back to camp, drunk—so beastly drunk he could scarcely sit on his horse. His friends desired him to be placed in one of the ambulances taken along to carry the meat. But I told them this would not be permitted; that if he chose to act in a disgraceful manner & could not ride his horse, he must be left behind. His friends then placed him in charge of a Cavalry Pvt. & sent him back to camp. Had I been on duty I should have placed him under arrest, but it was a social occasion. He became drunk before we were 3 miles from camp—to the surprise of the other officers, none of whom had been drinking. Our party killed 12 buffalo. The tongues were exhibited as evidence!"

"My danger in connection with the Indians was twofold," Elizabeth wrote later, recalling her ambivalent feelings about joining Armstrong. "I was in peril from death or capture by the savages, and liable to be killed by my own friends to prevent my capture. . . . I had been a subject of conversation among the officers—being the only woman who, as a rule, followed the regiment—and without discussing it much in my presence, the universal understanding was that anyone having me in charge in an emergency (where there was imminent danger of my capture) should shoot me instantly."

By force of passion, Custer's prudent sense of danger at times assumed an infantile state. Never doubting his own apparent indestructibility, he flattered himself that his wife enjoyed the same guardian angel.

On Saturday, May 18, Libbie and Eliza rolled into the Fort Hays cavalry encampment in a hospital wagon. Autie swept Libbie into his arms, hustled her into his log-and-canvas shebang.

"It seemed to me the end of all the troubles that would ever enter my life had come when I was lifted out of the ambulance into my husband's tent."

Despite desertions and discontent, fun and frolic fared well at Fort Hays. As was his wont, Colonel Custer turned Cavalry Headquarters into a zoo tenanted by wolves, coyotes, prairie dogs, jack rabbits, raccoons, porcupines, wildcats, badgers, rattlesnakes, owls, eagles, hawks, young antelopes, deer, buffalo calves—even a pelican—and an inevitable slew of hounds and horses. Eliza, saucily indulgent of Custer's idiosyncrasies, remarked: "Mercy sakes, Miss Libbie, one o' them pesky pets is as precious as if it was a goldmine!"

★7★

PLATTE RIVER:
THE CUSTER EXPEDITION

WHEN Hancock and Smith left
Hays for Department Headquarters at Leavenworth, there to receive further orders from Sherman, Custer was assigned temporary
command of the District of the Upper Arkansas. It became apparent that Old Eagle-Eye's demonstration was a *brutum fulmen*
when Cheyenne and Sioux dog-warriors resumed their unrelenting
raids in the Smoky Hill-Platte River country, burning settlements
and stage depots, attacking coaches and construction camps of the
Union-Kansas Pacific.

Governor Samuel J. Crawford, urged by two railroad presidents
and furious settlers, appealed to General Sherman for military
protection. Prior to planning and executing a decisive campaign,
Sherman ordered Custer to launch an expedition against the
hostile bands: to track them down, round them up, hold them for
the kill.

Custer's official instructions, soon to prove of great consequence
and controversy, were as follows:

"The Brev. Maj.-Gen'l Comdg. [Smith] directs that you proceed with your Command . . . to Ft. McPherson, at which point
you will find a large supply of rations & forage. . . . From Ft.
McPherson you will proceed up the South Fork of the Platte to
Ft. Sedgwick. . . . If every thing is found to be quiet & your
presence not required . . . you may come South to Ft. Wallace, at
which point you will find further instructions. The object of the
Expedition is to hunt out & chastise the Cheyennes, and that por-

tion of the Sioux who are their allies, between the Smoky Hill & the Platte. It is reported that all friendly Sioux have gone South of the Platte, and may be in the vicinity of Fts. McPherson or Sedgwick. You will (as soon as possible) inform yourself as to the whereabouts of these friendly bands, and avoid a collision with them."

Saturday, June 1, 1867. Colonel Custer and a 350-man squadron of the 7th Cavalry set out on their momentous scout to Fort McPherson, 175 miles northwest on the South Platte River, Nebraska Territory.

On June 8, thirty miles from the Platte, Armstrong penciled to Elizabeth: "The officers of the 7th—the entire camp—is wrapped in deep gloom by the suicide of Maj. Cooper while in a fit of delirium-tremens. . . . Another of Rum's victims! But for intemperance Maj. Cooper would have been a useful & accomplished officer, a brilliant & most companionable gentleman. He leaves a young wife, shortly to become a mother. One by one, all came to gaze on him who but a few minutes before had been the companion of our march. Actuated by what I deemed my duty to the living, I warned the other officers of the fate of him who lay there dead. I told them this was not the death of a soldier. All felt deeply—particularly his intimates, who shared his habits. May the example be not lost on them! I thank God my darling wife will never know anxiety thro' intemperance on my part. Would I could fly to her now! But a wise Providence decrees all."

The suicide of Major Wyckliffe Cooper, Custer's second-in-command, was only the first in a series of tragic episodes that would haunt the glory hunter till his dying day. Cooper, a Kentuckian who had served with distinction in the Federal cavalry, had been a manic-depressive and had drunk himself into a fool's paradise. That dreamworld was shattered when Custer confiscated his whiskey supply, threatening to have him court-martialed for dereliction of duty unless he straightened out. In a fit of desperation, Cooper took the downward path.

Certain officers of the 7th never forgave Custer for (as they judged it) having "killed" Major Cooper. And the teetotaler's stagy *verbum sapienti,* over Cooper's corpse, was rather distasteful to a hard-drinking lot: "Gentlemen, this is not the death of a soldier. It is unnecessary, standing as we do in the presence of such an example, that I should say more." Custer's field book reveals why the Cooper family later accused him of indirect homicide: "Funeral [at Fort McPherson] as quiet as possible, suicide not being entitled to military honors." From that fateful evening, Armstrong's peace of mind was ravaged by a war of nerves.

Custer and the 7th had reached Fort McPherson, on the Platte, during the afternoon of June 10. Cooper was buried on the eleventh. "Rec'd telegram from Gen'l Sherman, at Ft. Sedgwick, in regard to Indians & a movement against them. The Command is to move at 6 a.m. to-morrow [June 12]."

Enraged by reports of continued depredations by dog-warriors, Sherman the Terrible had wired General Grant on the tenth: "The only course is for us to destroy the Hostile, and to segregate the peaceful & maintain them." Grant agreed, though reluctantly. The wartime stigma of "Butcher" still haunted him. Sherman had a flexible conscience, a ruthlessly realistic understanding of "the inevitable," and instructed Custer to await marching orders. No mention was made of appeasement, compromise, conciliatory powwows with the "red devils." By their own actions, war to the death seemed predestined.

But not in Custer's mind. On his own initiative, the yellow-haired chief called a peace council with Pawnee-Killer's band of Sioux warriors, then in the vicinity. Custer had cause to regret his good will. "While protesting strongly in favor of preserving peaceful relations with us, the subsequent conduct of the chiefs only confirmed the suspicion that they had arranged the council not to perfect a friendly agreement with us but to spy out & discover, if possible, our future plans & movements. In this they were disappointed."

Sherman railed into McPherson from Sedgwick, 125 miles due west, on the following day. "Indian promises aren't worth a damn," he growled to Custer. "The redman must be taught a lasting lesson. All who refuse to obey the whiteman's law must be killed." Observing Custer's frown, Sherman waxed philosophical: "It's an inevitable conflict of races, one that must occur when a stronger is gradually displacing a weaker."

Sherman's verbal orders to Custer were peremptory: "I want you to clean out that Augean stable of hostiles along the Republican River. Capture or kill all you can. Written instructions will follow."

In Pawnee, the Republican was *Kîrârûtâ* (Shit Creek) because it was polluted by herds of buffalo. The stream spread over four hundred miles eastward out of Colorado Territory to join the Smoky Hill at Fort Riley. It cut a swath through rugged country, canyon-cleft and bluff-barricaded. Hunting Indians in such tablelands would be like trying to fetch water in a sieve. But Custer was game.

Southwestward the 7th pushed, heat-dazed and dust-crazed, driven to uncertain desperation by "Old Iron-Ass." Yet their awe of him transcended the severity of a Godforsaken region, and they followed him unflinchingly.

On June 24, 1867, the column lay bivouacked on North Fork of the Republican. In an unguarded moment between darkness and daylight, Colonel Custer was brought to his feet by the sharp crack of a carbine. Lieutenant Tom, officer of the day, poked his blond head through the tent flaps and shouted, "They're here!"

Seconds later, the still air was shattered by wild war whoops and brisk gunfire. Libbie learned from her waggish spouse that "Gen'l Custer on this occasion appeared in a beautiful crimson robe (red flannel robe-de-nuit) very becoming to his complexion. His hair was worn *au naturel,* and permitted to fall carelessly over his shoulders. In his hand he carried gracefully a handsome Spencer Rifle. It is unnecessary to add that he became the observed of all observers."

Custer had grabbed his carbine and burst out of the tent, dashing shoeless as well as hatless to the point where attack seemed to be concentrated. The first flush of daylight revealed several hundred mounted warriors intent on stampeding his *remuda* at the rear of the camp. Alertness saved the occasion; for every trooper was armed and out of his tent in short order, forcing the Indians back with carbine blasts.

When the attackers withdrew across North Fork, Custer sent forward one of his interpreters to arrange a parley, as "It was desirable that we should learn, if possible, to what tribe our enemies belonged." The hostiles agreed to meet the yellow-haired chief and six of his officers, on the riverbank. "To guard against treachery, I placed most of my Command under arms & arranged with Tom that a blast from the bugle should bring assistance to me if required."

Seven "long knives," accompanied by bugler and interpreter, dismounted on the grassy bank and gazed across the shallow stream at a savage procession threading through tall weeds and willows. Custer signaled his escort to unholster revolvers and tuck them in their belts. The bugler, who held their horses, was admonished: "Watch every move they make. Upon the first appearance of violence or treachery, sound the *Advance*."

"*Pawnee-Killer!*" Custer breathed, recognizing the head chief who waded on foot.

"That treacherous dog!" another muttered, fingering his revolver.

Custer said, "Hold your tempers. Let him speak his piece."

Pawnee-Killer, he thought, *who had overwhelmed us with the earnestness of his professions of peace; and who, after partaking of our hospitality under the guise of friendship, and leaving our camp laden with provisions and presents, returned to attack and murder us within a fortnight.*

Extended hands and the familiar salute of "*Hâo!*" greeted the scowling soldiers. According to Custer, "Pawnee-Killer & his chiefs met us as if they were quite willing to forgive us for interfering with the success of their intended surprise of our camp in the morning." Not mentioning the duel at dawn, the white chief attempted unsuccessfully to learn by verbal strategy the locality of

←48→

the Indians' village and their future movements. Equally unsuccessful were the red chief's subtle endeavors to penetrate Custer's plans. Indeed: "Suspicious of their intentions, I kept one hand on my revolver during the continuance of our interview."

The conference was about to end indecisively when a young brave, armed to the teeth, lunged out of the willows on the opposite bank and came splashing over with a throaty "*Hâo!*" He was soon followed by another, then another, until four bucks had swelled the red delegation to eleven.

"Do you forget the conditions under which we meet?" Custer snapped, indicating the newcomers. "You are violating your part of the agreement."

Pawnee-Killer smiled coldly, motioning with his leathery hand. "My young men feel well disposed toward you, Longhair. They came over only to shake hands and say 'Hello.'"

Custer raised his head in a half-nod, scowling. "No more of your men must come."

Pawnee-Killer shrugged, expressionless. The conversation was picked up, carried warily until another bunch of braves decided to cross the stream and pay their respects to *Pêhîhonskâ*: "Longhair" Custer. That was the limit of patience. "We all felt convinced that the coming-over of these warriors, one by one, was but the execution of a preconceived plan whereof we were to become the victims as soon as their advantage in numbers should justify them in attacking us."

Custer said pointedly, "Remember our agreement. We have observed *our* part of the bargain faithfully. *You* have not. So long as our talk continues, not another warrior of yours must cross the river." He called the chief's attention to his bugler. "If any more of your braves dare to cross over, I shall tell that man to sound the signal that will bring my entire command to my side in a few moments." He stared Pawnee-Killer straight in the eye.

The Indian's lips loosened in a cryptic smile. Eyes pantherlike, he at once waved to his braves on the other side to stay put.

The interview ended with a request for sugar, coffee, and ammunition—which Custer curtly refused, without explanation.

A standoff had been tacitly agreed upon, by virtue of Custerian bluff. An attempt to follow Pawnee-Killer failed. The Indian pony outdistanced the cavalry mount. Custer fretted. "God damn 'em, we'll track 'em to the ends of the earth!" That he would. It was the run-ragged 7th's greatest fear.

Reaching the North Republican riverhead, near the South Platte in Colorado, Custer telegraphed Sherman for further instructions. Fort Sedgwick lay about fifty miles northeast of Riverside Station, into which flashed a reply that dispatches were on the way. A temporary halt, and rest, was therefore in order.

Armstrong characteristically described his forced march up North Fork as "the painful journey, under a burning July sun, of 65 miles without a drop of water for our horses or draft-animals. This march was necessarily effected in one day, and produced untold suffering among the poor dumb brutes. Many of the dogs accompanying the Command died from thirst & exhaustion." No mention of *human* suffering! Not that "Old Hard-Arse" didn't care about his men. He cared they should follow him to Hell and then sleep. "Those unfortunate persons who have always been accustomed to the easy comforts of civilization, and who have never known what real fatigue or hunger is, cannot realize or appreciate the blissful luxury of a sleep which follows a day's ride in the saddle of half a hundred miles or more."

Receiving no written orders from Sherman, Custer again wired the fort and was surprised to learn that the Division Commander had long since dispatched Lieutenant Lyman S. Kidder and ten troopers of the 2nd Cavalry with letters of instruction. Colonel Custer immediately replied that nothing had been seen or heard of Lieutenant Kidder's detachment, and therefore requested telegraphic copies of the important dispatches:

"The instructions of Gen'l Sherman were for me to march my Command [southward] across the country from the Platte to the Smoky Hill River, striking the latter at Ft. Wallace. Owing to the low state of my supplies, I determined to set out for Ft. Wallace at daylight next morning."

Move he must. Yet one thing haunted him, made him hesitate.

"Great anxiety prevailed throughout the Command concerning Lt. Kidder & his party. . . . Knowing that the Indians would in all probability maintain a strict watch over the trail, to surprise any small party which might venture over it, I felt in the highest degree solicitous for the safety of Lt. K."

After careful consideration, Custer decided to put Kidder out of his mind and move as ordered. Nothing must stop him now. Not even mass desertion, which erupted in the predawn hours of July 7.

The causes of dissatisfaction and demoralization among the troopers were many, yet those for which Custer may have been responsible were few. Foremost was his indefatigability, and his assumption that others were (or rather should be) equal to such hard driving. An average of twenty-five miles a day, in rough terrain and raging heat, was torture to horse and man; but "If I can stand it, they can!" was the hell-driver's boast. "Iron-Ass Curly," they called him, and "Horse-Killer Custer."

"He was a dare-devil," one veteran writes, "but most of the men didn't like him. He was too hard on the men & horses. He changed his mind too often. He was always right. He never conferred enough with his officers. When he got a notion, we had to go. He wouldn't listen to the other officers."

Custer lays the blame for desertion upon "inferior & insufficient rations," and upon the golden lure of "our most valuable & lately discovered mining-regions [in Colorado]. The opportunity to obtain marvellous wages as miners, and the prospect of amassing sudden wealth, proved a temptation sufficiently strong to make many of the men forget their sworn obligations to their Gov't & their duty as soldiers." The legal penalty for desertion in time of war was death, but the desperate were not deterred by such knowledge in their attempts at escape to the mines.

Between thirty and forty desperadoes bolted to "freedom" during the night. "Let 'em go, God damn 'em!" Custer responded to the reporting provost marshal. "They won't get far in *this* country." The regiment marched at daybreak, as planned. Kidder and deserters be damned! No one, nothing, must stop the unrelenting pursuit of redskins.

"In the vicinity of the Platte River," Armstrong informed Elizabeth, "35 of my men deserted in 24 hrs. Was apprehensive for the whole Command, as we had (and still have) before us a long march thro' hostile country. When breaking camp, about 5 a.m. on the 7th [July], 13 of my men deliberately shouldered their arms & started off for the Platte—in the presence of the entire Command, in open day. Not knowing but that the remainder of the Command (or a considerable portion of it) might leave as well, I felt that severe & summary measures must be taken. I therefore directed Tom, Maj. Elliot, and Lts. Cooke & Jackson, with a few of the guard, to pursue the deserters & bring them back to camp—dead or alive. Seven of the deserters, being mounted on our best horses, made their escape. Six were brought back to camp. Three were shot down while resisting arrest; these only wounded. The remaining 3, by throwing themselves on the ground & feigning death, escaped being shot. Wounds were treated, but did not prove serious. Anticipate no further trouble."

Though Colonel Custer had been plagued by drunkenness and desertion ever since he took subordinate command of the 7th Cavalry, this incident was the last straw. Scurvy-haunted, gold-hungry troopers had been slipping away at an average of fifty a month; but the July 7 loss was the largest yet for a twenty-four-hour period.

Phil Sheridan, acting as Provost Marshal of the Division of the Missouri, had instructed Custer to shoot down all bounty jumpers without benefit of court-martial. Custer had not been so cold-blooded, preferring to pardon those who surrendered without a fight, but now he had lost all patience and pity.

When the three wounded runaways came jolting back to camp, tied belly-down across their saddles, they were yelling bloody murder. Custer was first to welcome them back. Pulling his revolver, he cocked and pointed it at each of them. "If you don't stop that Goddamn racket, I'll blow your brains out!"

That shut them up at once.

Custer then ordered the other three turntails to be shaved bald, stripped bare, and paraded through camp with bugles blaring "The Rogue's March":

> Poor old soldier, poor old soldier:
> He'll be tarred and feathered and sent to Hell,
> Because he would not soldier well!

All but two of Custer's "skinners," or herd-teamsters, had been arrested for mutiny or insubordination. According to his degree of individual guilt, each was horsewhipped or spread-eagled stark naked in the roasting sun (the prey of ants and flies and other plagues) till he cried "*Peccavi*." And several troopers, seized for mutinous conspiracy, were repeatedly doused in the Platte by being horse-dragged across a ford with lariats tied to their legs. "The effect was all that could be desired," Custer soon assured his wife. "There has not been another desertion."

Custer pushed on toward Fort Wallace, about a hundred miles to the south, there to provision and await further orders. "The march to Wallace from the Platte was a forced one." So reads Custer's field book for July, 1867. However, he still blamed wholesale desertion on "the gross neglect & mismanagement of the Commissary Dept.," which "subjected both officers & men to needless privations," Hardtack and bacon boxes, marked *1860*, were sources of scurvy and dysentery. Coffee and sugar were long-lost luxuries. "That desertions will occur under the most stringent & prohibitory laws I have no doubt," Custer reported to Headquarters, "and I am equally certain that many that have taken place can be attributed to the mismanagement of the Commissary Dept." This indictment did not endear him to military bureaucrats, who bitterly awaited the opportunity to discredit "Sir Brag."

July 12. The sun was high in the heavens, burning the very soul out of a heartless land, when Colonel Custer spotted the bloated carcass of a white horse lying spectral and ominous on the shimmering plateau. He and his escort spurred forward, dismounted to examine their disquieting find. The animal had apparently been shot within the past few days; and though it was stripped of trappings, the brand *U.S.* indicated "government property."

A shudder of recognition, and each was convinced that here lay one of the mounts belonging to Lieutenant Kidder's detail—apparently ahead of them on the trail to Fort Wallace.

The column pressed on at a slow trot. Two miles had melted away, into a blinding glare that rimmed the horizon with molten fire, when they came upon another dead cavalry horse, blistered and bursting in the Kansas furnace. Unshod pony tracks were everywhere, as were the prints of shod saddlers. The suspense, the anxiety, was almost maddening.

The pace quickened. Custer's imagination worked feverishly. *A running fight!* he thought, fretting. *A race for life!* He later fancied: "How painfully, almost despairingly exciting must have been this ride for life! A mere handful of brave men struggling to escape the bloody clutches of the hundreds of red-visaged demons who, mounted on their well-trained war-ponies, were straining every nerve and muscle to reek their hands in the life-blood of their victims. It was not death alone that threatened this little band. They were not riding simply to preserve life. They rode, and doubtless prayed as they rode, that they might escape the savage tortures, the worse-than-death which threatened them. Would that their prayer had been granted!"

Arrowing into a valley where tall grass shivered in a hot breeze, Custer and the 7th saw several large buzzards gliding lazily in circles to the forward-left of the trail. A familiar reek, sickening sweet, glutted an atmosphere already heavy with heat-stench and alkali dust. It reminded Armstrong of "the horrible sensations experienced upon a battle-field when passing among the decaying bodies of the dead."

Frantic curiosity spurred them on, through rushes and willows, until "a sight met our gaze which made my very blood curdle. Lying in irregular order, and within a very limited circle, were the mangled bodies of poor Kidder and his party—yet so brutally hacked and disfigured as to be beyond recognition save as human beings. Every individual of the party had been scalped and his skull broken—the latter done by some weapon, probably a tomahawk—except the Sioux chief Red-Bead [Kidder's guide], whose scalp had simply been removed from his head and then thrown down by his side. This, [Will] Comstock [Custer's scout] informed us, was in accordance with a custom which prohibits an Indian from bearing off the scalp of one of his own tribe. This circumstance, then, told us who the perpetrators of this deed were. They could be none other than the Sioux, led in all probability by Pawnee-Killer. Red-Bead, being less disfigured and mutilated than the others, was the only individual capable of being recognized. Even the clothes of all the party had been carried away. Some of the bodies were lying in beds of ashes, with partly burned fragments of wood near them, showing that the savages had put them to death by the terrible tortures of fire. The sinews of the arms and legs had been cut away, the nose of every man hacked off, and the features otherwise defaced so that it would have been scarcely possible for even a relative to recognize a single one of the unfortunate victims. We could not even distinguish the officer from his men. Each body was pierced by from twenty to fifty arrows, and the arrows were found as the savage demons had left them—bristling in the bodies. While the details of that fearful struggle will probably never be known—telling how long and gallantly this ill-fated little band contended for their lives—yet the surrounding circumstances of ground, empty cartridge-shells and distance from where the attack began, satisfied us that Kidder and his men fought as only brave men fight when the watch-word is victory or death."

Colonel Custer wrote to Lieutenant Kidder's father, "No historian will ever chronicle the heroism which was probably here displayed. We can picture what determination, what bravery, what heroism must have inspired this devoted little band of martyrs when surrounded & assailed by a vastly overwhelming force of blood-thirsty, merciless & unrestrained barbarians—and that they manfully struggled to the last, equally devoid of hope or fear."

Silently, sadly, men of the 7th dug a common grave for their fellow soldiers of the 2nd Cavalry. *Esprit de corps,* burnt out of the regiment by a terrible land and a tireless leader, was suddenly rekindled by sparks of indignation and vengeance. Custer exploited this new burst of energy, driving his men ever harder. On, on to Fort Wallace and fresh supplies and relentless campaigning —until every hostile was humbled in the dust.

⋆8⋆

FORT RILEY: ARREST

Sundown, July 14, 1867. Jogging dog-tired into Fort Wallace, a hodgepodge of dilapidated dugouts and tumble-down shebangs, Old Curly and his flying detachment found the garrison (Captain Albert Barnitz and two companies of the 7th) half dead from starvation and disease and repeated attacks. Marauding Cheyennes had cut off the stage lines and supply trains from Kansas City to Denver.

Custer also learned that a flash flood had washed out Fort Hays, causing a mass evacuation to Fort Harker. No news of Libbie! Only two postriders and no stagecoaches for weeks. No word from General Sherman, or even General Hancock! No telegraphic communication for weeks.

Famine, fever. Stage lines broken, telegraph wires cut. Washout, emergency evacuation. Hostiles, dog-warriors. Libbie . . . *Libbie!*

Armstrong turned to his aide and adjutant, Lieutenants Thomas W. Custer and William W. Cooke, and said excitedly, "Order out a 75-man detail on the best mounts we've got. All our empty wagons as well. We're riding to Harker for rations and medicine."

Monday, July 15. A blood-red sun sank into the purple sea of the Great Plains as Colonel Custer and his special detail—many called it a "forlorn hope"—cantered eastward out of Fort Wallace.

Custer forced-marched 150 grueling miles over the Smoky Hill Stage Road to Fort Hays. He made it in fifty-five hours, at 3 A.M.

of the eighteenth, stopping only long enough to water the horses and gulp down black coffee. Burnt-out stage and telegraph stations glared at him along the roadside. Stripped, scalped, mangled, and scorched corpses—some bloated and bursting, others torn apart by carrion birds and coyotes, all riddled with arrows—littered the blistered, cactus-studded flats with skeletons.

Only two of the seventy-five troopers had been lost, picked off by Cheyenne snipers. Custer later avowed: "Frequent halts & brief rests were made along our line of march," and "occasionally we would halt long enough to indulge in a few [*i.e.,* six] hours' sleep." Those who accompanied him swore otherwise: that he drove them like the devil, until the rear became a desperate confusion of slackers who fell prey to Indian ambush and they lost two of their number. Custer merely states that they had, without authority, "halted some distance behind"—but does not say why. The fact is, after a hundred miles of relentless riding, they were too stunned to go on.

Old Hard-Arse justified his doggedness by admitting, "It was far above the usual rate of a leisurely-made march, but during the same season & with a larger Command I marched 60 miles in 15 hours. This was officially reported, but occasioned no remark." He added, after citing a ninety-miles-in-twenty-four-hours forced march made during the War, that, in 1866, "I marched a small detachment 80 miles in 17 hours—every horse accompanying the detachment completing the march in as fresh condition, apparently, as when the march began." However, still no mention of the *human* condition! At any rate, 156 deserters from the 7th Cavalry between April 18 and July 13 was a fair record compared with other regiments on the frontier, whose scurvied and demoralized members were bolting by fifties and hundreds a month.

July 18, 3 P.M. Custer caught an hour of sleep, then pushed onward. Stragglers at flood-ravaged Fort Hays told him of an explosive outbreak of cholera at Harker. All those not on the sick list had been evacuated to Fort Riley. For all he knew, Elizabeth lay dying of cholera at Fort Harker!

Custer turned to his second-in-command, Captain Louis

McLane Hamilton, and muttered sharply, "Rest the men till day-break, then move out. I'm going ahead to Harker. Supplies will be ready to load when you arrive. If any of the men give you trouble, don't hesitate to shoot. Shoot to kill!" (Twenty of the escort had already deserted.)

Armstrong, Brother Tom, Adjutant Cooke, and two volunteer troopers swung into the saddle and galloped off to Fort Harker. They made it in less than twelve hours, a distance of sixty miles, by 2 A.M. of the nineteenth.

The post was deserted except for cholera patients, doctors and nurses, and a few bummers. At last word, Libbie was all right, had left with Eliza in an ambulance, under escort, to Fort Riley. *Thank God!* Armstrong heaved a sigh of relief; yet he was still apprehensive, fretting under the least delay. Nothing would satisfy him but to see his beloved wife alive and well.

Letters awaited him, full of anguish and anxiety that made him frantic.

It was the dead of night. Custer flashed telegrams to Forts Sedgwick and Leavenworth (Sherman and Hancock), announcing the fate of Kidder and his detachment. Then he dashed into head-quarters, rousing Colonel A. J. Smith from a troubled sleep.

After Custer had rattled off a brief report, bleary-eyed Smith pointed to his absent adjutant's bunk and drawled, "Well, here is Weir's bed. Lie down and take some sleep."

"No, General!" Custer blurted, addressing his superior by Civil War rank. "I'd like to go up to Riley and see my wife. How long can you give me?"

Smith knit his brow, motioning absently. "I can't spare you. You must remain."

Custer exploded: "God damn it, sir, I *shan't* remain. The train leaves at three, and I'll be on it."

"You damned fool. How dare you?"

Custer was cut down by Smith's retort. "But, General, I see no occasion for my presence until the supply train and escort are ready to return to Wallace. I beg of you: give me a day with

Libbie. It's been two months since I last saw her, and she may be dying—even dead!—of cholera."

Smith softened, moved by the desperation in Custer's eyes and voice. "Very well. But hurry back—hurry back. We shall want you directly."

Custer nodded, darted out the doorway.

"Wait a minute! I'll go on and get Weir. He'll show you over to the depot."

Custer glanced at his watch. "It's close to three now!"

"Have no fear. You'll make it."

When Colonel Smith had fetched Adjutant-Lieutenant Thomas B. Weir, on special duty at the telegraph office, a train whistle shrilled ominously.

Custer fussed. "We must get off at once in order to catch the train."

Weir handed him an official envelope. "Orders from G.H.Q., sir."

"Damn 'em!" Custer muttered, thrusting the dispatch in his jacket and striding forward. "To the depot!"

"Remember me to Mrs. Custer, and give my respects to the ladies!" Smith called after him, smiling to think that Custer had missed the train. But that didn't stop Old Curly.

Instructing Tom and Cooke to await Hamilton and the wagons, then load them with the needed supplies for Fort Wallace, he grabbed a fresh relay horse by the halter, dashed out of Harker, and spanked seventy-five miles across the desolate prairie to Riley. One thought, one hope and vision, spurred him on: Libbie.

It was just before noon, Friday, July 19, 1867. Elizabeth Custer was heartsick, in a daze, pacing the floor of her quarters on Officers' Row. Suddenly her heart lightened at a familiar sound: the clank of a saber, and with it those brisk, bounding steps she knew so well. The door flew open.

Autie and Libbie flung themselves into each other's arms. She wept with joy, and hugged him desperately; and he, tears in his eyes, caressed her with trembling hands. Eliza, half-crying, half-scolding, flitted about like a headless hen between the kitchen and the parlor, then finally settled down to fixing a meal.

It was one, long, perfect summer day; and it would be theirs for a lifetime.

"Certainly, General Custer is a good cavalry officer: brave, energetic, intelligent. He served brilliantly during the War, and accomplished a good deal against the Confederate cavalry. What has he done against the Indians? Nothing. Vainly he exhausted men & horses, pursuing the Indians without making contact with them, and his best reports amount to four or five men killed to one of the enemy."

So reads the journal of Colonel Philippe Régis de Trobriand, French military attaché in Dakota Territory and a colorful member of McClellan's staff during the Rebellion.

Custer's summer campaign was a failure, putting a lame and impotent conclusion to Hancock's punitive spring expedition. Phantom dog-warriors had scattered and vanished, melting into the fluid fire and abysmal shadows of the prairie. They had driven the yellow-haired chief to desperation, infecting his spirit with fury and fear. Completely elusive, they hit and ran through a phantasmagoria of depredations: raiding and wrecking the railroads, robbing and raping the settlements, enraging Sherman and Hancock with murders and mutilations at a cost to themselves of only six braves killed between March and September of '67. Surely no one was to blame, for the Army had much to learn about Indian fighting and psychology, but a scapegoat was straightaway and conveniently set upon to atone for the apparent sins of omission and commission.

After Custer's diplomatic encounters with Pawnee-Killer, in which the *beau sabreur* acted on his own hook, Sherman took a dim view of him whom he had described as "very brave even to rashness—a good trait for a Cavalry officer."

". . . He has not too much sense," the General decided, adding that Old Curly had "no excuses to offer for his attempt to act a political part."

Although "I can't well do without him," Colonel Smith merely regarded Custer as a "dandified young buck." General Hancock seemed to concur—still envisioning Armstrong as the slipshod, curly-pated, pink-cheeked, devil-be-damned maverick at Williamsburg who "was glad to aid Gen'l Hancock on that day" and who "captured a Captain & 5 men without any assistance, and a large Rebel flag!"

No sooner had Lieutenant Colonel Custer reached Fort Riley than he was handed a telegram from Colonel Smith, ordering him to return to Harker at once. It was as if Custer had left without permission! Accompanying the curt directive was a copy of Hancock's special orders of July 13, stating: "The Cavalry should be kept constantly employed."

Armstrong raced back to Harker by rail, demanding an explanation from Old Rawhide.

"Take your troubles to Hancock," Smith answered angrily. "You read the S.O. He wants you constantly employed, and I regret having let you go without his knowledge."

Custer, obedient to duty, acquiesced without an argument. What need? He had seen Libbie and comforted her. Yes, "There was in that summer of 1867 one long, perfect day." She worshiped him for it: his noble sacrifice, his *beau geste*. "It was mine, and—blessed be our memory, which preserves to us the joys as well as the sadness of life!—it is still mine, for time and for eternity." To a devoted wife this was sufficient justification for one of the biggest mistakes of her husband's life.

Sunday, July 28. Lieutenant Colonel George Armstrong Custer was placed under arrest, pending court-martial proceedings, by order of Major General Winfield Scott Hancock. Charges were preferred by Colonel Andrew Jackson Smith and Captain Robert M. West.

Yes, Colonel Smith had once said of Custer, "God damn that dandified young buck, I can't well do without him!" But when reprimanded by General Hancock for allowing Custer to abandon his command in savage territory, and at a dangerous and desperate time, Smith changed his mind and washed his hands of the whole affair. Why should he be held responsible for Custer's caprices? So he preferred charges to save his own skin.

And what of Captain West? How did he fit into this controversy? By now, all the officers of the 7th Cavalry were about equally divided for and against Old Curly. West happened to head the clique *against*.

"But why notice it?" Armstrong reasoned with an indignant Elizabeth. "Don't I know what *I've* been through to gain *my* victory! That fellow, you must remember, has fought and lost— and knows in his soul he'll go to the dogs if he doesn't hold up— and Libbie, he can't do it, and I'm sorry for him."

West had indeed lost! A brigadier general during the War, cited for valor at Five Forks, he had been "kicked downstairs" to captain. For Robert West, the record read: "Arrest for intoxication while on duty" and "Drunk & disorderly when on duty." Custer, who had precious little patience with boozers, was therefore hard on him, assigning him menial tasks worthy of a shavetail, in hopes of "straightening him out." West reveled in his revenge.

★9★

FORT LEAVENWORTH: THE TRIAL

THE accused was escorted a hundred miles east to Fort Leavenworth, there to stand trial. The accused's wife went with him on the train. Sheridan, then in Washinton, offered them his rent-free quarters. On military parole, Custer was not obliged to sit in jail.

From September through November, 1867, Custer kept up a steady correspondence with an old acquaintance, the noted lawyer-statesman Robert J. Walker, former Secretary of the Treasury and Governor of Kansas Territory. On September 30, Armstrong wrote: "I have obtained evidence that last spring, when desertions were so numerous, Gen'l Hancock telegraphed Gen'l Sheridan to shoot deserters down. Gen'l Sheridan has been summoned to testify that he ordered me to shoot without trial for the same offence. He himself called my attention to this, and urged me to introduce it in evidence. He assured me that in any & all circumstances I could count on him as my friend, and that the authorities in Washington regard my trial as an attempt by Hancock to cover up the failure of the Indian expedition. Capt. West is drinking himself to death—has delirium-tremens, to such an extent the Prosecution will not put him on the witness-stand!"

Libbie wrote to her anxious father-in-law: "How little the trial troubles us! It is progressing finely for Aut. . . . Autie took a leave himself, knowing none would be granted him, and Gen'l Hancock ordered his arrest. It sounds quite solemn to unaccustomed ears, but officers look on it as an ordinary occurrence—

especially when one has done so little worthy of punishment as Aut has. When he ran the risk of a court-martial in leaving Ft. Wallace, he did it expecting the consequences. But he did it for *me,* above all else; and we are quite determined not to live apart again, even if it means he must leave the Army otherwise so delightful to us."

Captain West, leading witness for the prosecution, eventually testified he heard Colonel Custer issue the following orders to Major Elliot on the day three deserters were shot down: "Stop those men! Shoot them where you find them. Don't bring in any alive."

Captain Frederick W. Benteen, another anti-Custerite, gave evidence he heard his commanding officer shout to Lieutenants Custer, Cooke, and Jackson, "Bring back none of those men alive." He then elaborated: "It was like a buffalo hunt. The dismounted deserters were shot down, while begging for their lives, by General Custer's executioners: Major Elliot, Lieutenant Tom Custer, and the executioner-in-chief, Lieutenant Cooke. . . . Three of the deserters were brought in badly wounded, and screaming in extreme agony. General Custer rode up to them, pistol in hand, and told them if they didn't stop making so much fuss he would shoot them to death."

Both West and Benteen said that when the regimental surgeon dared to approach the three wounded runaways, Custer stopped him and said, "Doctor, don't go near those men. I have no sympathy for them."

Dr. I. T. Coates, a personal friend of his commanding officer, later testified that Custer gave such an order only as a threat to potential deserters—that none, if wounded in flight, would receive medical treatment—for soon thereafter, Coates added, Custer whispered to him, "My sympathies are not with those men, but I want you to give them all necessary attention. I'll have them placed in a wagon, out of sight. You may attend them after a while."

The prisoners were subsequently treated in full at Fort Wallace, where pure water could be had for dressing wounds. One of them died there on July 17, allegedly of "bad treatment."

Hard-drinking Fred Benteen had a studied contempt for Custer that dated back to their first meeting at Fort Riley, in the winter of '66. Benteen, like West, had been a distinguished brigadier of volunteer cavalry during the War; and he had shared his fellow officer's fate of having been reduced to captaincy and subordinated to "the most self-appointed general in this man's army." A staunch cynic-realist, disenchanted and embittered by personal tragedies, Benteen could stand no "romantic nonsense" in the dirty game of war. For this reason, Old Curly was, in his jaundiced eyes, a detestable farce.

Benteen, with sardonic deliberation, bore witness to Custer's brutalization of his troops: "The gang of prisoners were marched through company streets, preceded by trumpets sounding *The Rogue's March*. Their heads were then shaved, and the poor devils were spread-eagled on the plain until they cried 'peccavi.' I reported this to Department Headquarters. . . . On arrival at Fort McPherson, the same orders issued at Hays were carried out. Men of the command arrested were soused in the Platte River—a lariat having been tied to their legs—and this repeated till they were nearly drowned. This also I reported to D.H.Q." In conclusion, Benteen accused Custer of evicting sick and foot-sore troopers from the hospital wagons to make room for his sick and footsore dogs. The courtroom rumbled with laughter.

Charges of "excessive cruelty" and "illegal conduct" were challenged when Sherman's, Sheridan's, and Hancock's official orders to shoot or otherwise punish all bounty jumpers and mutineers were placed in evidence.

Custer explained away the forced-marching charge to the amusement of all but the accusers. He said: "Forced marching is one of the necessary evils of war. Sinful? Yes. But scarcely unorthodox!"

The charge of lost government mounts was laughed out of court when Custer offered to pay for them out of his own pocket. No one seemed to know exactly how many were lost! "Only seven, so far as I know," Custer testified. "Surely I can't be held accountable for them! I should first have to find the seven deserters who took them, and even that is no guarantee they are all still in unlawful possession of seven United States horses!"

The two troopers whom Custer allegedly "allowed to be killed" were sniped by Indians at Downer's Station, about fifty miles west of Fort Hays. "These men had halted without authority some distance behind the command, when they were jumped by twenty-five or thirty Indians. Had they kept in the ranks, or even offered any defense, this would not have occurred. Instead, they put spurs to their horses and attempted to escape by flight. Two of them were killed in the running. Lost in the line of duty? I should think not! If desertion was their game, they paid dearly for it."

But Custer was also accused of abandoning their bodies without burial, of not pursuing the attackers or even halting long enough to investigate the incident. He answered that the station patrol buried them, and that time and circumstances did not allow chasing a few snipers like will-o'-the-wisps. But Custer was still a murderer in Benteen's eyes.

The most serious accusation, that of being A.W.O.L. from Fort Wallace, wasn't so easily rationalized. But Custer forged ahead regardless.

"As to my leaving Fort Wallace without permission: I had to leave Fort Wallace and get to Fort Harker—the nearest point of open communications—in order to obtain permission to leave Fort Wallace, where I vainly expected to find General Hancock or due instructions from General Sherman. Finding neither, I was obliged to place myself in a position of discovery." He then added emphatically: "Without fear of contradiction, I assert that had I failed to report at Harker or the nearest point of direct communication—and had General Hancock been there awaiting me, as I then supposed he was, and had any misfortunate result in the campaign ensued—had this been the case, I assert without fear of contradiction that I would have been court-martialed for disobedience of orders. And yet, for obeying those orders—

which, it seems to me, could not be mistaken—I am being court-martialed today."

Custer stated that on June 14, while he was at Fort McPherson, General Sherman arrived from Fort Sedgwick, giving him a free hand to hunt hostiles along the Republican River. "Don't confine yourself to orders if your better judgment leads you elsewhere. Go to Denver City, if you wish. You can even go to Hell, if you want to!" These were Old Tecumseh's characteristic words as Custer recalled them.

Custer's defense counsel, one-time fellow cadet at the Point, Major Charles C. Parsons, produced in evidence General Hancock's dispatch of July 13, 1867: "To Gen'l Smith, Comdg. Dist. of Upper Arkansas: The Maj.-Gen'l Comdg. desires you to give instructions to Gen'l Custer's Command, which it is understood will arrive at Ft. Wallace about the 17th inst., that until further orders it will operate thro' Ft. Wallace as a base & between the Arkansas & the Platte. He will habitually draw his supplies from Ft. Wallace, but a sufficient quantity of supplies has been placed at Fts. Hays, Dodge, Larned & Lyons, in order that if he should find it necessary to visit these forts he will be able to obtain ample supplies. . . . The Cavalry should be kept constantly employed."

Parsons rightly contended that the defendant had obeyed these orders to the letter; that he had reached Fort Wallace only to find it in a state of siege and privation, and that in order to keep his command "constantly employed," he found it necessary to visit Fort Hays for "ample supplies." His trips to Forts Harker and Riley were justified by General Sherman's wire of June 27: "I don't understand about Gen'l Custer being on the Republican, awaiting supplies from Ft. Wallace. If this be so, and he finds that all the Indians have gone south, convey to him my orders that he proceed with all his Command in search of the Indians towards Ft. Wallace & report to Gen'l Hancock, who will leave Denver for same place to-day."

When Custer arrived at Wallace, expecting to find "further orders," he found that Hancock had passed on toward Leavenworth (Dept. Hd.-Qrs.) without a word to anyone. Duty therefore obliged Custer to "report to Gen'l Hancock," wherever he may have been! And that duty took him all the way to Riley—and Libbie.

Sherman's directing Custer to report at once to Fort Wallace and await further orders had been supplemented by a communiqué from Hancock, signed by Smith's adjutant. When Weir testified for the defense, Custer presented it as evidence:

> Hd.-Qrs., Dist. Upper Ark.
> In the Field, Ft. Harker, Kas.
> July 16th, 1867

Bvt. Maj.-Gen'l G. A. Custer, Comdg. 7th U.S. Cavalry
General:

The Bvt. Maj.-Gen'l Comdg. [Smith] directs me to forward to you the accompanying communication from Dept. Hd.-Qrs. [Hancock] for your information & guidance, and to say that he expects you to keep your Command as actively employed as the condition of the animals will permit. You will see by the communication referred to that you are not restricted in your movements to the vicinity of Ft. Wallace, but are to operate wherever the presence or movements of Indians may lead you.

I am, very resp't'y, y'r obed't Serv't,
> *T. B. Weir*
> 1st Lieut. 7th Cav., A.A.A.Gen.

The official catch, however, lay in those last words: "wherever the presence or movements of Indians may lead you." No such presence or movements led Custer all the way to Fort Harker. But he had a damned good excuse, he thought. With all communications cut off, the garrison at Fort Wallace was on its last legs for want of food and medicine. Such a critical state of affairs made this "last, lone outpost" vulnerable to Indian attack. He therefore determined to save the garrison from certain death by disease, starvation, and massacre by running the gantlet for relief supplies. And that he did, without leaving the fort unprotected in his temporary absence!

But what justified his making that lone, hard ride to Fort Riley—and Libbie? Oh, he was looking for General Hancock! Not finding him at Harker, Custer reckoned he must be at Riley. He wished to report to him in person for detailed instructions concerning the perilous situation at Wallace. Unfortunately, the General wasn't to be found at Riley. He was in Leavenworth at the time. And even more unfortunate—for no sound, logical reason whatsoever!—Colonel Smith then preferred charges, Captain West ardently supported them, and General Hancock ordered Colonel Custer's immediate arrest.

Major Joel H. Elliot, followed by other members of the so-called Custer Gang, substantiated their commanding officer's testimony: "Not finding General Hancock at Fort Wallace, General Custer said that he was ordered by General Sherman to report to Hancock and was disappointed at not finding him there. In the absence of further instructions, General Custer told me he felt it his duty to follow General Hancock to Fort Harker, report to him, and ascertain what orders—if any—were awaiting him. . . . When General Custer left Fort Wallace, it was my opinion—and, so far as I can testify, that of all the other officers—that the command would not be engaged, or in condition to be actively engaged, for at least three or four weeks. The horses were nearly all barefoot, and required shoeing; and the first horseshoes in sufficient quantities for issuing to the command reached Wallace about the fourth or fifth of August, by a train escorted by Captain Hamilton. My energies were therefore fully employed, for nearly a month, in recuperating the command and preparing it for the field. Without supplies, and without shoes, the cavalry could hardly have been kept constantly engaged as ordered by General Hancock, who was nowhere to be consulted."

Enough said!

On Sunday, October 13, Libbie wrote to Pop Custer: "The Court closed yesterday. The final decision may not be heard for some time, from Washington, but Autie will hear by telegram from Gov't friends. The trial has developed into nothing but a plan of persecution for Autie. I can't write much! In two days

this (last) week I copied about 50 pages of foolscap for the
defence—a labor of love, of course."

Custer remarked to Parsons: "The court is packed against me.
That's easy to see!"

Captain Robert Chandler, Hancock's aide-de-camp, acted as
judge advocate. The tribunal numbered Smith's and Hancock's
friends. The die was cast.

On November 8, the Washington Bureau of Military Justice
issued a "Review of the Trial of Gen'l G. A. Custer" to War
Secretary Lorenzo Thomas:

> Bvt. Maj.-Gen'l G. A. Custer, Lt.-Col. 7th U.S. Cavalry, was
> tried in Sept. & Oct. last by Gen'l Court-Martial convened at
> Ft. Leavenworth, Kansas, by order of the General-in-Chief,
> under the following Charges:
>
> I. Absent without leave from his Command
>   Finding: *Guilty*
>   In that Accused did, at or near Ft. Wallace, Kans., on
> or about July 15th last, absent himself from his Command
> without proper authority & proceed to Ft. Harker, Kans., a
> distance of about 275 miles: this at a time when his Com-
> mand was expected to be actively engaged against the
> Indians.
>
> II. Conduct to the prejudice of good order & military disci-
>   pline
>   Finding: *Guilty*
>   1. Finding: *Guilty.* In that Accused, immediately after
> his Command had completed a long & exhausting march,
> and when the horses belonging thereto had not been rested
> & were unfit for service, did select a portion of said Com-
> mand (namely 3 Comdg. Officers & about 75 men, with their
> horses) and did execute a rapid march from Ft. Wallace to
> Ft. Hays: the said march being upon private business & with-
> out authority, and damaging the horses of the detachment.
>   2. Finding: *Guilty,* but attach no criminality. In that
> Accused, while executing an unauthorized journey on private
> business from Ft. Wallace to Ft. Riley, did procure certain

mules belonging to the U. S. for the conveyance of himself & part of his escort: this July 17th, 1867.

3. Finding: *Guilty*. In that Accused, when near Downer's Station, Kans., July 16th, 1867, after receiving information that a party of Indians had attacked a small party detached from his escort near said station, did fail to take proper measures for the repulse of said Indians, or the defence or relief of said detachment; and further, after the return of such detached party with report that 2 of their number had been killed, did neglect to take any measures to pursue such Indians or recover or bury the bodies of those killed.

Addit'l Charges (Conduct prejudicial to good order & military discipline)
Finding: *Guilty*

1. Finding: *Guilty*. In that Accused, while en route commanding & marching a column of his Regt. (6 Companies strong) from the Valley of the Platte River to the Valley of the Smoky Hill River, did, when ordering a party of 3 Officers & others of his Command in pursuit of supposed deserters who were then in sight leaving camp, also order the said party to shoot the supposed deserters dead & to bring none in alive: this on "Custer's Cavalry Column Trail," 15 miles south of Platte River, 50 miles S.W. of Ft. Sedgwick, Col. Terr., July 7th, 1867.

2. Finding: *Guilty*. In that Accused did order enlisted men of his Command to be shot down as deserters, but without trial, and did thus cause 3 men to be severely wounded: this July 7th, 1867.

3. Finding: *Guilty*, but attach no criminality. In that Accused, after 3 of his Command had been shot down & wounded by his order, did order said men to be placed in a Gov't wagon & hauled 18 miles, neglecting & refusing to permit them to receive medical treatment: this July 7th, 1867.

4. Finding: *Guilty*. In that Accused did order & cause the summary shooting as a deserter, but without trial, of one Priv. Chas. Johnson, Co. E, 7th Cav.; whereby said Johnson was so severely wounded that he soon after (to wit, on

the 17th July, 1867, at or near Ft. Wallace, Kans.) did die: this July 7th, 1867.

The Accused pleaded "Not Guilty" under all the Charges & Specifications.

The conclusion unavoidably reached . . . is that Gen'l Custer's anxiety to see his family at Ft. Riley overcame his appreciation of the paramount necessity to obey orders which is incumbent on every military officer, and that the excuses he offers for his act of insubordination are after-thoughts.

The Court find the Accused as indicated in the margin of each Specification, . . . and sentence him:

Sentence: To be suspended from rank & command for one (1) year, and forfeit his pay proper for the same time.

Wednesday, November 20. Libbie broke the news to Pop Custer: "Father, the sentence is unjust as possible. Autie merits acquittal. . . . It does not disturb us, tho', for now we can be together. . . . Autie & I are the wonder of the garrison, we are in such spirits!"

"Custer was the most convenient scapegoat [for the "ridiculous failure" of Hancock's campaign]," says Whittaker; "so they degraded him, on a flimsy pretence," because it seemed "necessary to punish some one to silence public sneers." However, convicted of being absent without leave from Fort Wallace, Custer received a commuted sentence of temporary rather than permanent suspension. President Johnson, Secretary Thomas, and General Sheridan each had a hand in saving him from a "bobtail" or dishonorable discharge by the Judge Advocate General's Office.

General Grant noted in his official endorsement: "The reviewing officer, in examining the testimony in the case, is convinced that the Court, in awarding so lenient a sentence for the offences of which the Accused is found guilty, must have taken into consideration his previous services."

Colonel Custer dropped a line to his friend and adviser, Mr. Walker: "All with whom I have conversed deem the verdict not sustained by the evidence, as I have been adjudged guilty on some specification on which the Judge-Advocate declined to take testimony; viz., my journey to Ft. Riley 'on private business.' However, I have written Gen'l Sheridan to make no effort to obtain a remission of any portion of my sentence. I would not accept it. . . . I am like Micawber, 'waiting for something to turn up.' "

Something turned up soon enough. The ghost of Major Wyckliff Cooper, kingpin of the anti-Custer ring before his suicide. Smarting at not having succeeded in busting Custer to an inglorious civvy, Captain West and his coterie ("a crew of drunken pickpockets," as Old Curly called them) received the vociferous and venomous support of Cooper's friends and family in blaming Custer for his disgraceful death, officially listed as "from excessive drinking." They besieged the War Department for satisfaction; and when that failed, they hinted the "yellow peacock" had paid Brother Tom (who first found the body) to shoot the Major.

Captain Benteen openly asserted: "Major Cooper was out of whisky when he shot himself because that damned fool Dr. Coates, acting under orders from Custer, wouldn't even give him a drink to straighten out on." But he was the only anti-Custerite prudent enough not to accuse "*le grand poseur*" of staging a suicide.

The Bureau of Military Justice, prodded by certain pressure groups, suggested that Custer be tried for murder—the "murder" of Trooper Johnson—but deigned to leave such a decision to President Johnson and General Grant. Not wishing to be embroiled in further controversy, the unpopular Chief Executive washed his hands of the whole affair. And the General-in-Chief merely commented (*pro forma*) that "the leniency of that sentence, considering the nature of the offences of which Gen'l Custer is found guilty, is to be remarked on."

On January 3, 1868, the tree of vengeance bore fruit. Colonel Custer and Lieutenant Cooke were arrested on a civil charge of murder. Accused of having caused the death of a teamster, by flogging and exposure, they were arraigned on the eighth by Judge Adams of Leavenworth. When it could not be proven that the skinner died of a sunstroke induced by brutalization, the defendants were discharged. Thus, a last-ditch effort at "nailing"

Custer "before a court of competent jurisdiction" failed miserably.

According to anti-Custerites, the so-called Custer Clan ("those damned cormorants" to Captain Benteen) was a gang of murderers, thieves, liars, and "arrant, rascally, beggarly, lousy knaves." And "there were many officers in the 7th who wouldn't have believed Gen. Custer on oath!" Worst of all, the great stickler was himself an insubordinate. "From Hancock, Custer performed his first 'cutting loose' act. Hancock didn't relish it, and rounded him up."

Armstrong didn't trouble himself to answer his accusers in kind. Though even General Hancock had turned against him to save face, which seemed more justifiable than grinding an ax, Custer had no regrets. Not as long as he had Libbie. And his brilliant war record. These they could never take from him.

⋆10⋆

INDIAN TERRITORY:
BATTLE OF THE WASHITA

Monroe, Michigan. Thursday evening, September 24, 1868. Armstrong and Elizabeth had just sat down to dinner at the Emanuel H. Custer residence when the doorbell jingled. A moment later, kid-brother Boston rushed into the dining room waving a telegram. Armstrong ripped it open and read:

> Hd.-Qrs., Dept. of the Mo.
> In the Field, Ft. Hays, Kans.
> Sept. 24th, 1868
>
> *Gen'l G. A. Custer*
> Monroe, Mich.
> Gen'ls Sherman, Sully & myself, and nearly all the Officers of your Regt., have asked for you; and I hope the application will be successful. Can you come at once? 11 Cos. of your Regt. will move about the 1st of Oct. against hostile Indians, from Medicine-Lodge Creek toward the Wichita Mts.
> *P. H. Sheridan*
> Maj.-Gen'l Comdg. Mil. Dept. Mo.

Could he come at once! Too excited to eat, Armstrong kissed his wonder-stricken wife and dashed down to the telegraph office. An answer flashed over the wires to Sheridan, Hancock's successor, at Fort Hays: "Will start to join you by next train."

Even before official confirmation of his reinstatement, Custer was racing southwestward to the Great Plains, just as fast as the iron horse could carry him. Libbie would follow, as soon as she finished packing, bearing with her that document.

Custer later wrote that he did not regard his arrest and trial "in a fault-finding spirit. I have no fault to find. It is said that blessings sometimes come in disguise. Such proved to be true in this instance."

A fellow officer regarded Custer as "a natural optimist. He took rose-colored views of everything." More aptly fatalistic, *Beau Sabreur* flattered himself: "It is a happy disposition that can content itself in all phases of fortune by saying that 'that which cannot be cured must be endured.' I had frequent recourse to this and similar consoling expressions in the endeavor to reconcile myself to the separation from my Command."

If the disgrace of "rustication" had no profound effect upon him, inactivity certainly had rankled Custer's restless spirit. A man who could rationalize his chastisement as a blessing in disguise—as an "unintentional favor" on the part of those "who, whether intentionally or not, had been a party to my retirement"— must have pretended that he was "living in involuntary but unregretful retirement from active service."

In any case, according to Sherman, Custer was "ready & willing now to fight the Indians, instead of visiting his wife & ruining his Regt."

"We ask only to be let alone," proclaimed Black-Kettle (*Mô-katâvatâ*), Chief of the Cheyenne Nation. "All we want is that you yellowfaces keep out of our country. We don't want to fight you. This is *our* country. The Great Spirit gave it to us. Keep out, and we will be friends."

White America was trekking west, but Black-Kettle shut his eyes to the handwriting on the wall. And the proudest of his people, with blood in their eyes, vowed to hold the white wolf by the ears.

War parties of Cheyenne, Arapaho, Kiowa, Comanche, Plains Apache, and Sioux continued to terrorize white settlements in

Kansas, Colorado, and Texas. In less than two months at one period, 124 homesteaders were burned out and killed.

On August 17, 1868, Governor Crawford wired President Johnson: "I have just returned from N.W. Kansas, the scene of a terrible Indian massacre. On the 13th & 14th inst., 40 of our citizens were killed & wounded by hostile Indians. Men, women & children were murdered indiscriminately. Many of them were scalped, and their bodies mutilated. Women, after receiving mortal wounds, were outraged & otherwise inhumanly treated in the presence of their dying husbands & children."

Crawford demanded immediate government action; and his appeals, piling up with those of railroad officials and army officers, resulted in "Executive Clemency" for Colonel Custer.

Black-Kettle, though understandably malcontent, was no troublemaker; and his token efforts for peace with the white intruders did not endear him to his old associates, headed by Kiowa Chief Satanta (White-Bear). Though not directly responsible for the evil elements in his midst, Black-Kettle encouraged them by his appeasement and double talk. But with Indian law so loose, and each tribe a stratocracy of independent powers, the old Cheyenne was obliged to ignore, if not to indulge, the worst of his people.

A firm believer in "our manifest destiny," Sherman declared: "Either the Indians must give way or we must abandon all west of the Missouri River & confess that 40,000,000 whites are cowed by a few thousand savages. . . . I have stretched my power & authority to help them; but when they laugh at our cordiality, rape our women, murder our men, burn whole trains with their drivers to cinders & send word they never intended to keep their treaties, then we must fight them." He added pointedly: "When we come to fight Indians, I will take my code from soldiers & not from civilians." A loud-resounding slap at what Custer called "well-meaning but mistaken philanthropists" and "pretended but not disinterested friends of the Indians"!

Colonel Wynkoop, Agent for the Cheyennes and Arapahoes, was foremost among the profiteers who insisted that arming the Indians was tantamount to befriending them. Indian Affairs Commissioner N. G. Taylor replied: "If you are satisfied that the issue of arms & ammunition is necessary to preserve the peace, and that no evil will result from their delivery, let the Indians have them."

The Colonel did—about 240 pistols and rifles, with ample powder and lead—and the result was one of the most bloody outbursts of red savagery ever experienced in the Missouri Division. In August of '68, a war party of 260 "braves" abandoned Wynkoop's Fort Larned Reservation and perpetrated a series of murders, rapes, plunders, and burnings that caused Governors Crawford and Hall to declare Kansas and Colorado a disaster area.

Indian Affairs Superintendent Thomas Murphy notified Commissioner Taylor of unprovoked depredations, adding, "I earnestly recommend that the Indians who have committed these gross outrages be turned over to the Military, and that they be severely punished. When I reflect that at the very time these Indians were making such loud professions of friendship at Larned, receiving their annuities, &c., they were then contemplating & planning this campaign, I can no longer have confidence in what they say or promise. War is surely upon us."

General Sherman, in a communiqué to Secretary of War John M. Schofield, supported Murphy's recommendation and disposition: "All the Cheyennes & Arapahoes are now at war. Admitting that some of them have not done acts of murder, rape, &c., still they have not restrained those who have; nor have they on demand given up the criminals as they agreed to do. The treaty made at Medicine-Lodge [in 1867] is, therefore, already broken by them. . . . No better time could be possibly chosen than the present for destroying or humiliating those bands that have so outrageously violated their treaties & begun a devastating war without one particle of provocation; and after a reasonable time given for the innocent to withdraw, I will solicit an order from the President declaring all Indians who remain outside of their lawful reservations to be outlaws, and commanding all people—soldiers & citizens—to proceed against them as such."

But the innocent would not withdraw, and so they would suffer with the guilty. Sherman's policy was approved by General Grant: "Our settlements, &c., must be protected—even if the extermination of every Indian tribe is necessary to secure such a result." Even General C. C. Augur, liberal member of the Indian Peace Commission ("The Olive-Branchers" or "Quakers"), admitted that "the Indians must be terribly whipped before they can appreciate kindness."

In September and October, 1868, Sherman advised and apprized Grant and Schofield: "No better time could possibly be chosen than the present for destroying or humbling those bands that have so outrageously violated their treaties. I hope he [Sheridan] may get hold of them & obliterate them. . . . I will urge Gen'l Sheridan to push his measures for the utter destruction & subjugation of all who are outside [the Reservation] in a hostile attitude. I propose that he shall prosecute the war with vindictive earnestness against all hostile Indians, till they are obliterated or beg for mercy."

Red-faced General Sheridan slammed his fist down on the field table. "The only good Indians I ever saw were dead!"

Red-faced General Sherman nodded. "Yes; and the more we can kill this year, the less we'll have to kill next year. For the more I see of these Goddamn red devils, the more convinced I am that they all have to be killed or be maintained as a species of paupers. Their attempts at civilization are simply ridiculous. We have tried kindness, till it is construed as weakness. Now we must deal with 'em on their own terms."

Custer listened in patient silence. He did not hate "redskins," but it wasn't his job to love them. He understood the Indian—even sympathized with him—but it wasn't his duty to tolerate. He was obliged to return evil for evil, and no flexible conscience was needed in the light of Indian atrocities.

Lieutenant Colonel Custer rode out of Fort Hays for Fort Dodge, seventy-five miles southwest on the Arkansas River, there to join his command. It was Sunday, October 4, 1868. Before he left, he breakfasted with Little Phil and received his first instructions.

"Custer, I rely on you in everything. You're the only man that never failed me. That's why I'm sending you on this expedition without special orders, leaving you to act entirely on your own judgment. Since nothing positive is known as to the exact whereabouts of Black-Kettle's lodges, any instructions I might give would have to be general in terms. Just scout out the winter hidingplaces of hostiles, and settle the score wherever you find 'em."

Custer reached Fort Dodge in a couple of days—"rather good for some one out of practice!"—and found Brigadier General Alfred Sully (commanding the Upper Arkansas District) with a punitive force consisting of the 3rd U.S. Infantry (five companies), the 19th Kansas Volunteer Cavalry (Ex-Governor and Colonel S. J. Crawford commanding), and eleven troops of the notorious 7th U.S. Regular Cavalry.

Custer's estimation of Sully as a soldier was anything but favorable, for Sully was one of those "featherbed generals" whose habits placed him "comfortably stowed away in his ambulance" while on campaign. Custer, the inexhaustible man of action, had little patience for or understanding of age-induced infirmities. So a clash was inevitable.

Sully's column, with Custer and the 7th spearheading it, pulled out of Fort Dodge on November 12. Their destination was Indian Territory, that unrevealed mystery south of the Arkansas. A week later found them establishing a base of operations on North Fork of the Canadian River, seventy-five miles south of Dodge. This was Camp Supply. Sheridan, commanding the Missouri Military Department "in the field," arrived soon thereafter with last-minute instructions for Sully and Custer.

Armstrong noticed that Phil, with advancing age, had taken on the aspect of "a low-comedy man"—to borrow the expression of one reporter—and that his squatty hulk and careless attire, close-cut iron-gray hair and ruddy weatherworn face composed a "grotesque figure," a true "guy." But he was still the fire-eater of the

Shenandoah, Sheridan the Bold, and his orders were explicit: "You will proceed south in the direction of the Antelope Hills, then toward the Washita River, the supposed winter seat of the hostile tribes. You will destroy their villages and ponies, kill or hang all warriors, and bring back all women and children alive."

Jim Bridger, celebrated pioneer-scout, spoke up: "Ginral, you cain't hunt Injuns on the Plains in winter; for blizzards don't respect man or beast."

"All the better for us!" Custer answered. "We can move; the Indians can't. If we attempted to fight 'em in a warmer season, as was our old mistake, we should yield to them the advantages of climate and supplies, of bountiful forage for their ponies, immense herds of game for their war parties, allowing them to move freely from point to point. We should then be meeting them on ground of their own selection. Winter will hold 'em down for the kill."

Custer then persuaded Sheridan to leave the infantry behind, and with them General Sully. "They'll only hamper our progress in tracking the hostiles, and I'm firmly confident the 7th Cavalry is equal to any band of Indians on the Plains."

Indeed, Old Iron-Arse had licked his eight hundred troopers into perfect shape, and had introduced inspiriting competition by organizing a company of sharpshooters under the command of crack-shot Lieutenant Cooke. He even instituted a "coloring of the horses," whereby each company was distinguished for its breed of mount, the better to promote *esprit de corps*. "There is no need of fluttering guidons & stirring trumpet-calls to identify them," noted one observer. "Something in the snap & style of the whole regiment stamps them at once. I know the 7th Cavalry at a glance."

What need of "Old Featherbed" Sully and his footsloggers? What need, indeed, for Colonel Crawford and his omnium-gatherum of ill-mounted and ill-trained volunteers? Leave 'em all behind! "The 7th can handle anything it meets."

Sheridan nodded. "I believe it can. The field is entirely yours."

Custer was ecstatic. That night, the 7th Cavalry's band serenaded General Sheridan. Sully retired to Fort Dodge in disgust. Phil's pet, "like Balaam's ass," had stolen his thunder.

On Sunday evening, November 22, Armstrong dashed off a letter to "My Sweet Little Army Crow" at Fort Leavenworth: "Some of the officers think this may be a campaign on paper, but I know Gen'l Sheridan better. We are going into the heart of Indian country, where white troops have never been before. . . . My official actions shall not be tarnished by a single unjust or partial act. I do not long for glory or fame; I only long for my little girl. My reward is centered on ending this trying separation as soon as possible."

Daybreak, November 23, 1868. Bundled in buffalo robe and fur cap, full-bearded Colonel Custer made a last-minute inspection of his wagon train, and rode up to General Sheridan's tent for the usual farewell.

"So long, old boy," Phil said with a hearty handshake. "Take care of yourself. Keep me informed if anything turns up. And good luck!"

Custer saluted. "If this white stuff stays on the ground a week, I promise you—we'll get our Indians." His sharp voice shattered the brittle air. "Trumpeter, sound *To Horse!* . . . Seventh Cavalry, prepare to mount! *Mount!* . . . Seventh Cavalry, by column of twos, forward *ho!*" The "Advance" blared, instantly muffled by the gray-horsed band booming *"The Girl I Left Behind Me"*;

> Then to the West we bore away
> To win a name in story,
> And there where sets the sun of day
> There dawn'd our sun of glory . . .

Compass in hand, Old Curly pranced far out in front—beyond the scouts and guides, into the blinding storm, his horse knee-deep in frosty flakes. He was again in his element.

Thursday, November 26, 1868. 10 P.M. The sharp crunching of hoofs on the hard crust of frozen snow blanketing the Washita

River valley, Indian (Oklahoma) Territory, was a ghostly sound in the vast sepulchral stillness. A long ribbon of wraithlike forms snaked steadily southward by moonlight. Camp Supply, about sixty miles away to the north, now seemed like part of a lost world. Custer and his 7th Cavalry were piercing the heart of Redman's Land. Looming up on either hand were the majestic and forbidding Antelope Hills, "those boundless solitudes—so silent that their silence alone increases their grandeur."

Chief Little-Beaver, head of the Osage scouts, stalked along on foot beside the yellow-haired chief. Suddenly he stopped, sniffing the cold air.

Custer checked his mount, raised his hand for a halt. "What's the matter?" he whispered, glancing at the shadowy terrain ahead.

"Me don't know," Little-Beaver gestured with frosty breath, "but me smell fire."

Yellowhair perked up his foxlike nose. "I don't smell anything." He looked back and swung his arm. "Let's keep moving."

A half-mile later, Little-Beaver pointed to the black belt of timber on their left. "Look," he muttered. "Me told you so."

Custer saw a handful of glowing ashes on the edge of the woods. He grinned. "Redman has better nose than whiteman. That fire must have been set by ponyboys. A sure sign we're near our game." Yellowhair slipped off his horse. "Little-Beaver, you and Hard-Rope follow me. We'll go up on that rise and have a look."

The two Osages nodded, gliding after him like panthers. Just before they reached the crest of the ridge, Little-Beaver motioned for Custer and Hard-Rope to hang back while he took a cautionary look.

Custer watched intently as the gray-haired chief crept forward to the top of the pine-clustered hill and gazed out into the valley beyond. Little-Beaver instantly flicked his hand up above his eyes—a sign that he saw something—then crouched down and came creeping back.

"What is it?" Custer asked with bated breath.

Little-Beaver pointed. "Heaps Injuns down there."

Custer crept up to the crest, the two Osages at his heels. Keeping low, so as not to be seen in the moonlight, he peered over the brow of the hill and sighted a huge dark mass on the flats below—about a half-mile away.

Custer looked long and hard, then whispered to Little-Beaver: "What makes you think that's Black-Kettle down there? Could be a herd of buffalo, or even wild horses."

Little-Beaver grunted. "Me heard dog bark." Seconds later he mumbled, "Injun pony herd," as if to convince himself.

Custer waited quietly, breathlessly, to be convinced. Moments seemed like hours, but he was soon rewarded for his patience. All three of them heard the barking of a dog in the heavy timber off to the right of the mysterious herd. Then the tinkling of a pony bell echoed faintly, and Custer was now convinced that this was an Indian *remuda*. Black-Kettle's village must lie a short distance beyond the herd, along the Washita River. *Hallelujah!*

Just as Custer turned to retrace his steps back to the anxiously waiting troopers, another sound (vibrant in the crisp atmosphere of the valley) caught his ears. It was the cry of an infant.

Yellowhair glanced at Little-Beaver. "We attack at dawn."

Leaving the two Osages to keep a sharp lookout, Custer made tracks back to his command and called a council of war. It was now close to midnight. When all the senior officers were huddled in a small circle, Custer told them in a low tone what he had seen and heard. Then he detailed his plan of action:

"We're going to employ the hours between now and daylight to completely surround the village. Needless to say, I want complete silence to be observed when this movement is taking place. At daybreak, or as soon as it's barely light enough for the purpose, we'll attack the Indians from all sides. Since we number about eight hundred, I'm dividing the regiment into four battalions of equal strength. By this disposition it's hoped we'll prevent the escape of every Indian in the village. Major Elliot, I want you to take Companies G, H, and M, move downstream to the left, and circle behind the village. Captain Thompson, take B and F, and strike the village from the right-rear in connection with Major Elliot. Captain Myers, you shall take E and I and strike from the timber on the right. Captains Hamilton and West and I will go in from here with two squadrons of the remaining four companies. I shall expect every detachment to be in position, ready for the attack, by daylight. Elliot and Thompson will therefore move out immediately, as they have the longest route to cover. There's plenty of time, so we needn't rush. And remember: everything hinges on the element of surprise. We've got to catch 'em napping. That necessitates a concerted assault. The signal to close in will come from the band. When you hear 'em strike up *Garry Owen,* sound the *Charge* and do your job. All I can say now is good going and good luck."

The night grew stinging-cold, but no fires were allowed. The troopers were even ordered not to stamp their feet or pace back and forth to keep warm. The crunch-crunch of solid snow might sound the alarm to Black-Kettle's braves. So the men had to be satisfied with swinging their arms, shaking their legs, and swaying to and fro; many gently slapped their horses with gloved hands to keep them from freezing.

Pulling the cape of his fur-lined greatcoat over his head, Custer huddled on warm buffalo robes with his pack of staghounds and drifted off to sleep for about an hour. When he awoke, he reached for his pocket watch. It was two hours before dawn. The moon had vanished; they were now shrouded in blackness.

Custer stretched to his feet and stalked slowly about the bivouac. He found the troopers hunched together in squads of three and four at the feet of their horses. Soon he spotted the ten Osage warriors, with their chiefs Little-Beaver and Hard-Rope. They were sitting cross-legged in a circle, wrapped in their shaggy buffalo blankets, dragging languidly on long white clay pipes. Close by crouched Joseph E. ("Californie Joe") Milner, Custer's chief of scouts. "Half-man, half-horse, half-alligator," this giant ridge-runner sported magnificent red whiskers, a flaming curly mane, and a huge black sombrero. He rode a mule named Maud, looking like a pair of tongs on a chairback, and a stubby old brierwood pipe was always sticking out the corner of his mouth. Milner, who despised all discipline, nonetheless respected Custer as a "hoss man" instead of an "ambulance man." His first question on meeting Old Hard-Butt, "D'you b'lieve in cotchin' Injuns in ambulances er on hossback?", was an obvious slap at old General Sully, who campaigned against Indians "on wheels, jist as ef he war goin' to a town fun'ral in the States, an' stood 'bout as much chance o' cotchin' redskins as a six-mule team would o' cotchin' a pack of thievin' ki-o-tees!"

Custer's attention was suddenly attracted by a remarkable sight in the paling sky. For a second he felt a thrill of apprehension. Above the black etching of the ridge ahead, in bold relief against the purplescent canopy of heaven, a small ball of golden fire slowly ascended. Everyone stared in blank astonishment. And the higher it rose the bigger it swelled in brilliance, radiating the most gorgeous blend of colors.

"Bejaisus." Californie Joe gaped, scratching his ginger mop. "How long it hangs fire! Why don't it explode?"

"What is it, anyhow?" asked another white scout.

Custer breathed more freely. "No mystery, gentlemen," he said, gazing at the phenomenal sparkle in the frosty sky. "You are now looking at the brightest and most beautiful of morningstars."

The "Star of the Washita," like Napoleon's "Sun of Austerlitz," became proverbial; and Old Curly would henceforth be immortalized in Cheyenne legend as "Son-of-Morningstar."

A white, still dawn was breaking over the dark crest ahead as Colonel Custer led his 7th Cavalry slowly up the pine-dotted slope. It was freezing cold, but the troopers were obliged to leave behind their overcoats and haversacks so as to have free play for fast action. The sharp crunching of hoofs on crusted snow might have alerted the Indians were it not for their huge pony herd, which was now stomping and blowing for fodder.

The cayuses began to scud off nervously into the timber as a long cavalcade of bluecoats came inching down into the icy valley. Birch-bark lodges stood like tall white sentinels among the bare trees skirting the icebound Washita. Custer saw whiffs of smoke curling up from their conical peaks. The entire village was steeped in silence.

Armstrong shivered, as much from nerves as from the cold. This was his lucky break, his chance to regain past glory. All other considerations bowed before this ruling passion. It was now or never, neck or nothing, triumph or disgrace. He would stand the test at any cost to anyone.

Colonel Custer was about to turn in the saddle and signal the attack when a rifleshot cracked on the far side of the village. Dogs began to bark, and there was a rustle of life in the tepees. Major Elliot had been spotted, but it was too late now for Black-Kettle and his tribe.

"Let 'er rip!" Old Curly cried; and at once the brass band burst out with its raucous regimental air, "Garry Owen":

> We'll break windows, we'll break doors,
> The watch knock down by threes and fours,
> Then let the doctors work their cures
> And tinker up our bruises!

The famed Irish quickstep, soon to legendize the 7th as "The Garryowens," blasted across snow-blown flats till saliva froze in the instruments. "Platoons, front into line! Gallop *ho!*" Cheers echoed in a continuous roar, and bugles blared the "Charge," as all four cavalry units plowed hell-for-leather into the village.

Half-naked braves popped out of their tepees, sounding the war whoop. Grabbing their rifles, bows and arrows, they sprang behind frosted trees or bounded over the frozen banks and into snow-choked gullies. Armstrong and Tom Custer picked them off with their revolvers as they weaved in and out of the trees and pounded around the lodges, scattering mud and slush, shouting like buffalo hunters riding down game.

Blood splashed and splattered over trampled snow, and bodies leaped and sprawled. Squaws screamed, ponies squealed, troopers swore, arrows whirred, and carbines crackled. It was a hell of sound and slaughter.

The first victims were Black-Kettle and his wife, shot dead in front of their tepee at the initial volley. Sub-chief Little-Rock died too, defending his family against the inevitable. Nude Indians, male and female, plunged into numbing water—to be slashed by broken ice. Children were trampled under raging horses, and pockets of braves were killed in gullies by Cooke's sharpshooters. One squaw, attempting to escape with a captive white boy, was surrounded by several troopers. When she pulled a knife and ripped open the little lad's stomach, "retributive justice reached her in the shape of a well-directed bullet."

Not until the sun was high and hot did the last shot ring out over the valley. Dozens of dead and dying Indians cluttered the ground. The rest had fled to tall timber downstream, abandoning their small band of women and children to the longknives.

Colonel Custer rode over to the field hospital, where Dr. Morris J. Asch and his assistant surgeon were treating a dozen wounded troopers. Brother Tom had been winged in the hand. Captain Louis McLane Hamilton lay stone-dead, shot in the back, some said by Lieutenant Cooke. Hamilton, grandson of the great Alexander, had been a Custer man. After the court-martial, he had become a loner, associating with neither faction. "When my time comes," he had said, "I hope I'll be shot through the heart in battle." His hope was almost fulfilled.

Custer spied a little bugler boy sitting on a pile of buffalo robes near where Dr. Asch was bandaging Tom's hand. The lad's face was smeared with blood, which was trickling down his cheek from a wound in his forehead. At first glance, Custer thought a bullet had pierced the boy's skull.

"What happened to you, sonny?" he said.

"Oh, an Injun shot me in the head with a steel-pointed arrow, sir!" the bugler answered matter-of-factly.

"Well, that's sure an odd-looking arrow wound!"

"The arrow struck me just above the eye here; and when it hit the skull it glanced under the skin and came out here near my ear, making it look like it went right through my head!"

"Well, who pulled it out? *You?*"

"Oh, no, sir! I was afraid to. It just stuck there till I got here. The arrow was barbed, and it couldn't be pulled out all at once, so Doc had to cut off the steel point first. He's letting the bad blood drain out and the skin stretch back in place before he dresses it."

"Well now, young fellow, you certainly bear your suffering manfully! By the way, did you see the Indian who pegged you?"

The bugler boy shoved a hand deep down in his trousers pocket and fished up the fresh scalp of a Cheyenne. "If anybody thinks I didn't see him, sir," he said nonchalantly, "I want 'em to take a look at that!"

The death chant rose in full chorus, unnerving in its horror, as women and children were rounded up and placed under protective guard. "This was quite a delicate mission," Custer noted later, "as it was difficult to convince the squaws & children that they had anything but death to expect at our hands."

On Sunday morning, November 29, Californie Joe burst into Phil Sheridan's tent at Camp Supply.

"Well, Joe"—the General cracked a frowning smile—"what brings you back so soon? *Running away?*"

The frontiersman snorted. "By Jeese, I've jest made that thar ole critter o' mine out thar git up an' dust fer the last thirty-six hours! I tell yer it's a big thing, an' we jest made them red devils git."

Sheridan's ruddy face glowed. "So you've had a fight!"

"Weel," Joe drawled, scratching his beard with the stem of his pipe, "we've had suthin'! *You* may call it fightin', but *I* calls it wipin' out the varmints. Yass, an' sech a one as they won't have agin, I tell ye!"

Sheridan glanced at Custer's semi-official report and dashed off an immediate personal reply: "The Battle of the Washita River is the most complete & successful of all our private battles, and was fought in such unfavorable weather & circumstances as to reflect the highest credit on Yourself & Regt."

When Californie Joe came back to camp on the Washita, after

carrying the good news to Little Phil, Adjutant W. W. Cooke proudly read the following document to officers and men of the Fighting 7th:

> Hd.-Qrs., Dept. of the Mo.
> In the Field, Depôt on N. Canadian
> At Junction of Beaver Creek
> Ind. Terr., Nov. 29th, 1868

Gen'l Field Orders No. 6:

The Maj.-Gen'l Comdg. announces to this Command the defeat, by the 7th Regt. of Cavalry, of a large force of Cheyenne Indians under the celebrated Chief Black-Kettle, re-enforced by the Arapahoes under Little-Raven & the Kiowas under Satanta, on the morning of the 27th inst., on the Washita River, near the Antelope Hills, Indian Territory, resulting in a loss to the savages of 103 warriors killed (including Black-Kettle), . . . the complete destruction of their village & almost total annihilation of this Indian band. . . .

The energy & rapidity shown during one of the heaviest snow-storms that has visited this section of the country, with the temperature below freezing-point, and the gallantry & bravery displayed, resulting in such signal success, reflect the highest credit upon both the officers & men of the 7th Cavalry; and the Maj.-Gen'l Comdg. . . . desires to express his thanks to the officers & men engaged in the Battle of the Washita, and his special congratulations are tendered to their distinguished commander, Brev. Maj.-Gen'l G. A. Custer, for the efficient & gallant services rendered, which have characterized the opening of the campaign against hostile Indians south of the Arkansas.

By Command of

Maj.-Gen'l P. H. Sheridan

Major Joel H. Elliot and nineteen troopers were missing. Custer was told they had charged off in pursuit of runaway Indians, with Elliot shouting, "Here goes for a brevet or a coffin!" There was now little chance of their ever being found alive. Elliot was a glory hunter, and such men spun the thread of their own fates. Custer styled him "a young officer of great courage & enterprise." According to Benteen: "Elliot, like myself, was 'pirating' on his own hook. . . . Elliot . . . had, in underhand ways, been 'peppering' Custer, thinking he was not aware of it—but he was."

The ghost of Joel Elliot would haunt Armstrong Custer as malignantly as that of Wyckliff Cooper, for the Hero of the Washita was soon accused (by Benteen and West) of having abandoned the Major to his fate.

Over eight hundred cayuses were corraled by Captain Benteen and his troop. Custer ordered them all to be slaughtered. They were of no use to the cavalry, but the Indians must never get hold of them again. "If we retained them, they [the Indians] might conclude that one object of our Expedition against them was to secure plunder—an object thoroughly consistent with the Red-man's idea of war. Instead, it was our desire to impress upon his uncultured mind that our every act and purpose had been simply to inflict deserved punishment upon him for the many murders and other depredations committed by him."

While 875 ponies were being slaughtered, the village of seventy-five lodges was burned to the ground. Retribution was complete.

★11★

WASHITA: MEYOTZI

Fifty-three squaws and papooses were brought before "Strong-Arm" and "Buffalo-Calf," as Armstrong and Thomas were called by the Plains Indians. Californie Joe acted as interpreter.

Having assured them that they would be treated with all due respect, and that he was no fork-tongued butcher of women and children, Big Chief Yellowhair (*Hâyotzi*) was immediately surrounded by grateful squaws clamoring to shake his hand.

After the adulation, a queenly middle-aged woman spoke up in her native tongue: "I am Mawissa, sister of Chief Black-Kettle. You claim to be a chief. This man [she pointed to Californie Joe] says you are the big chief of longknives. If this is true, and you are what he claims, show that you can act like a great chief and secure for us that treatment which the helpless are entitled to."

Joe translated to Custer; and Mawissa's petition met with the hearty approval of her female companions, who grunted their assent.

Before Custer could ask what was her pleasure, Mawissa stepped into the gathering of squaws, took a timid young Cheyenne girl by the hand, and led her over to him.

"This is Princess Meyotzi," she said, "daughter of Chief Little-Rock. He too was killed by your longknives; but when he lived, Little-Rock was second in rank to my dead brother Black-Kettle. Meyotzi is seventeen summers. She is now without father and mother; but the fruit is ripe for a great warrior to pluck and eat, so she will no longer need a father or mother."

Mawissa then placed the young girl's hand in that of Yellow-hair, shut her eyes, and began to mumble a singsong of Cheyenne formulas. Custer was flabbergasted. He stood in respectful indulgence, holding Meyotzi's hand, while the gray-haired matron cast up her eyes in trancelike reverence and moved her hands slowly down over his and the girl's face, moaning, "*Mânito! Mânito!*"

Knowing that Manito was the Great Spirit of Magic Potency, Custer's curiosity got the better of his silence. He turned to an old squaw-man and whispered, "What's this woman doing, Joe?"

With a broad grin on his face, Milner replied, "Why, she's marryin' you to that thar young squaw!"

Custer blanched, then reddened. "You damned fool," he muttered. "You know damn well I'm already married. If this is your idea of a joke . . . !"

Still flushed with anger and embarrassment, Custer blurted at Milner: "Tell this woman I appreciate her kindness, but according to the whiteman's laws I can't marry her young friend. Now tell her!"

Joe shrugged and relit his pipe. "No use in that now, Ginral. You an' her is already hitched!"

"Is that so?" Custer snapped. "Well, since you seem so damned pleased, perhaps you'd like to explain this woman's motives."

"That thar's easy enough t'onnerstand, Ginral. Married—as *they* call it, mind ye—to that thar squaw, she'll tell ye all the rest of 'em is her kinfolks; an' as a nateral sort o' thing, you'll be 'spected to kinda provide an' take keer o' yer wife's relations. That thar's jist as I told ya, fer don't I know! Didn't I go an' marry a young Cheyenne squaw, an' give her ole pa two o' me best ponies fer 'er, an' twarn't a week till every tarnal Injun in the village—young an' old—come to my lodge! An' didn't me squaw try to mek me b'lieve they was all relations o' her'n, an' that I oughta give 'em some grub; but I didn't do nothin' o' the sort."

"Well, then, how did you get out of it?"

"Git out of it! Why, I jist took all me ponies an' traps, an' the fust good chanct I lit out. That thar's how I got out of it! An' lemme tell ya; I was satisfied to marry one er two of 'em, but when it come to marryin' a whole dern tribe"—he shook his shaggy head—" 'scuse me!"

Mêyotzi: "Yellow-Sprout," or "Young-Grass-that-Shoots-in-Spring." Like so many Indian names, enchantingly poetic. And Meyotzi was a vision of lyric beauty. Custer described her as "an exceedingly comely squaw possessing a bright cheery face, a countenance beaming with intelligence, and a disposition more inclined to be merry than one usually finds among the Indians. . . . Added to bright laughing eyes, a set of pearly teeth and a rich complexion, her well-shaped head was crowned with a luxuriant growth of the most beautiful silken tresses rivalling in color the blackness of the raven and extending, when allowed to fall loosely over her shoulders, to below her waist."

Did he taste the forbidden fruit of the wilds? And in so tasting, did he dream of Libbie? How simple and pure was his husbandly love? If in the least sophisticated, the least egocentric, did it make Meyotzi the fanciful fulfillment of a lonely soldier's yearning for the girl he left behind him? Because Yellowhair was so kind and respectful, Meyotzi loved him. Her love was Indian—the duty-bound dedication of squaw to buck—but it was also free, from the heart.

To Tom Custer, Buffalo-Calf, Meyotzi was "Sally-Ann"—just another convenient and compliant wench. She submitted to him because he was Yellowhair's brother, and that was the proper thing to do. But Tom abused his fraternal rights, and everyone knew it. It was a standing joke among the senior officers. As Fred Benteen put it, "Custer winks at being cuckolded by his kid-brother. That relieves him of his own blanket duty!"

There is much speculation as to whether Custer consummated his "marriage" to Meyotzi, known also as "Mo-nah-see-tah." The Indians, with a kind of halfhearted pride, claim he did; but the question to be considered is whether they confused Armstrong with

Tom, who dressed and looked somewhat like his older brother. Meyotzi seems to have kept silence concerning the whole affair, perhaps in deference to her own dignity "as belonging to the cream of the [Cheyenne] aristocracy, if not to royalty itself."

Custer said: "Although never claimed as an exponent of the peace policy about which so much has been said and written, yet I entertained the most peaceable sentiments toward all Indians who were in a condition to do no harm nor violate any law. And while cherishing these friendly feelings, and desiring to do all in my power to render our captives comfortable and free from anxiety regarding their future treatment at our hands, I think even the most strenuous and ardent advocate of that peace policy (which teaches that the Indian should be left free and unmolested in the gratification of his simple tastes and habits) will at least not wholly condemn me when they learn that this touching and unmistakable proof of confidence and esteem offered by Mahwis-sa, and gracefully if not blushingly acquiesced in by the Indian maiden, was firmly but respectfully declined."

★12★
FORT COBB: THE GLORY
OF THE WASHITA

DECEMBER 2, 1868. With band
crashing ("Ain't I Glad to Git Out o' the Wilderness") and colors
flying, Old Curly and his Fighting 7th paraded into base camp on
the North Canadian River. Custer saluted Sheridan with a saber
flourish, and Phil, with an Irish grin, waved his battered old billy-
cock hat.

"In speaking of the review afterwards," Autie wrote Libbie:
"Gen'l Sheridan said the appearance of the troops, with the bright
rays of the sun reflected from their burnished arms & equipments
as they advanced in beautiful order & precision down the slope, the
Band playing & the blue of the soldiers' uniforms slightly relieved
by the gaudy colors of the Indians (both captives & Osages), the
strangely fantastic part played by the Osage guides—their shouts,
chanting their war-songs & firing their guns in air—all combined
to render the scene one of the most beautiful & highly interesting
he remembered ever having witnessed."

"Bully for you, my boy!" Sheridan roared in the G.H.Q. tent,
slapping Custer on the back. "You've wiped out the disgrace of
two futile years of campaigning. Christ knows, I was damned
worried about the safety of your command in this cold and snow!
But I kept in mind that the immediate effect of a signal victory
would be to demoralize the hostiles and expedite our ultimate success."

On December 1, Sheridan informed Sherman that Custer had
"wiped out old Black-Kettle & his murderers & rapers of helpless

women." Sherman wired his congratulations from St. Louis, following this communiqué from the War Department and Secretary Schofield: "I congratulate you, Sheridan, and Custer on the splendid success with which your campaign is begun."

Sherman esteemed the Washita affair a "great success which I regard as decisive & conclusive," and Sheridan assured him: "One month more will let us out of this country with a fair settlement of the Indian troubles on the condition that punishment should always follow crime."

"The same spirit who, in the Shenandoah Valley campaign of 1864, had so successfully inaugurated the 'whirling' movement, was now . . . determined that . . . re-enforced by the biting frosts of winter we should continue to 'press things' until our savage enemies should not only be completely humbled, but be forced by the combined perils of war and winter to beg for peace and settle quietly down within the limits of their reservation." So Custer stated in his memoirs.

Accordingly, on December 7, General Sheridan and Colonel Custer marched southward with eleven companies of the 7th U.S. Regular Cavalry and ten of the 19th Kansas Volunteer Cavalry. Destination was Fort Cobb on the Washita, over a hundred miles southeast of Camp Supply, and objective was to round up all "strays" (hostiles) not dealt with on November 27. Accompanying the expedition as guides and interpreters were Mawissa (Black-Kettle's sister), Meyotzi (Little-Rock's daughter and Yellowhair's "left-hand wife"), and a Sioux squaw whose identity is unknown. The inevitable Californie Joe went along too.

Friday, December 11, 1868. While scouting the Washita battleground, Colonel Custer and a hundred-man patrol found the bodies of Major Elliot and sixteen troopers. They were stripped and frozen stiff, savagely mutilated and bristling with arrows. It was a saddening, sickening spectacle.

In the words of *Herald* correspondent D. R. Keim, "a scene was witnessed sufficient to call forth the rebuke of every benevolent

& enlightened mind against the darkened intellects of the so-called philanthropists."

"No words were needed to tell how desperate had been the struggle before they were finally over-powered," Custer recorded. "Seeing the hopelessness of breaking thro' the line which surrounded them—and which undoubtedly numbered more than 100 to 1—Elliot dismounted his men, tied their horses together & prepared to sell their lives as dearly as possible."

The official report of Dr. Henry Lippincott (Assistant Surgeon, 7th Cavalry), who examined the corpses, is illustrative of the "good medicine" practiced by dog-warriors. As a grim testimony to "the Red-man's blood-thirsty & insatiable vengeance," we read that Major Joel H. Elliot suffered "2 bullet-holes in head, 1 in left cheek; right hand cut off, little finger of left hand cut off, left foot almost cut off, private parts cut off; deep gash in right groin, deep gashes in calves of both legs; throat cut." The body of Sergeant-Major Walter Kennedy, whose head was partly cut off, revealed twenty-one bullet wounds. Others were scalped, completely decapitated; "right ear cut off," "skull fractured," "penis cut off," *ad infinitum, ad nauseam.*

"In addition to the wounds & barbarities reported by Dr. Lippincott," Custer informed Sheridan, "in the deserted camp lately occupied by Satanta with the Kiowas, my men discovered the bodies of a young white woman & child—the former apparently about 23 yrs. of age, the latter probably 18 mos. old. . . . Upon our attacking & routing Black-Kettle's camp, her captors (fearing she might be re-captured by us & her testimony used against them) had deliberately murdered her & her child in cold blood. The woman had received a shot in the forehead; her entire scalp had been removed & her skull horribly crushed. The child also bore numerous marks of violence."

When word of these atrocities reached the settlements, frontier newspapers began printing such solutions to the Indian problem as: "Offer a reward of $500. for each Indian's scalp brought in, and in less than six months we will have an end of the Indian war and will have peace with the red devils on a permanent basis."

Fortunately for the advancement of American civilization, the Army did not subscribe to this so-called solution. The New York *Times* suggested: "We must come back to the old army policy of reservations—peace for the Indian on the reservation, war for his hostilities outside the reservation." The Chicago *Tribune* agreed, adding: "The first thing that the savages need is so much war and of such kind as shall result in their settlement on reservations. . . . When the War Dept. has done this, . . . then philanthropy can have its turn."

Sheridan wrote to Sherman from Fort Cobb: "I do not care one cent, as far as I am concerned myself, whether they [the hostile Indians] come in or stay out. If they stay out, I will make war on them winter & summer as long as I live, or until they are wiped out. They cannot come in here & make peace with me now, and then commence killing white people again in the spring. If I make peace with them, I want it to be a peace which will last; and if they commit robberies & murders afterwards, they must be punished."

"You must all come in," Custer warned them. "Not only the chiefs and squaws, but braves as well. This reservation is now the only ground left for the Indians. All other ground is bad."

Sheridan added: "I am not a bad chief, nor is my friend Yellowhair. We are not bad men. If you come in here and do as we say, I will not be a bad chief to you."

December 19. Late that night, Armstrong wrote to Elizabeth: "The Cheyennes, Kiowas & Arapahoes are hastening in to give themselves up. They are sick of war since the Battle of the Washita. So am I. I am as impatient as a crazed animal to have them come in, so that I can start on my homeward journey rejoicing." Two weeks later she got the glad word:

Ft. Cobb, Ind. Terr.
Jan. 2nd, '69

My Darling Girl,
The last remaining tribes of hostile Indians—Apaches & Comanches—have sent in their head chiefs to beg pity from us.

Yesterday (what a Happy New Year!) a grand council was held near my tent. All the head chiefs of the Apaches, Kiowas, Comanches, Cheyennes & Arapahoes were assembled. I was alone with them except for one officer, who took stenographic notes of the speeches. (I now understand sign-language!) . . . The arrogance & pride is whipped out of the Indians. They no longer presume to make demands of us; on the contrary, they have surrendered themselves into our keeping. As in the case of the tribes here now, no promise or inducement has been held out. I have made no pretense to be friendlily disposed. Whatever I have asked the tribes to do, or accede to, has been in the form of a demand. They have, from the commencement of this campaign, been treated not as independent nations but as refractory subjects of a common gov't. . . .

Almost at once, there arose a scandalous uproar back East about what was fondly called "Custer's Washita Massacre." Gunrunners and dollar do-gooders in the Indian Bureau (Department of the Interior) stood behind the swarms of "sobbyists" that stormed Washington, ballyhooing the Vanishing American's inalienable rights. None of these seemed concerned with Indian atrocities, or with a realistic means of preventing them. Apparently, only white men were on the warpath, wantonly wiping out their red brethren, who were nobly defending their sacred land with shiny new Winchester carbines generously supplied by Indian agents "for hunting purposes only."

The imputation of having deliberately slaughtered innocent Indians—men, women, and children—was all a part of the "get Custer" campaign. But when his faithful friends in the War Department threatened to expose a few confidential records—"Arrest for intoxication while on duty," "Arrest for disorderly conduct & excessive drinking," etc.—chronic bellyachers and troublemakers like Captain West kept their mouths shut.

All of them, that is, except one. And he, for a while, would remain anonymous.

"Before setting out on the last Expedition," Custer explains in his memoirs, "I had stated to the officers in a casual manner that all parties engaged in the conduct of the contemplated campaign against the Indians must reconcile themselves in advance, no matter how the Expedition might result, to becoming the recipients of censure and unbounded criticism; that if we failed to engage and whip the Indians, labor as we might to accomplish this, the people in the West (particularly along and near the Frontier, those who had been victims of the assaults made by Indians) would denounce us in unmeasured terms as being inefficient or luke-warm in the performance of our duty; whereas if we should find and punish the Indians as they deserved, a wail would rise up from the horrified humanitarians throughout the country, and we would be accused of attacking and killing friendly and defenceless Indians.

"My predictions proved true. No sooner was the intelligence of the Battle of the Washita flashed over the country than the anticipated cry was raised. In many instances it emanated from a class of persons truly good in themselves and in their intentions, but who were familiar to only a very limited degree with the dark side of the Indian question, and whose ideas were of the sentimental order. There was another class, however, equally loud in their utterances of pretended horror; who were actuated by pecuniary motives alone, and who (from their supposed or real intimate knowledge of Indian character and of the true merits of the contest between the Indians and the Government) were able to give some weight to their expressed opinions and assertions of alleged facts. Some of these last described actually went so far as to assert not only that the village we had attacked and destroyed was that of Indians who had always been friendly and peaceable toward the whites, but that many of the warriors and chiefs were partially civilized and had actually borne arms in the Union Army during the War of the Rebellion. The most astonishing fact connected with these assertions was not that they were uttered, but that many well-informed people believed them."

He adds that despite all outcries of indignation, honestly or otherwise evoked, the U.S. Government "was in earnest in its determination to administer proper and deserved punishment to the guilty." Indeed, the Government had no choice. Its duty was to protect United States citizens, whose votes were very important to those in office.

The "Glory of the Washita" was assailed on many fronts. One of the most vociferous assailants was crusader Wendell Phillips, so-called Prophet of Liberty, who delivered the following diatribe to an enraptured audience of self-righteous indignationists:

"I blush today at the swords of the Republic, crimsoned and disgraced by blood better than theirs. Sheridan—*Sheridan*—sends Custer out, with his sword ready-drawn against the Indians; and Custer sends a letter to Sheridan, 'I have had a glorious victory,' and Sheridan heads a dispatch: 'A brilliant victory.' You read on, and Custer says: 'I came on a Cheyenne village—silent as night, careless as children, unheeding danger. I descended on the sleeping group, and slew men and women; and when the sun rose, I found myself in possession of 875 head of horses; and as I could not carry them, I shot them.' Oh, the American soldier descended on a peaceful village, filled with agriculture and industry and property, sleeping in peace under the flag of the Republic; and like a ruthless savage, he trod it out in blood. (*Shame! shame!*) You send your generals, fresh from the great war that taught the nation that we had no eye to see race, to herald that victory to Washington as a brilliant success. Oh, it was a coldblooded butchery!"

The cry went up that Custer had wantonly slaughtered women and children. Cheyenne fugitives (who certainly weren't there to see for themselves) informed Indian agents that a rumored twenty-five innocents had been slain on that terrible morning, but did not comment on how or why.

Custer stated his case thus: "Savages though they were, and justly outlawed by the number and atrocity of their recent murders and depredations on the helpless settlers of the Frontier, I could not but regret that in a war such as we were forced to engage in the mode and circumstances of battle would possibly prevent discrimination. . . . Before engaging in the fight, orders had been given to prevent the killing of any but the fighting strength of the village; but in a struggle of this character it is impossible at all times to discriminate—particularly when, in a hand-to-hand conflict such as the one the troops were then engaged in, the squaws are as dangerous adversaries as the warriors; while Indian boys between ten and fifteen years of age were found as expert and determined in the use of the pistol and bow and arrow as the older warriors."

Sherman and Sheridan defended Custer on grounds that the death of any women and children, after the precautionary issuance of such a prohibitive order, was purely accidental or due to individual acts of cruelty for which Custer could not be held accountable. "Did we cease to throw shells into Vicksburg or Atlanta because women & children were there?" Sherman reasoned. "War is cruel, and you cannot refine it."

The charge that Custer had attacked a friendly village, massacring innocent Indians in their beds, was also dismissed by the Division Commander in a letter to Sheridan (December 23, 1868): "This you know is a free country, and people have the lawful right to misrepresent as much as they please—and to print them—but the great mass of our people cannot be humbugged into the belief that Black-Kettle's camp was friendly with its captive women & children, its herds of stolen horses & its stolen mail, arms, powder, &c.—trophies of war. I am well-satisfied with Custer's attack, and would not have wept if he had served Satanta & Bull-Bear's band in the same style. I want you all to go ahead—kill & punish the Hostile, rescue the captive white women & children, capture & destroy the ponies, lances, carbines, &c. &c. of the Cheyennes, Arapahoes & Kiowas. Mark out the spots where they must stay, and then systematize the whole (friendly & hostile) into camps with a view to economical support until we can try to get them to be self-supporting like the Cherokees & Choctaws."

But allusions to "the murdered Black-Kettle" persisted. According to Yale ethnologist George Bird Grinnell, who lived with the Cheyennes, "Black-Kettle was a striking example of a consistently friendly Indian who, because he was friendly and so because his whereabouts were usually known, was punished for the acts of people whom it was supposed he could control."

"I have worn the uniform of my country 55 years," wrote Major General William S. Harney, member of the Indian Peace Commission, "and I know that Black-Kettle was as good a friend of the U.S. as I am."

Sherman and Sheridan laughed at such assertions. Accusations that they were carrying on a war of extermination were also dismissed with patient scorn. "As to 'extermination,' " Sherman wrote, "it is for the Indians themselves to determine. We don't want to exterminate or even to fight them. At best it is an inglorious war, not apt to add much to our fame or our personal comfort; and for our soldiers, to whom we owe our first thoughts, it is all danger & extreme labor—without a single compensating advantage. To accuse us of inaugurating or wishing such a war is to accuse us of a want of common sense, and of that regard for order & peace which has ever characterized our Regular Army. The injustice & frauds heretofore practised on the Indians, as charged, are not of our making; and I know the present war did not result from any acts of ours." Reiterating that "Indian wars never bring honors or reward" ["War is hell; its glory is all moonshine"], Old Tecumseh declared: "I will say nothing & do nothing to restrain our troops from doing what they deem proper on the spot, and will allow no more vague charges of cruelty or inhumanity to tie their hands. . . . I feel certain that the great mass of our people sustain us fully, but we cannot silence those who have an interest in keeping up an eternal war on the Plains; for 'None are so blind as those who will not see.' "

Ft. Cobb, Ind. Terr.
Feb. 9th, '69

Dear Little Durl,

To-day is our wedding anniversary! I am sorry we cannot spend it together, but I shall celebrate it in my heart.

None of us feel that we could or ought to leave here until the Indian question is settled. Without delicate handling by persons

of experience in Indian affairs, we are liable to lose all the
benefits of the winter campaign & be plunged into another war
with the southern tribes. . . .

I have been very strict with the officers. Have no favorites
where duty is concerned! I have had Tom in arrest, also Yates,
for drunkenness & disorderly conduct. George is "huffy," but I
hope will soon get over it. Tom is cuter than ever, but he is
becoming a little wild. A few more nights in the guard-house
should tame him down. Nevertheless, his conduct grieves
me. . . .

Custer spent a couple of months settling the "Indian question"
by co-signing peace treaties, relocating tribes on special reservations, and running down renegades who refused to bury the
hatchet. Sherman ordered him to "*kill* all hostiles," but Custer
was not now desirous of shedding blood arbitrarily; so he wielded
the weapons of diplomacy whenever possible.

He performed a Herculean task, despite the well-meaning in-
terference of Major General William B. Hazen, Superintendent
of the Southern Indian District and special Peace Commissioner
for the Indian Bureau. Custer vividly remembered him as "Old
Hazer" Hazen, who had arrested him at the Point in '61 for
"conduct unbecoming an officer and a gentleman" and for "in-
citing to riot." After distinguishing himself in the Civil War, Hazen
was appointed to the unenviable post of protecting poor Indians
from bloodthirsty cavalrymen. When his mission of peace and
charity came to nought, the Indian Bureau and the War Department called a temporary truce—so long as the shady interests of
neither could be served by further competition.

The trouble began with Sheridan's telegram to Sherman (December 2, 1868): "Something should be done to stop this anomaly.
I am ordered to fight these Indians & Gen'l Hazen is permitted to
feed them."

Five months before, Major General John Pope had written General Sherman: "I know no task more hopeless than the attempt to
keep the peace in Indian country under the operations of the or-

ganized system of fraud & rascality known as the 'Indian System' & administered by the Indian Bureau."

On October 1, 1868, the New York *Herald* ascribed the Indian embarrassment "to the bad management of the Interior Department, and to the correlative fact that the Government is the ally of the Indian and furnishes him the means to murder our soldiers."

"If Gen. Sherman shall succeed in crushing out the Indian contract and Interior Dept. thieves who swarm on our Indian frontier," the *Tribune* proclaimed, "he will perform a service no less glorious than he has heretofore rendered the country."

Proposed transference of the Indian Bureau (Department of the Interior) to the War Department was one of the most hotly contested issues of Manifest Destiny. Secretary of War or Secretary of the Interior: who could best be trusted to control this vital and controversial bureau?

Custer wrote: "The Army as a unit, and from motives of peace & justice, favors giving this control to the Sec'y of War. Opposed to this view is a large, powerful & at times unscrupulous party, many of whose strongest adherents are dependent upon the fraudulent practices & profits of which the Indian is the victim . . . practices & profits which only exist so long as the Indian Bureau is under the supervision of the Interior Dept. . . . It seems almost incredible that a policy which is claimed & represented to be based on sympathy for the Red-man, and a desire to secure to him his rights, is shaped in reality & manipulated behind the scenes with the distinct & sole object of reaping a rich harvest by plundering both the Govt. & the Indians."

He shrewdly concluded: "To do away with the vast army of agents, traders & civilian employees (which is a necessary appendage of the civilian policy) would be to deprive many members of Congress of a vast deal of patronage which they now enjoy." Then he asked: "Who ever heard of a retired Indian-agent or trader in limited circumstances? How do they realize fortunes upon so small a salary?" The answer was that both agent and trader worked hand in glove to defraud both the Government and its wards; that between agent and Indian "there is no system of accountability"; that "the agent, instead of distributing to the Indians all of the goods intended for them by the Govt., only distributes one-half & retains the other half"; and that the dishonest agent then providently transferred "the unissued portion of the annuities from his Govt. store-house to the trading-establishment of his friend the trader," thereby reaping a harvest of kickbacks from illegal sales.

And Custer added pointedly, "Is it to be wondered at that Army Officers (who are often made aware of the injustice done the Indian yet are powerless to prevent it, and who trace many of our difficulties with the Indians to these causes) should urge the abolishment of a system which has proven itself so fruitful in fraud & dishonest dealing toward those whose interest it should be their duty to protect?"

In *Report of the Joint Special Committee on the Condition of the Indian Tribes* (January, 1867) there is a statement: "While it is true many agents, teachers, and employees of the Government are inefficient, faithless, and even guilty of peculations and fraudulent practices upon the Government and upon the Indians, it is equally true that military posts among the Indians have frequently become centers of demoralization and destruction to the Indian tribes; while the blunders and want of discretion of inexperienced officers in command have brought on long and expensive wars the cost of which, being included in the expenditures of the Army, are never seen and realized by the people of the country."

When Sheridan and Custer reached the Washita twenty miles above Fort Cobb on December 16, 1868, General Hazen insisted by special courier "that all the camps this side of the point reported to have been reached [by Sheridan and Custer] are friendly, and have not been on the war-path this season."

These "friendly" camps belonged to Satanta and Lone-Wolf, two of the bloodthirstiest Kiowas ever to terrorize the Plains. Custer and Sheridan contended, from Indian-captive reports, that Kiowa hostiles had been encamped below Black-Kettle on the

Washita that fateful morning of November 27. Hazen disagreed, producing evidence to the contrary.

Custer's contention was based on the testimonies of Mawissa, and other Indians present during the battle. Hazen relied on his own knowledge and that of his subordinates, both civil and military, who stated that very few if any Kiowas were encamped on the Washita with Black-Kettle; that they had, as a tribe, come to the Fort Cobb reservation a week before the fight; and that all the chiefs were asleep in Hazen's tent on the night of the twenty-sixth.

Hazen would write that Custer "erred greatly in his statement that the Kiowa Indians (as a tribe) were in the Battle of Washita, and that I was wrong in not permitting his Command (20 days after) to fall upon them—men, women, and children—and destroy them, when gathered together in promised security under my charge. . . . That the Kiowas have at all times richly deserved the severest punishment, I have constantly maintained; but punishment under such circumstances as it was desired to inflict it on the 17th day of December, 1868, while they were resting under the most sacred promise of protection, I could never assent to."

However, Hazen had written Sherman on December 7: "I have never had faith in Satanta [chief of the hostile Kiowas]; and if he finally gets a drubbing with the rest, it will be better for everybody. I think by large presents of coffee & sugar he might have been bought for peace, but not for a valuable & lasting one. . . . The prevailing sentiment reported of the people [i.e., half of the Kiowas under Satanta] who have gone out to the hostile camp [of Arapahoes, Cheyennes, and Comanches] is no doubt war-like, and altho' professing peace, will likely be found in the next fight. I am more strongly of the opinion than ever that Gen'l Sheridan should do his work thoro'ly this winter, and that it will then be lasting. . . . To suppose the late battle decisive, and cease offensive operations, would be very unfortunate."

On Hazen's urging, Satanta and Lone-Wolf rode out of Fort Cobb on December 16 to parley with Custer and Sheridan under a white flag supplied by the Superintendent. Custer, true to form, spurred far beyond the column to meet them with a small escort of officers and scouts. Such demonstrations of daring were sure to awe "savages" into discretion. He confronted the Kiowa chieftains, acutely aware that "Large parties of their warriors could be seen posted in the neighboring ravines & upon the surrounding hill-tops. All were painted & plumed for war; and nearly all were armed with one rifle, two revolvers, bow & arrow—some of their bows being strung—and their whole appearance & conduct plainly indicating that they had come for war."

"Our hearts are good; our tongues are straight," Satanta asserted, but Yellowhair nonetheless refused to take his outstretched hand. The chief thereupon jerked it back, pounded his chest, roared, "Me Kiowa!"

Custer was not impressed—least of all when Lone-Wolf caressed his buckskinned arm and rumbled, "Heap big nice son-a-bitch! Heap son-a-bitch!"

Learning that the rest of the tribe had fled southward at his approach, Custer threatened to hang Satanta and Lone-Wolf unless they returned—which they did directly. Meanwhile, Custer amused Satanta by engaging in a series of shooting matches with his twenty-year-old son, purportedly the tribe's greatest marksman. Custer's luck and skill won out; and indeed, "I attached no little importance to these frequent & friendly meetings between Satanta's son & myself. Any superiority in the handling or use of weapons, in horseback exercises, or in any of the recognized manly sports, is a sure stepping-stone in obtaining for the possessor the highest regard of the Red-man."

Custer boasted that regard.

★13★

WICHITA MOUNTAINS: THE ROUNDUP

"T HE Indian question, so far as the Kiowas are concerned, is regarded as settled—at least for the time being—and it becomes our next study how to effect a similar settlement with the Cheyennes & Arapahoes, who fled after the Battle of the Washita & are supposed to be somewhere between the Wichita Mts. & the western border of Texas." So Armstrong wrote to Elizabeth on February 16, 1869. Shortly thereafter, he devised a plan whereby war might be averted and the renegades persuaded into peaceful return to their reservations. "There are those who would have the public believe that the Army is at all times clamorous for an Indian war," and that General Custer was a glory-hunting Indian hater, but he would make them eat their words at a time when successfully drastic measures could have won him considerable *éclat*.

Custer laid his plan before General Sheridan: "We have some fifteen hundred troops, a force ample to cope with all the Indians on the Plains. But since the Washita campaign, it would be extremely difficult if not impracticable to move so large a body of troops near their villages and expect 'em not to scatter like grouse. It would also be impracticable to move upon them stealthily, as they're more than ever on the alert. If we must intimidate them into a state of reason, it should be by moral rather than military power. I believe, Phil, that if I can see the leading chiefs of the two hostile tribes and convince them of the friendly desire of the

Government, they might be induced to return to their reservation."

Sheridan scowled, rubbed his grizzled mustache. Was this Custer talking? Sounded like a Quaker! Lost in wonder, he muttered, "You don't mean to go alone?"

"Certainly not! I fear I'm not sufficiently orthodox as a peace commissioner to believe what so many of that order preach but fail to practice: that I could take an olive branch in one hand, the plan of a schoolhouse in the other, and unaccompanied by force, visit the Indian villages in safety. No; with your approval, Phil, I should like to select forty men, two officers, and a medic from the 7th, with Chiefs Little-Robe [Cheyenne] and Yellow-Bear [Arapaho] as guides, and set out in search of the hostile camp."

"Well," Sheridan ventured with uneasiness, "the nature of your proposition is such that I won't order you to execute it; but if you volunteer to go, I'll give you the full sanction of my authority and every possible assistance to make this mission a successful one. However, let me order you to exercise the greatest caution against the treachery of these red devils, who might be only too glad to massacre your party in revenge for their smashup on the Washita."

Custer providently chose Lieutenant Cooke's sharpshooters as his escort, accompanied by Captain Tom Custer, Captain Sam Robbins, and Dr. Renick. Neva, a trusty Blackfoot who had been one of Frémont's scouts and was Kit Carson's son-in-law, served as interpreter. "I need not say that in the opinion of many of our comrades our mission was regarded as closely bordering on the imprudent, to qualify it by no stronger term."

Indeed, none other than Captain Benteen ("one of the most prudent officers of my Command") was so convinced of Custer's folly that he contrived to slip a loaded derringer into his hand on departure, remarking dryly, "You'd better take it, General. It may prove useful to you."

Custer later confessed: "It was given me under the firm conviction that the Indians would overwhelm & massacre my entire party; and to prevent my being captured, disarmed & reserved for torture, that little pistol was given me in order that at the last moment I might become my own executioner—an office I was not seeking, nor did I share in my friend's opinion." Benteen was always good for a grim joke, at which Custer was never amused.

Southwestward they rode, toward the Wichita Mountains.

On January 24, 1869, a fretful Phil Sheridan cautioned his "pet": "My dear Custer, . . . Keep close watch to prevent Cheyennes & Arapahoes from getting the advantage of you."

Phantoms of worry were dispelled when Sheridan received glad word from Custer that Little-Raven's Arapaho village had been entered without incident, and that a friendly council produced the promise (immediately fulfilled) that all Arapahoes would return to their reservation without fear of intimidation or punishment by the bigknives.

When informed that the Cheyennes were nowhere to be found, Sheridan replied (January 31): "If the Cheyennes do not come in at once, I will move out against them. I hope this will not be necessary, but if so let me know. I will make them feel lightning."

Raw weather and scant supplies forced Custer back to base camp without locating the Cheyennes. It was a hunger-haunted march of eighty miles in sixteen hours, during which the forlorn detachment devoured horseflesh *faute de mieux*.

"I did not tell you of my intentions," Autie informed Libbie on February 8, "fearing that you might be anxious; but I am now back safe & well. We have been to try & bring in the Indian villages, and have had what some people would term a rough time. . . . But I enjoyed it all, and often thought of the song:

> The bold dragoon he has no care
> As he rides along with his uncombed hair.

He added, recalling the powwow with Little-Raven: "I wish you could see with what awe I am held by the Indians. A sound drubbing, you know, always produces this. They have given me a name, 'Mon-to-e-te,' which means 'Strong-Arm. . . .' Tell Eliza I am tired of living on roast horse & parched corn, and will soon be

←113→

at home & want soup every day. . . . Gen'l Sheridan . . . said again, for the 50th time, that I could go East at the earliest possible moment; but I tell him, as I always have, that I would not go till the work was all done."

Camp Wichita, Medicine-Bluff Creek, I.T.
Mar. 1st, '69
. . . I am going to march over a portion of the country to which everyone is a stranger & the distance unknown. . . . I shall be glad to get on the move again. I have remained in camp until I am tired of it. I seldom care to stay in one camp over 2 or 3 days. I am almost as nomadic in my proclivities as the Indians themselves! . . .

Tuesday, March 2, 1869. Lieutenant Colonel G. A. Custer, with fifteen hundred men of the 7th U.S. Cavalry and the 19th Kansas Cavalry, moved westward "in quest of the recalcitrant Cheyennes"—to "administer to them such treatment as their past conduct might merit & existing circumstances demanded." Another object of this punitive expedition was to secure the release of two white girls held captive by the hostiles since before the Washita campaign.

Sheridan had refused to ransom a Mrs. Clara Blynn and her little son Willie, later brutally murdered by Arapahoes (Custer claimed the Kiowas, on Mawissa's authority) during the Washita rout. "After having her husband & friends murdered, and her own person subjected to the fearful bestiality of perhaps the whole tribe, it is mock humanity to secure what is left of her for the consideration of 5 ponies." So Sheridan reasoned, assuring Sherman that "the red fiends, one after another, ravish the [captive white] women until they become insensible." He makes no mention of children, though it is to be assumed that repeated abuse would also render them unworthy of civilized consideration.

Custer thought far differently from his superior, and one of his greatest hopes was to rescue white prisoners—particularly women and children—at any cost.

The Frontier Custer, 1868.

Custer, The Indian Fighter, 1868.

Custer and a "King of the Forest."

A Photo Studio Expedition: Custer and Grand Duke Alexis, 1872.

Colonel Custer, 1872.

Custer: Evening Dress, 1874.

Lieutenant Colonel G. A. Custer, 1876.

Captain Thomas W. Custer, 1876.

Custer and Indian Scouts. Dakota Territory, 1876.

Staff and their wives. Dakota Territory, 1874. Custer is standing, third from left.

The Lone Survivor. "Comanche," 1887.

Custer's Last Stand by V. Mercaldo.

Battlefield Cemetery. Little Big Horn, Montana.

When, after a long and exhausting hunt, he and his Osage trackers finally located the hostiles, Custer's first thoughts were for the safety of the captives. "I knew that the first shot fired on either side would be the signal for the murder of the two white girls. While knowing the Cheyennes to be deserving of castigation, and feeling assured that they were almost in our power, I did not dare to imperil the lives of the two white captives by making an attack on the village—altho' never before or since have we seen so favorable an opportunity for administering well-merited punishment to one of the strongest & most troublesome of the hostile tribes."

With the head of the column over a mile behind him, Yellowhair sought a truce. Advancing toward the village in a zigzag manner, he guided his horse in a series of circles betokening a desire to powwow. Now and then he glanced furtively to the rear, measuring the column's approach with as much concern as he observed the enemy's disposition before him.

A dozen warriors spurred forward to honor his intentions, but drew rein a short distance away. They shook their lances menacingly, affecting fierce scowls and spitting freely. With revolver in left hand and right hand held aloft, Custer signaled for the spokesman to meet him midway.

Pro forma, white man and red exchanged monosyllabic greetings and clasped hands. In the course of the conversation that followed, Custer learned to his unrevealed satisfaction "that the village of the entire Cheyenne tribe was located on the stream in front of us, and that Medicine-Arrow (the head chief of the Cheyennes) was in the group of Indians then in view."

"Send for Medicine-Arrow," Yellowhair motioned. "I wish to talk with the head chief."

The spokesman grunted, turned aside, hailed one of his companions, who dashed back for Medicine-Arrow. The big chief soon came galloping up with his lieutenant, Little-Robe, and about twenty braves in paint and feathers.

"Hâo!"—*"Hâo!"* and handshakes opened the confrontation, during which Medicine-Arrow was advised that Yellowhair had

come with enough longknives to avenge any contemplated act of treachery.

"The women and children of our people will be much excited and alarmed by the presence of so many bigknives," the chief rattled. "To put them at ease, I urge you to accompany me into the village at once and show them that no attack will be made."

Custer nodded, signing for them to go on.

"At a gallop!" Medicine-Arrow invited, to which Yellowhair responded favorably by digging his heels into his horse.

"Some may regard this movement on my part as having been anything but prudent, and I will admit that viewed in the ordinary light it might seem to partake somewhat of a foolhardy errand. But I can assure them that no one could be more thoroughly convinced of the treachery and blood-thirsty disposition of the Indian than I am, nor would I ever trust life in their hands except it was to their interest to preserve that life; for no class of beings act so much from self-interest as the Indian, and on this occasion I knew (before accepting the proposal of the Chief to enter his village) that he and every member of his band felt it to be to their interest not only to protect me from harm but to treat me with every consideration."

The great conclave in Medicine-Arrow's tepee is enriched by legend. Seated cross-legged on a buffalo robe to the right of the chief ("the post of honor") and to the left of the Cheyenne medicineman, full-bearded Yellowhair in fringed buckskins received the pipe of peace from the weirdly incantating Keeper of the Sacred Medicine Arrows, who clasped Custer's right hand to his heart: ". . . by which, no doubt, it was intended to neutralize any power or proclivity for harm I may have been supposed to possess."

For a moment, Armstrong puffed away "with as great a degree of nonchalance as a man unaccustomed to smoking could well assume." But when the medicineman solemnly insisted on his retaining the pipe till the end of invocation, Custer grew anxious at making "a miniature volcano" of himself. "I pictured to myself the commander of an important expedition seated in solemn council with a score & a half of dusky chieftains, the pipe of peace being passed, and before it had left the hands of the aforesaid commander, he becoming deathly sick—owing to lack of familiarity with the noxious weed or its substitutes. I imagined the sudden termination of the council, the absurdity of the figure cut, and the contempt of the chiefs for one who must, under the circumstances, appear so deficient in manly accomplishments."

Fortunately for Custer's peace of body and mind, "divine tobacco" worked no devilish mischief. Not so the shaman, who was (unbeknownst to his victim) putting a curse on the yellow-haired chief.

While he mumbled and grumbled the appropriate formulas, Medicine-Arrow addressed Custer in the Cheyenne tongue: "You are a treacherous one, O Creeping-Panther; but if you come with a bad purpose, to do harm to my people, you will one day be killed with all your men."

"Then [according to G. B. Grinnell] the arrow-keeper with a pipe-stick loosened the ashes in the pipe and poured them out on the toes of Custer's boots, to give him bad luck." The curse was complete.

Late that evening of March 15, during a powwow held at Custer's headquarters, it was learned that the Cheyennes planned to steal away while the yellow-haired chief was thus diverted. Custer, equal to any emergency, had skillfully seized four of the sub-chiefs and held them as hostages pending unconditional surrender of the two white girls and an immediate return to the reservation near Camp Supply.

Several days passed, during which Medicine-Arrow made a play for time while slowly moving his tribe away. He promised to give up the white captives, but only after Custer had given up his own prisoners; to which Custer replied that unless the girls were released by the following sunset, the four chiefs would be hanged and hostilities opened—"cost what it might."

The ruse worked. The two girls were released at sunset. "Men whom I have seen face death without quailing found their eyes filled with tears, unable to restrain the deep emotion produced by this joyful event."

In a letter dated March 24, Armstrong told Elizabeth the story of the two girls. "It is that of hundreds of other women & girls whose husbands, fathers, or brothers take their lives in their hands & seek homes on the Frontier. They had been traded repeatedly from the hands of one chief to those of another; and they had suffered daily outrages at the hands of the young men, who deem it a test of manhood to forcibly abuse a captive female in gangs, to the exhaustion & insensibility of all—the last warrior to survive the assault being considered the most manly. Besides indignities & insults far more terrible than death itself, the physical suffering to which the two girls were submitted was too great almost to be believed. They were required to transport huge burdens on their backs, large enough to have made a load for a beast of burden. They were limited to barely enough food to sustain life; sometimes a small morsel of mule-meat, not more than an inch square, was their allowance of food for 24 hrs. The squaws beat them unmercifully with clubs whenever the men were not present. Upon one occasion, one of the girls was felled to the ground by a blow from a club in the hands of one of the squaws. Their joy therefore at regaining their freedom after a captivity of nearly a year can be better imagined than described."

Writing from the Washita battleground, Autie had proclaimed in the same letter: "I have been successful in my campaign against the Cheyennes. I out-marched them, out-witted them at their own game, proved to them they were in my power, and could & would have annihilated the entire village of over 200 lodges but for 2 reasons. 1st.—I desired to obtain the release of the two white women held captive by them, which I could not have done had I attacked. 2nd.—If I had attacked them, those who escaped (and absent portions of the tribe also) would have been on the war-path all summer; and we would have obtained no rest. These reasons alone influenced me to pursue the course I have; and now, when I can review the whole matter coolly, my better judgment & my humanity tell me I have acted wisely. You cannot appreciate how delicately I was situated. I counselled with no one; but when we overtook the Cheyenne village, and saw it in our power to annihilate them, my Command (from highest to lowest) desired bloodshed. They were eager for revenge, and could not comprehend my conduct. They disapproved & criticized it. I paid no heed, but followed the dictates of my own judgment—the judgment upon which Gen'l Sheridan said he relied for the attainment of the best results. He had authorized me to do as I pleased, fight or not. And now my most bitter enemies cannot say that I am either blood-thirsty or possessed of an unworthy ambition. Had I given the signal to attack, officers & men would have hailed it with a shout of gratification. I braved their opinion & acted in opposition to their wishes; but to-day not one but says I was right, and any other course would have been disastrous. Many have come to me & confessed their error." As for the Cheyennes, "I think we have rendered them sick & tired of war."

Lieutenant Colonel Horace L. Moore, who had replaced Governor Crawford in command of the 19th Kansas, styled Custer's order not to attack the village "a wet blanket saturated with ice-water." His volunteer troopers, many of whom had lost loved ones by Indian atrocities, branded Old Curly "a coward and a traitor." But Custer did what Sheridan probably would never have done: substituted diplomacy for force of arms, in favor of two miserable creatures "unworthy of rescue."

On March 6, Sheridan scratched a note to Custer from Camp Supply: "Just rec'd wires from Gen'ls Sherman & Grant, requiring me to report at Washington without delay. I start to-morrow. . . . I will push your claims on the subject of promotion as soon as I get to Washington; and if anything can be done, *you may rely on me* to look out for your interests. . . . *P.S.*—I feel very anxious to hear from you."

Sheridan heard from Custer: good news, but also bad. According to a Kansas cavalryman, "Custer fed us on one hard-tack a day & *The Arkansaw Traveller*." On March 1 of '69, Autie informed Libbie that "My Command has been living on quarter-rations of bread for 10 days. Gen'l Sheridan has been worried almost to distraction. I wish some of those responsible for this state of affairs, who themselves are living in comfort & luxury, could be made to share the discomforts & privations of troops serving in the field."

Now, the situation was no better: "Have I told you how shamefully the Commissary Dept. has treated the Command? Gen'l Sheridan is terribly enraged at Gen'l Van Vleit [Chief Quartermaster, Department of the Missouri] & curses him not a little. . . . We feel that troops undergoing the severities & unusual hardships of a winter campaign, such as ours, should receive every comfort the Gov't can give. . . . If Gen'l V. could only hear the execrations heaped on his head!"

Custer and his column marched back to base camp on a diet, as usual, of mule and horse and parched grain. *God damn all government drones and profiteers!*

Two footnotes to the campaign are of controversial interest. While at Fort Sill, below the Washita and at the foot of the Wichita Mountains sixty miles south of Fort Cobb, Captain Tom and several other officers of the 7th Cavalry "Custer Gang" took the mercurial cure for venereal disease. Fort Sill medical records (January–February, 1869) listed as treated those who had entertained sexual contact with infected squaws. Apparently, Armstrong's observation that Tom "is becoming more profane & a little vulgar" was more meaningful than meets the eye. And his careless remark that Meyotzi (Sally-Ann) "had become a great favorite with the entire Command" would justify Benteen's sneer that Yellowhair, symbolically married to Meyotzi, had been cuckolded not only by Brother Tom but by any number of the Custer Clan. It is alleged that these same medical records (now missing) bore G. A. Custer's name, by virtue of the curse of Venus, which poses several possibilities.

Camp Wichita, Fort Sill. Friday evening, February 19, 1869. "Officers' Call" had been sounded from regimental headquarters, and all but one of Colonel Custer's staff hurried into his big Sibley tent. There they saw him sitting cross-legged on the bench of his field table, tapping the sole of his boot with the handle of a rawhide riding whip. He motioned for them to squat around the inside walls, then stood up straight. His face was slightly flushed in the flickering glow of lanternlight, and it was easy to see that he was smoldering.

Custer paced back and forth, switching his buckskinned legs with the "hide-tickler." "It has been reported to me," he announced, "that some one of you has been belittling the Washita campaign, and therefore making a fool of the regiment. Now if I hear any more of this dangerous nonsense, and find out who has been disgracing his regiment, I'll horsewhip him!" Custer cracked his quirt, then snatched up a newspaper from the table.

At that moment Captain Fred Benteen came sauntering up to the entranceway. He was a short and slim "Dutchie" with a ruddy clean-shaven face, bright blue eyes, and a shock of wavy gray hair. He was puffing on a meerschaum.

Custer darted a glance at Benteen, then looked at the newspaper and said, "This letter I am going to read first appeared in the St. Louis *Democrat* of February ninth. Here it is now in the New York *Times* of February fourteenth." Custer read aloud with bitter sarcasm:

"Fort Cobb, I.T., Dec. 22, 1868

". . . On the 11th we camped within a few miles of our 'battle of the Washita'; and Gens. Sheridan and Custer, with a detail of one hundred men mounted as escort, went out with the view of searching for the bodies of our nineteen missing comrades, including Maj. Elliot.

"The bodies were found in a small circle, stripped as naked as when born, and frozen stiff. Their heads had been battered in, and some of them had been entirely chopped off; some of them had had the Adam's apple cut out of their throats; some had their hands and feet cut off, and nearly all had been horribly mangled in a way delicacy forbids me to mention. They lay scarcely two miles from the scene of the fight. . . .

"Who can describe the feeling of that brave band as, with anxious beating hearts, they strained their yearning eyes in the direction whence help should come? What must have been the despair that, when all hopes of succor died out, nerved their stout arms to do and die? . . .

"And now, to learn why the anxiously looked-for succor did not come, let us view the scene in the captured village scarce two short miles away. . . . Does no one think of the welfare of

Maj. Elliot and party? It seems not. . . . Officers and soldiers are watching, resting, eating, and sleeping. . . . The commander occupies himself in taking an inventory of the captured property. . . . That which cannot be taken away must be destroyed.

"Eight hundred ponies are to be put to death. Our Chief exhibits his close sharp-shooting and terrifies the crowd of frighted, captured squaws and papooses by dropping the straggling ponies in death near them. Ah! he is a clever marksman. Not even do the poor dogs of the Indians escape his eye and aim as they drop dead or limp howling away. . . . The work progresses! The plunder, having been culled over, is hastily piled; the wigwams are pulled down and thrown on it, and soon the whole is one blazing mass. . . . Surely some search will be made for our missing comrades. No, they are forgotten. Over them and the poor ponies the wolves will hold high carnival, and their howlings will be their only requiem. . . .

"Two weeks elapse; a larger force returns that way. A search is made and the bodies are found strewn round that little circle, frozen stiff and hard. Who shall write their eulogy? . . ."

Colonel Custer slammed the paper down on the table. His reddened face was taut with rage. "That's the Goddamndest thing I ever read in my life," he sputtered, "and it could only have been written by an officer of the 7th." He snapped his rawhide. "By Jesus, that man deserves to be horsewhipped; and if he's here now, I want him to step forward."

Custer glared about the tent. No one moved or dared utter a sound.

No one, that is, but Captain Benteen. He shifted his revolver to a handy position on his belt, unsnapped the holster flap, strode forward into the tent. "All right, General, I guess I'm the man you're after. You can start your horsewhipping here and now. I wrote that letter."

Custer smirked. "How noble of you, Captain. Sorry, but I want the saddle to go just where it fits."

"Well, here's your horse, General. While I can't back all the blame, still I'm ready for the whipping you promised."

"*Ha!* Calling my bluff, eh? Stand where you are, Captain. The rest of you are dismissed."

When the other officers had left the tent, Custer and Benteen stood alone face to face. Custer flicked his whip against his leg, and Benteen patted his holster. They stared at each other with wry smiles, then Custer said dryly: "I'll see you again on this matter, Captain. You're dismissed."

Benteen nodded and swung out of the tent. Those were the last words ever said by either man to the other on the subject of that notorious letter. Benteen ran and told reporter Keim (who then informed Sheridan) of Custer's horsewhipping threat, and Sheridan hastened to advise Custer to drop the whole scandalous matter. By that time, Custer had cooled off and was in a better mood to forgive and forget.

Benteen later wrote: "I wasn't ashamed of it [the letter], didn't care a damn for Custer, and owned straight up that I was the miscreant who had given it to the world. . . . Sheridan gave Custer a piece of his mind about the matter. . . . Everybody—I mean most of the captains & all of the subalterns in the 7th—seemed to be positively afraid of Custer. . . . I never fought Custer in any but the most open-handed manner, always going face-to-face for it . . . and showed him thro' all the history of the 7th Cav. that I was amply capable of taking care of myself. . . . Being in a Regt. like that, I had far too much pride to permit Custer's outfit driving me from it."

The character of Frederick William Benteen, who was not in the Army "for glory-going purposes" and who remained Custer's staunchest enemy, is worthy of note.

"He was rather a singular character, proud & a little vain perhaps," commented General E. A. Garlington, then a lieutenant in the 7th. "He was not an habitual drinker, but once or twice a year he would begin & keep it up for days. . . . It was during such periods that he became abusive & insulting to those whom he disliked or disapproved of. He was much liked by most of the officers in the regiment, and they took care of him in such periods." (These annual drunken fits were apparently brought on by his wife's misfortunes: "I lost 4 children in following that brazen trumpet around." With a weak constitution that subjected her to constant illness, Trabbie Benteen was hard pressed by frontier living.)

According to Colonel (then Lieutenant) C. A. Varnum, "Benteen drank & played poker, and when under the influence of liquor would utter sneering remarks. He was a law unto himself, and a soldier of undoubted courage."

It was inevitable that two rugged individualists, the one a romantic and the other a cynic, should clash as if the cherished identity of one depended upon the elimination of the other.

Captain Robert M. West resigned his commission on March 1, 1869. Reason: ill health. He lived seven months, then dropped dead, a victim of alcoholism. Colonel Andrew J. Smith was pensioned off the Army Register on May 6. Custer was glad to be rid of them. But a fresh thorn was thrust in his side when Major Marcus A. Reno arrived to replace Captain West. Custer knew Reno to be an old acquaintance of General Hazen. He smelled a rat. Was his regiment being infiltrated with Indian Ring agitators or informers?

The reason for Sheridan's sudden recall to Washington is found in Sherman's telegram to him of March 6, 1869: "Grant has been inaugurated [President of the United States]. He has just nominated me for General & you for Lieutenant-Gen'l." Custer was thrilled, for Phil's promotion and heightened influence would surely add feathers to his own nest. The beloved chief's promise echoed in his mind: "I will push your claims on the subject of promotion as soon as I get to Washington; and if anything can be done, *you may rely on me* to look out for your interests."

Though "damned with faint praise," Custer (in Whittaker's words) "had done what no other officer in the American Army had yet succeeded in doing. . . . In seven months he had closed the campaign which commenced in 1867, when Hancock let the Cheyennes slip from between his fingers. . . . Custer had ended the whole war and placed the frontier in peace, alone and unassisted, *just because he was given his own way. . . .*"

NEW YORK:
FORTUNE HUNTING

M<small>ID-SPRING</small>, 1869. All quiet on the Western Frontier. Colonel Custer and his 7th Cavalry marched 250 miles northward, out of Indian Territory and into Kansas, back to the Union Pacific railhead at Fort Hays. Mcyotzi, her womb swollen with child, accompanied the column in an ambulance requisitioned for her by the yellow-haired chief.

When Custer reached Hays on April 7, he read with delight a wire from Sheridan in Chicago: "I am very much rejoiced at the success of your expedition, and feel very proud of our winter operations & of the officers & men who bore privations so manfully. I presume you will want a leave, and so spoke to Gen'l Schofield; and if you desire such, you can have as long as you please."

Armstrong hopped a lightning express to Fort Leavenworth, where he raced into Libbie's arms.

With Colonel Smith on the retired list, Major General Samuel D. ("Old Buckskin") Sturgis was assigned commanding officer of the 7th Cavalry. Custer considered this a slap in the face, "the unkindest cut of all." His exploits and accomplishments had won him a public reputation of being the best Indian fighter on the Plains, but self-interested officialdom dared not act upon its reluctant recognition of the fact. Instead of rewarding him with what he had earned by virtue of sagacious enterprise, "the powers that boodle" advised the "wild man" to rest on his laurels as field chief of the famed Garryowens. Sheridan, apparently, could do nothing. His hands were tied by bureaucratic red tape.

Sam Sturgis, finding himself the innocent pawn of this controversy, filed a strong bid to bow out as nominal head of the Fighting 7th:

> Hd.-Qrs., 7th Cavalry
> Camp near Ft. Hays, Kas.
> August 13th, 1869

To the Adjutant-Gen'l, U. S. Army:
. . . In forwarding this communication, I respectfully ask for favorable consideration of Gen'l Custer's worth & former services; of the arduous and important services rendered by him against the Indians of this Dept., while in command of the 7th Cavalry. There is, perhaps, no other officer of equal rank on this line who has worked more faithfully against the Indians, or who has acquired the same degree of knowledge of the country & of the Indian character. If, however, it should be deemed impracticable to give him the command he desires, I would respectfully recommend that he be permitted to accompany the Hd.-Qrs. of the Regt.

> *S. D. Sturgis*
> Col., 7th Cav.
> Bvt. Maj.-Gen. U.S.A. Comdg. Regt.

Application unsuccessful. "We deem it impracticable. . . ."

Late August, 1869. According to medical records, a fair-haired boy was born to Meyotzi in the stockade at Fort Hays. She named him Yellow-Bird. It has been assumed, by many Cheyennes and anti-Custerites, that the child was sired by Yellowhair; but the weight of evidence seems to rest on Brother Tom. Autie and Libbie certainly wanted a child, and their disappointment in this desire raises a significant question.

Indian testimony, though generally revealing, is particularly apocryphal. "When my mind darkened with thoughts of Meyotzi's disgrace, I spilled dead ashes from the peacepipe on Yellowhair's boots, thus cursing him unto eternity." So spoke Brave-Bear, Cheyenne war chief, when in fact it was Medicine-Arrow's shaman who enacted this devilish deed. His comments on Meyotzi are interesting if not reliable: "She was a proud woman; she kept silence as the child of the soldier-chief grew in her womb. Finally, when the soldier-chief was talking peace with us, Meyotzi told him she was happy to bear his child. After that, he shunned her like a plague."

Yellow-Bird was therefore ignored and abused—as was his mother, who later left the tribe with Mawissa to join the Sioux, some said in an attempt to be near her "Son-of-Morningstar," others to be with a people not so prejudiced in their pride. Whatever the truth, such is the stuff of which legends are made.

"The Indian war has ended." This was Keim's final report from Fort Hays in the spring of '69. "There is not a hostile Indian within the limits of the Missouri Dept. The refractory tribes have been entirely subdued." Several years later, Custer informed the American public: "From and after the Washita campaign the frontiers of Kansas have enjoyed comparative peace and immunity from Indian depredations. No general Indian war has prevailed in that part of the country."

As Lieutenant General, Philip H. Sheridan was assigned command of the Military Division of the Missouri, with headquarters in Chicago. Arriving at Hays City en route to the depot, Colonel Custer dispatched a message to Sheridan in which he repeated what he had written his wife during the winter powwows: "Without delicate handling of the Indian question by persons of experience in Indian affairs, we are liable to lose all benefit of our last winter's campaign & be plunged into another general war with the southern tribes. I think this can be avoided."

President Grant, in his Inaugural Address of March 4, declared: "The proper treatment of the original occupants of this land—the Indians—is one deserving of careful study. I will favor any course toward them which tends to their civilization and ultimate citizenship."

Sherman left St. Louis for Washington, there to assume general-ship, with a dark outlook: "If I was an Indian, I'd behave worse than the Indians do. The whiteman has no business in this God-forsaken country."

The summer of '69 found Armstrong and Elizabeth at Fort Hays, enjoying the hospitality of Colonel and Mrs. Nelson A. Miles. Miles, whom the Indians called "Buffalo-Soldier," was a first-rate officer and hunting companion: a broad-shouldered six-footer with steel-blue eyes and Prussian mustachios, who had been awarded the Congressional Medal of Honor for valor during the Civil War. Libbie Custer and Mary Miles were purportedly the first (and perhaps the last) white women to hunt buffalo with their husbands. Miles appraised Custer as "ambitious and enterprising," one of the most fearless cavalry leaders the Civil War produced.

Though enterprise could be enacted on the Great Plains, it was ambition (and boredom of routine) that prompted Custer to write General of the Army W. T. Sherman on June 29, requesting the position of Commandant at West Point. Application was denied. The Army apparently had better use for its golden-haired hero— or, more likely, dared not entrust a post of high executive re-sponsibility to one so wild and unpredictable. In any case, Custer accepted the disappointment with philosophical indifference. If he were meant for the job, destiny would have ruled in his favor. Custer's Luck worked in strange and fitful ways.

In late autumn, 1869, Custer abandoned his wild life on the Plains and began to enjoy an extended leave of unlimited term back East. Dropping Libbie off in Monroe, he railed over to Chicago for a get-together with Sheridan. His old gang went with him. He wrote "the Old Lady" on December 2: "Tom & the rest of the staff are enjoying what they think a good joke—at my expence. We had seen a performance of Lydia Thompson's 'Blondes' at the Opera House, and the *Times*—a bitter, Copper-head sheet—informed the public that I was pursuing blondes now instead of the dusky maidens of the Plains."

Three days later, on Sunday, George Armstrong Custer encountered his thirtieth birthday. "To-day added another year to my calendar," he penned wistfully. "I hope I may profit by the experience it carries with it." Some twinge of conscience now prompted him to form a resolution that "From the 1st of Jan., and for ever, I cease (so long as I am a married man) to play cards or any other game of chance for money or its equivalent." In so resolving, "I experience a new-found joy. I breathe free'er, and I am not loath to say I respect my manhood more." Apparently, the cardsharps of Chicago had had a field day with the impulsive cavalier.

The year 1870 was an uneventful one for the Custers, with routine duty at Fort Hays. The summer of 1871 found Armstrong fortune hunting in New York City, Elizabeth visiting the folks in Monroe. Virtual inactivity had driven Custer to a desperation burdened with fears of oblivion and anxiety as to his financial future. He seemed to be going nowhere, doing nothing of note. All prospects now seemed to lie in the East. He sought the phantom of sudden wealth—and was led a merry chase.

"Few wealthy people seem to enjoy their married life," he informed "Dear Old Stand-by." "I have yet to find husband & wife here who enjoy life as we do." Several days later, "Darling Stand-by" learned that banker August Belmont and wife "speak very highly of me—Mr. B. most encouragingly of my business prospects. Is it not strange to think of your Bo meeting to confer with such men as Belmont, Astor, Morton & Bliss?"

Some sense of satisfaction must have prompted Custer to add that "Capt. [Robert] Chandler (formerly of Gen'l Hancock's staff), who was Judge-Advocate at my trial, is now in an insane asylum in Washington."

All-night conferences with stockbrokers and financiers, eager to use Custer to advantage, aroused linen-closet gossip in the Metropolitan Hotel. "The old Irish servant who takes care of my room looks at me with suspicion when I return—sometimes not till morning, the bed not having been touched. I think she believes I do not pass my nights in the most reputable manner. In fact, circumstances (as she sees them) are against me."

Having served as official observer in the Franco-Prussian War, General Sheridan arrived in New York to say, "Custer, I wish you had been with me!" and "Custer, you with that 3rd Division could have captured King William six times over!" Generals Merritt and Torbert joined the reunion at the Fifth Avenue Hotel, where Torbert insisted that Custer pay him a visit in Delaware.

Among other escapades, financiers Larry and Leonard Jerome escorted Custer to Belmont Park at Saratoga, where he watched the races ("in the midst of enjoyment") but refrained from betting. Larry Jerome, through daughter Jennie, was destined to become Sir Winston Churchill's grandfather.

Between sporting with Colonel Jerome Napoleon Bonaparte and James Gordon Bennett II, Custer attended the lavish dinner parties of such "talented & distinguished men" as Horace Greeley ("whom I once threatened to horse-whip!") of the New York *Tribune,* writer-adventurer Bayard Taylor, journalist Whitelaw Reid, poet-stockbroker E. C. Stedman, and Charles A. Dana of the New York *Sun.* Stedman, for one, "told me that during & since the War [in which he had served as correspondent for the *World*] I had been to him—and, he believed, to most people, the beau ideal of a Chevalier Bayard, 'knight *sans peur et sans reproche*'; and that I stood unrivalled as the 'young American hero. . . .' I was so complimented & extolled that, had I not had some experience, I should have been overwhelmed!"

While dining at Delmonico's with *arbiter elegantiae* and "King of the Lobby," Uncle Sam Ward, Custer was seriously advised "that our natures partake of the characteristics of whatever fish, flesh, or fowl we eat." In other words, "You are what you eat!"

Custer's eyes twinkled. "Well now, Mr. Sam, what effect would the rattlesnake have on a fellow? I've enjoyed that dish for the past six years." Ward suddenly lost his appetite.

Like his friendship with the great dramatic actress Clara Morris, and even his intimacy with Lawrence Barrett, Custer's platonic relationship with the attractive and celebrated dramatic soprano, Clara Louise Kellogg, is characteristically Victorian. "Miss Kellogg cannot endure affectation in man or woman," Libbie learned.

And "Miss Kellogg is very dainty in regard to gentlemen." Walks on Broadway, evenings at the theater or opera, lunch at Delmonico's; such were the simple pleasures.

"Ghosts will always rise up in my recollection of Custer—the 'Golden-Haired Laddie,' as his friends called him." So Clara Louise Kellogg says in her memoirs. "He was a good friend of mine; and after the war was over he used to come frequently to see me and tell me the most wonderful, thrilling stories about it, and of his earliest fights with the Indians. He was a most vivid creature; one felt a sense of vigour and energy and eagerness about him; and he was so brave and zealous as to make one know that he would always come up to the mark. I never saw more magnificent enthusiasm. . . . When on horseback, riding hard, with his long yellow hair blowing back in the wind, he was a marvellously striking figure."

Renowned Washington sculptress, Vinnie Ream, a child prodigy who enobled Lincoln in marble, begged Custer to come to the Capital and sit for a marble bust. The boy general begged off:

My Dear Vinnie,
. . . You are young, and have obtained a foot-hold upon the ladder of fame far in advance of your years—to attain which others in your profession of acknowledged genius have been compelled to devote a lifetime. Go on, dear friend, conquering —and to conquer. Your victories are lasting and, unlike mine, are not purchased at the expence of the life-blood of fellow creatures—leaving sorrow, suffering, and desolation on their track.
                                Faithfully yours,
                                G. A. Custer

★15★

KENTUCKY: SPECIAL DUTY

AFTER a financially unfruitful season of *divertissement* in New York, Custer was ordered back to active service in Kentucky, where the 7th Cavalry had been sent by President Grant to smash up the Ku Klux Klan and moonshining rackets.

It was now September, 1871. Custer was stationed at Elizabethtown—"Betsy," he dubbed it—and Libbie sped down from Monroe by rail to join him. Without his wife to brighten the dullness, special duty in the Bluegrass State would have been an insufferably humdrum existence for the world-famous Indian fighter.

"Autie would like to be on the Frontier," Libbie wrote to Pop Custer, "but spends his leisure reading & writing." Custer's literary labor of love was a series of articles for *Galaxy,* entitled "My Life on the Plains, or Personal Experiences with Indians."

Detailed in Louisville to purchase remounts for the regiment, Gen'l Custer soon fell in with all the slick "hoss-traders" of this horsy state. But lucky in love and war didn't necessarily mean lucky in the racing racket, and a run of sour luck caused Old Curly to swear off the sport of kings for the rest of his married life. Word has it that he lost $10,000 in racing three thoroughbreds (his own) that were drugged or overweighted.

Another reason for leaving "L'ville" was Colonel Blanton Duncan, an "Unreconstructed Reb" who (during a political debate) alluded to Colonel Custer as "a lackey of nigger-loving carpetbaggers." Custer jumped to the platform and slapped

Duncan's face, demanding immediate satisfaction; but friends separated them before a duel could be arranged. A similar incident had occurred at Austin in '66, where a newspaper editor who had referred to forage agent Emanuel H. Custer as "a remnant of Sherman's Bummers" was nearly horsewhipped by Old Iron-Butt. And to make matters worse, Armstrong's ferocious staghounds slaughtered a slew of domesticated dogs and pigs in the Louisville area—which resulted in a petition for his removal.

"Personally I should have preferred the Plains, but for your sake," husband informed wife. "Duty in the South has somewhat of a political aspect, which I always seek to avoid."

Custer was perhaps even more out of place as a teetotaler. "When the gentlemen ask him what he will take—Everybody in Kentucky drinks!—he says 'A glass of Alderney [milk]' & toasts in that while they take whiskey, brandy, wine." But "How grateful I am Autie does not drink."

Custer worked feverishly on his *Galaxy* articles, hoping they might in some measure reclaim his old glory, fearing to remain merely "one long-haired cavalryman in serviceable condition." *My Life on the Plains; or, Personal Experiences With Indians* began serialization in May of '72 and saw book form in 1874. Its success was immediate, making G. A. Custer as much a literary lion as a national hero, but its repercussions were far-reaching.

One to react was W. B. Hazen, who composed a pamphlet entitled *Some Corrections to "My Life on the Plains,"* wherein he took exception to Custer's criticism of his conduct at Fort Cobb. Hazen wrote: "His exceptionally brilliant record, his fame, which was so justly and splendidly earned, and the long and admiring acquaintance which I have had with him, makes it impossible for me to believe that he could intentionally write or speak otherwise than with perfect regard for truth and justice." Benteen, however, always referred to his superior's effort as "My Lie on the Plains."

January, 1872. Generals Custer and Sheridan, with 5th Cavalry scout Colonel William F. ("Buffalo Bill") Cody, played host to

Czar Alexander II's third son, twenty-one-year-old Grand Duke Alexis (Aleksei Aleksandrovich) Romanov, on a grand buffalo hunt in southern Nebraska.

The excursion was a spectacular success, and sharpshooters Armstrong and Alexis were duly photographed together in their respective sporting outfits. Custer impressed the prince with his fluent profanity, and Cody advised him to gargle with whiskey every morning instead of brushing his teeth.

Lawrence Barrett observed that Custer's "truly American characteristics gained him a friend whose quick eye discerned the depths of that genuine nature and valued it. The friendship which arose between the Russian Grand Duke and General Custer . . . was very honorable to both. The polished courtier discerned in the young Democrat those sterling qualities of manhood which maintained their individuality in the midst of ceremonies and flatteries, and the correspondence which passed between them upon the return of the Grand Duke to Russia was highly gratifying to Custer."

Custer continued to feel the agony of inactivity, of exile, in Elizabethtown. It was unlike him to be moody, to lack interest in his reading and writing, to speak of his lot as that of an outcast. He had failed in New York, failed as a civilian; but what hope did the life of a soldier yet hold for him? Fortune hunting had gone the way of glory hunting, and there seemed to be little left but to follow the beaten path to oblivion. The glory trail had vanished. *Where*? It agonized his sense of enterprise that he could not find it, that it would not reveal itself, that it had been a mocking illusion all these years of ecstasy and anguish.

Libbie saw the curtain of despair ringing down about him, and she was powerless to prevent its darkening envelopment. Only force of circumstance could lift the pall, would guide the clouded luminary into a blaze of glory.

In the spring of '72, Custer welcomed a new brother-in-law and staff officer, Lieutenant James Calhoun: a handsome, golden-haired, six-foot Buckeye. It was hard to believe that sandy-haired,

freckle-faced kid sister Maggie (Margaret Emma) was married—
and to the "Adonis of the Fighting 7th"! Aye, the so-called Custer
Gang (or Clan) was steadily growing into one big happy family
—the better to protect itself from Benteen & Co.!

February, 1873. Armstrong burst into the house, hoisted Eliza-
beth onto the dinner table, tossed a chair into the kitchen. Aunt
Eliza poked her head through the doorway and squealed, "Land
sakes alive, Gin'l! Chairs don't grow on trees in these here parts!"
   "Bid good-riddance to these here parts, 'Liza gal!" Custer said
gleefully, swinging a screaking Libbie off the table and around the
room. "We're heading West: lock, stock, and barrel!"
   "But where——?"
   "Dakota Territory! The Yellowstone country! The Northern
Pacific Railroad wants to push through the Badlands; and it shall
be our job to escort surveyors through country seen by only a
handful of whites, and to protect construction crews against
Indian resistance. Y'know, Bunkie, the Sioux don't want any iron
horses racing across their happy hunting-grounds—and I can't say
I blame 'em!—but who can stand in the way of progress and
civilization? They'll have their own way, whether I and those
poor savages like it or not. So if all adventurous Americans are
bent on and destined to head West, tame the wild frontier, and
extend the States to the Pacific Coast, I can't see but why I
shouldn't be one of the first to lead the way and cut the Gordian
knot."
   Except for her husband's discontent, Elizabeth Custer had been
happy and secure in the domestic tranquility of Kentucky. But
happiness and security were not all hers to claim, and she yielded
to the beckoning of Manifest Destiny. Her diary reads: "This
removal to Dakota means to Autie a reunion with his Regt. &
summer campaigns against Indians; to me it means months of
loneliness, anxiety & terror. But I shall honor my Father's dying
words: 'Follow him everywhere. It is your Destiny to make him
happy.' "

16

DAKOTA TERRITORY:
THE BLIZZARD

YANKTON, on the Missouri, capital of Dakota Territory. The Custers detrained on the open plain skirting the James River, about a mile east of town. While Camp Sturgis was being erected by the 7th Cavalry, Old Curly unloaded his litter of dogs, his thoroughbreds, cages of mockingbirds and canaries, and other traveling companions of the Custer Menagerie. When Autie suggested that Libbie should follow the officers' wives into Yankton, where a comfortable hotel awaited them, she chose to remain with her husband in a tent—"and fortunately for what followed I did so."

It was mid-April, but what the Custers never realized is that Yankton suffered "eight months of winter and four of very-late-fall." A blizzard fell upon them unawares, driving them into a deserted cabin that seemed little better than those ramshackle dugouts or shebangs endured by the Army of the Potomac. Exhausted from overexertion and the excitement and anticipation that impelled him like a human dynamo, Custer became deathly ill—and was forced to bed by weakness and his wife's urgings. Snowblasts penetrated every crack and cranny in the shack, creating a suffocating illusion of being buried alive.

When Adjutant Cooke reported for evening orders, Custer instructed him to break camp and direct the troopers into Yankton: there to be sheltered in houses, sheds, stables, and any other available room.

"And you, General?"

"I shall remain here."

"But Mrs. Custer———"

"I shall stay with my husband," she replied, administering a strong dose of medicine to her patient.

Cooke saluted and fought his way out the door, through torrents of wind-driven flakes; and "In a short time the camp was nearly deserted. . . . The townspeople, true to the unvarying Western hospitality, gave everything they could to the use of the Regt. . . . The sounds of the hoofs of hurrying horses flying by our cabin on their way to town had hardly died out before the black night closed in & left us alone on that wide, deserted plain."

Those thirty-six hours of storm-wrought imprisonment were one long nightmare for Elizabeth Custer. The wind shrieked like a thousand demons released from hell, rocking and shaking the little house with their frozen claws and blowing fury. Armstrong was too ill even to speak, so she found no comfort in his reassuring voice—only horror in his wild rambling fits. She administered medicine with benumbed fingers, constantly shaking encrusted snow from blankets and clothes as it sifted in like Kansas sand sprays.

A dull crash jolted her out of a delirium, and she saw a half-dozen bewildered troopers pry open the snow-banked door and in dazed motions indicate that two of their number were badly frozen. "Their sufferings were intense, and I could not forgive myself for not having something with which to revive them. Autie & I were both so well always that we did not even keep liquor for use in case of sickness."

Libbie looked in terror at that deadly stupor which betokens hopelessness, when suddenly she recalled a bottle of alcohol that was kept to fill the lamps. The victims revived, but "Poor fellows! they afterwards lost their feet, and some of their fingers had also to be amputated."

Morning came like evening, dimmed by drifts and swirling gusts; and "I grew more & more terrified at our utterly desolate condition. . . . When night came again & the cold increased, I believed that our hours were numbered." Unearthly sounds rose above the roar of Nature. A drove of fear-crazed mules dashed against the cabin, seeking shelter and warmth, and their brays were fraught with sepulchral horror. They kicked and pushed and huddled, then rushed madly away in desperation—"and were soon lost in the white wall of snow beyond. All night long the neigh of a distressed horse, almost human in its appeal, came to us at intervals. I pried the door open once, thinking it might be some suffering fellow-creature in distress. The strange, wild eyes of a horse—peering in for help—haunted me long afterwards. Occasionally a lost dog lifted up a howl of distress under our window, but before the door could be opened to admit him he had disappeared in the darkness. When the night was nearly spent, I sprang again to the window with a new horror; for no one, until he hears it for himself, can realize what varied sounds animals make in the excitement of peril. A drove of hogs, squealing & grunting, were pushing against the house; and the door which had withstood so much had to be held to keep it from being broken in."

Were it not that she was kept so busy, Libbie may well have lost her senses. Sleep came in refreshing fits, disturbed by dreadful noises and the need to attend her delirious husband and the distressed soldiers. "To be in the midst of such suffering, and yet have no way of ameliorating it—to have shelter, and yet to be surrounded by dumb beasts appealing to us for help—was simply terrible. Every minute seemed a day—every hour a year."

Armstrong was able to eat at daybreak, for the breaking of his fever so revived him that he began to make light of the danger in order to quiet Elizabeth. "The snow had ceased to fall; but for all that it still seemed that we were castaways & forgotten, hidden under the drifts that nearly surrounded us. Help was really near at hand, however, at even this darkest hour. A knock at the door, and the cheery voices of men came to our ears. Some citizens of Yankton had at last found their way to our relief."

Libbie collapsed, although "I tried to smother the sobs that had been suppressed during the terrors of our desolation." Autie comforted her "by tender words," but "reminded me that he

←138→

would not like any one to know I had lost my pluck when all the danger I had passed thro' was really ended."

With Colonel Sam Sturgis recalled to St. Paul for staff duty at Headquarters, Department of Dakota, Lieutenant Colonel G. A. Custer assumed full command of the 7th Cavalry during its 250-mile mud-trek up the Missouri River to Fort Rice, below the Northern Pacific railhead at Bismarck.

Strikingly attired in green riding habits, Libbie Custer and Maggie Calhoun rode at the head of the regiment with their husbands. Frolic-dashes over the plains, potshots at game on the run, and the usual Custer Clan banter filled those toilsome hours of marching.

Libbie penciled in her diary: "It often happens that my travelling-waggon is the hospital for an ill or foot-sore dog. Autie has to stop very often to attend to wounded paws, but experience is teaching the dogs to make their way very skillfully where the cactus grows. . . . It is of no use trying to keep the dogs out of my tent. They stand around & eye me with such reproachful looks if I attempt to tie up the entrance & leave them out. If it is very cold when I return from the dining-tent, I find dogs under & on the camp-bed—and so thickly scattered over the floor that I have to step carefully over them to avoid hurting feet or tails. If I secure a place in bed, I am fortunate! Sometimes, when it has rained & all of them are wet, I rebel. The steam from their shaggy coats is stifling; but Autie begs so hard for them that I teach myself to endure the air at last. . . . Fortunately, in pleasant weather, I am let off with only the ill or injured ones for perpetual companions."

The column paraded into Fort Rice on June 10, band blasting "Garry Owen":

> We are the boys that take delight in
> Smashing the Limerick lights when lightin',
> Through the streets like sporters fightin',
> And clearing all before us!

Elizabeth and Margaret soon proceeded to Bismarck under escort, and from there they railed to Monroe. There was no place for women on a dangerous mission. Besides, Rice was not conceived to accommodate army wives. There was barely enough room and sustenance for officers and men, who were obliged to share common quarters; a rather degrading necessity in those days of sharply drawn lines of martial caste.

So it was separation again, made painful by compulsion. Separation scarcely bearable but by the grace of letters and prayerful expectation.

★17★
MONTANA TERRITORY: THE YELLOWSTONE EXPEDITION

F RIDAY, June 20, 1873. Dressed in a flaming-red blouse, buckskin breeches, and a white felt hat, Colonel Custer led his 7th Cavalry out of Fort Rice and westward into the forbidden Yellowstone country.

Major General David S. Stanley commanded the two-thousand-man expedition. Custer knew him to be an incompetent sot, a featherbed infantry officer who liked "being comfortably stowed away in his ambulance." Well, the teetotaler had had enough of drunkards in uniform; and he favored no intentions of letting Stanley ruin the enterprise.

Nor had Stanley any inclination to let Custer run the show. He knew the man by rumor and report, and this unfavorable information was confirmed in his mind by a characteristic incident that took place on the tenth. The 7th Cavalry had reached the river point opposite Fort Rice, where Captain Joseph Lafarge met them with his transport steamer.

"Gen'l Stanley has directed me to ferry yer troops across, Colonel," the old salt said.

Custer nodded. "Very well. Repair to the wheelhouse. I shall take charge of the proceedings."

Thus began a heated dispute between sailor and soldier, the one insisting on his right to stevedore the regiment onto his own boat, and the other challenging that right on the opinion: "That damned washtub couldn't hold but two companies without sinking!"

Insulted, Lafarge stalked back to his boat and steamed across without Custer, hooting, "For all I care, youse can start swimmin'!"

Seeing the 7th stranded, Stanley demanded an explanation from Lafarge, who cursed Custer roundly as an arrogative imbecile.

"Take me across," the General said. "*I* shall supervise the proceedings."

And so he did, much to Custer's and Lafarge's mutual dissatisfaction.

Accompanying the expedition as official observer was Captain Frederick Dent Grant, the President's oldest son and Sheridan's new aide-de-camp. He had been offered to Sherman for a goldbrick's desk at the War Department, but Old Cump wouldn't have him. "Grant has fallen into the hands of the Indian Ring, and I'll be Goddamned if I admit a spy to Army Headquarters!" So Sheridan took him, without choice, then appointed the youth as Stanley's A.D.C. and recalled Sturgis to fill the vacancy. All in all, a neat shuffle!

> Camp on Heart River, D.T.
> June 26th, '73

My Darling Sunbeam,

. . . Our march has been perfectly delightful. I never saw such fine hunting! We have encountered no Indians. . . .

The day we arrived here I was lying half-asleep on a buffalo-robe in my tent when I heard "Orderly, which is Gen'l Custer's tent?" I sprang up. . . . It was my old friend Gen'l Tom Rosser, now Chief Engineer for N. Pacific R.R. I spread the buffalo-robe under the fly of the tent; and stretched out in the moonlight, we listened to one another's accounts of the battles in which we had been opposed. It seemed like the time when we were cadets together, huddled under one blanket, discussing our dreams of the future. Rosser said the worst whipping he ever had was the one I gave him at "Woodstock Races" (well I remember it!), when I captured everything he had—including that uniform of his now in Monroe. Rosser (I call him "Tex") asked if you did not accompany me almost everywhere; so you see what an extensive reputation for campaigning you have! And, do you know, he tells me he thinks I am anxious to get back to you. But I did not tell him I was already counting the days! . . .

The officers (Tom & Mr. Calhoun included) have been sitting night & day, playing cards, since we left Ft. Rice. . . . I congratulate myself daily—as often as the subject enters my mind—that I have told Satan to get behind me so far as poker is concerned. You often said I could never give it up. But I have always said I could give up anything—except you. . . .

Yellowstone River, Montana Terr.
July 19th

My sweet Rosebud,

Well, here we are at last—encamped on the banks of the far-famed & to you far-distant Yellowstone! How I have longed for you during our march into what seems a new world, a wonder-land! . . . No artist—not even a Church or a Bierstadt—could fairly represent the wonderful country we passed over; while each step of our progress was like each successive shifting of the kaleidoscope, presenting to our wondering gaze views which almost appalled us by their sublimity. . . . What would you think to pass thro' thousands of acres of petrified trees, some of which are 12 ft. in diametre, with trunks & branches perfect! No country equals this region in the number & character of its petrifactions. . . . I am making a rare collection of the fossils that the country is rich in—animal, vegetable & mineral specimens. I intend to give them to the college [Michigan University] at Ann Arbor. . . .

How I wish that some of our home-boys who possess talent & education, but lack means & opportunity, would cut loose & try their fortunes in this great enterprising Western country, where the virile virtues come out in full-fledged manhood. It is such a pleasure when I can help young men who evince a disposition to help themselves. I never forget those who gave me my first encouragement in life. It is such a comfort to me to feel independent. In this country, no man need fail in life if determined to succeed. . . .

Custer now told of official troubles, beginning June 27. On that day he and the 7th rode through thirty miles of badlands to where the Little Missouri crosses Heart River, there to aid the railway engineers and their cavalry escort in constructing a pontoon bridge of wagon frames and water barrels over a stream 30 feet wide and 10 feet deep. "I superintended & planned it, and about 180 men worked to complete it . . . in about 2 hrs.—over which the whole Command & waggon-train passed [on July 1]." Custer added: "The Engineers have been escorted daily by the Cavalry, so find themselves progressing far more rapidly than when dragging along with the 'Web-Feet' [infantry] as heretofore. Gen'l Rosser cannot speak too highly of the 7th."

It seems, however, that Old Curly "cut loose" without consulting Stanley—and left infantry and supply train fifteen miles in the rear: "stuck in the mud, they say—but probably thro' lack of energy; for Capt. Smith took our waggons back to the main line for supplies, and returned with them loaded. . . . Gen'l Rosser considers this Expedition too unwieldy to perform the work well, and I agree with him." In their opinion, Stanley and his "webfeet" need never have come—were quite unnecessary and a drag on Northern Pacific wheels. Besides, from all appearances, "Rosser & I do not think we are going to have any serious Indian troubles." Were it not for Custer's cavalry, Rosser declared openly, the job of surveying would never get done according to schedule. And so the Custer-Stanley controversy began.

"Gen'l Stanley is acting very badly—drinking, as usual—and I anticipate official trouble with him. I should greatly regret this, but fear it cannot be avoided. Rosser has told me how badly Gen'l S. behaved last year, some days being so overcome that the [first and unsuccessful] expedition could not go on. [This initial enterprise failed because of Stanley's incapacitation, thus necessitating a second survey with teetotaler and taskmaster Custer along.] One morning, the Engineers started at the appointed hour; but Rosser, looking back from a high bluff, saw that the Infantry camp was still standing. On going back, he found the officers searching for the Gen'l—but in vain. Finally Maj. Worth told Rosser confidentially that, having found Gen'l S. dead-drunk on the ground outside the camp, he had carried him into his own tent (tho' he & the Gen'l were not on good terms) for the honor of the Service. He was then lying there in a drunken stupor.

"Rosser said he told Gen'l Stanley in St. Paul (before starting) that he would have a different man to deal with this year, in command of the 7th Cav.; one who would not hesitate, as Second-in-Command, to put a guard over him (Stanley) if incapacitated. Gen'l S., Rosser said, acknowledged that he knew this & would try to do better. But whiskey has too strong a hold on him.

"Our officers are terribly down on him. One day when intoxicated, after leaving Rice, he abused Mr. Balarian [the 7th's Own Sutler] in such coarse terms—calling him foul names like 'dirty Jew bastard' & 'damned thieving foreigner'—and threatened to hang him should he seek to come into camp at any time. Why? Because Balarian (who ignores Gen'l S.) sells whiskey cheap only to those who can hold it! Now Mr. B., who is a great favorite with our officers, asked me what he should do. I bade him come into camp with me, whiskey & all, and no one has been hanged as yet! Gen'l Stanley, in one of his fits of ill-humor, ordered Capt. Grant to go to the 7th Cav. & inspect Mr. Balarian's waggons & stores, and if he found any spirituous liquors there, to take an axe & spill the contents of barrels. This would have injured Mr. B. financially, as he had thousands of dollars' worth on hand. Capt. Grant was greatly mortified (being fond of whiskey himself), but fortunately Mr. B.'s waggons were so far in the rear it was hours before they arrived. So, after chatting with me on pleasant topics, Capt. G. said, 'Well, my tent leaked last night; so I guess I'll go back & take a nap. By that time the waggons may be in. And I hope the Sutler will have anything of the kind hidden before I come to inspect.' Our officers regarded Gen'l S.'s order as persecution, and were eager to help. So Mr. B. loaded his drinkables into one waggon & made the rounds of our temperate officers—leaving with each a keg of brandy, case of rum, or barrel of Bourbon, for temporary keeping. Never were temperate officers so well provided with intoxicants! Then Gen'l S.

re-considered (fearing he might be cutting his own throat, I suppose) and cancelled his order to Capt. G. to inspect. But fearing this might be a trap, the officers retained their keep for a few days till the excitement was over."

Benteen summarized: "Stanley got drunk, so the game was thrown into Custer's hand, and thus he 'got away with Stanley.' "

Autie's letter continued lightheartedly: "I am prouder & prouder of the 7th, Libbie. Not an officer or man of my Command has been seen intoxicated since the Expedition left Ft. Rice."

In the meantime, pot-valiant General Stanley was writing to his wife (June 28): "I have seen enough of Custer to convince me that he is a cold-blooded, untruthful & unprincipled man. He is universally despised by all the officers of his Regiment, excepting his relatives & one or two sycophants. He brought a trader [Balarian] in the field without permission, carries an old negro woman & a cast-iron cooking-stove, and delays the march often by his extensive packing-up in the morning. As I said, I will try, but am not sure I can avoid trouble with him."

And July 1: "I had a little flurry with Custer, as I told you I probably would. . . . Without consulting me, he marched off 15 miles, coolly sending me a note to send him forage & rations. I sent after him, ordered him to halt where he was, to unload his waggons & send for his own rations & forage, and never presume to make another movement without orders. . . . He was just gradually assuming command, and now he knows he has a Commanding Officer who will not tolerate his arrogance."

On August 15, Stanley reported that Custer "behaves very well since he agreed to do so." For all of a week, the 7th Cavalry had brought up the rear of the column and its commander held in nominal arrest. "You are the most insubordinate and troublesome officer I have ever dealt with," Stanley had sputtered on July 1. "You may consider yourself under arrest, and take your station in the rear." Now, on Rosser's insistence, Custer was back in the lead with his troopers, riding far ahead like the great pathfinder he was, guiding that massive mission through canyons and coulees like deep livid scars on the green and yellow hide of nature.

> Yellowstone River, above Powder River
> July 31st, 4 P.M.

Good-Morning, my Sunbeam!

Soon you will be counting our separation by weeks instead of months, and will be on your way to a Post on the frontier of Dakota. . . . The mail brought many newspapers with allusions to the Expedition & references to your "Boy General." I send you an extract from the *Chicago Post* calling him the "Glorious Boy." . . . The officers & men of the 7th are behaving admirably, while scarcely a day passes without one seeing an Infantry officer too intoxicated to be fit for duty. . . . You have no idea how whiskey alone has delayed the Expedition & added to Gov't expenses. Gen'l Rosser says it's a disgrace to the Service, and I (needless to say!) agree. . . .

P.S.—Tell Maggie Mr. Calhoun makes a splendid Adjutant.

Monday, August 4, 1873; 11 A.M. Colonel Custer and a ninety-man scouting party were bivouacked in a cottonwood grove on the banks of the swift-flowing Yellowstone, near the mouth of the Tongue River.

It was a breathless, cloudless day—hot enough to roast a mule. Old Curly sat in the sweltering shade of his tent, stripped down to his long white underwear, scrawling a letter to Libbie.

Suddenly there was heard the cracking of carbines and a frantic outburst: "Indians! Indians!"

Adjutant Calhoun darted into the headquarters tent. "Indians are galloping this way, sir!"

Custer jumped to his feet. "How many of 'em?"

"About a dozen, sir! From the way they're yelling and waving blankets, I reckon they mean to stampede the horses."

Custer grabbed his Remington sporting rifle and dashed out of the tent. "Bring in your horses, men!" he yelled to his troopers. "Bring in your horses!"

Instantly a swarm of cavalrymen raced over to the picketlines and led their mounts into the bivouac.

Custer turned to the bugler. "Sound *Boots and Saddles!*" Then to Captain Myles Moylan, Calhoun's brother-in-law: "Mount the squadron and move out in pursuit!" Custer lurched into the saddle, brandishing his rifle. "Jim, Tom, Bloody-Knife—follow me!"

Custer clapped heels to his horse and charged off after the swirling cluster of hostiles. Sprinting far ahead of Moylan's skirmish lines, he chased yelping Sioux across the yellow plain to within several hundred yards of another cottonwood grove upriver. He then checked his steed and raised his rifle for the horsemen behind him to halt where they were.

Custer signed to Bloody-Knife, his fierce-looking young Arikara scout, who loped up alongside. "We're being decoyed into a trap."

The Arikara grunted gravely. Each eyed the timber with nervous intensity.

Custer turned in the saddle and waved his Remington. "Dismount! *dismount!* Prepare to fight on foot!"

A torrent of screaming braves gushed from the trees, their breechloaders barking. Custer's horse reared and tumbled to the ground. He leaped clear, shouting to Bloody-Knife, "Pick off the chief!"

Custer jerked up his rifle, drew a bead on the head buck. Bloody-Knife leveled at the same warrior, a half-naked savage with painted physique, fluttering war bonnet, and feathered lance. Both fired at once. Man and pony collapsed in a flying spill. Struck with alarm, his several hundred whooping followers swung off to attack Moylan, were met with a murderous volley, and bolted away.

Leaping into the saddle behind Bloody-Knife, Custer "rode as only a man rides whose life is the prize"—back to the dismounted triangle of troopers.

Setting fire to sun-scorched grass, the Indians charged behind a flaming veil, whirling in fitful spurts, shrieking and shooting.

"*Now,*" Custer said to Moylan, "let's mount and drive 'em off!"

Taking advantage of their own curtain of smoke, Custer countercharged the Indians and scattered them like sheep. "Had they been willing (as white-men would have been) to assume greater risks, their success would have been assured." Outnumbered three to one, and almost completely surrounded, Custer and his detachment would have been wiped out but for a presence of mind that enacted the dictum: "Attack is the best defense."

Rosser, in a letter to Elizabeth, declared that "I thought him then one of the finest specimens of a soldier I had ever seen."

Custer says: "The only satisfaction we had [from the fight] was to drive at full speed for several miles a force out-numbering us 5 to 1." The Indians, however, were satisfied in having slain Veterinary Surgeon Holzinger and Sutler Balarian, who had wandered off (unarmed) ahead of the main column in search of fossils. Flattering themselves for being safe between Stanley and Custer, they were surprised by several warriors fleeing Moylan's first volley. Holzinger's bald head was smashed by a tomahawk, his stout body riddled with arrows. Balarian, whose hair was clipped close, escaped scalping; but his genitals were mutilated, his thighs gashed. Both had been stripped and robbed. The Fighting 7th vowed terrible vengeance, for the jolly old men had been "great favorites."

"So far as the troops attacked were concerned," Custer adds in his report to Stanley, "the Indians (to offset their own heavy losses) had been able to do us no damage except to wound one man & two horses."

For the next several days, Custer shadowed red phantoms over rock-ribbed hills, down dark-timbered dells, across sage-and-cactus flats, exchanging long-range volleys with bunches of Sioux on the opposite bank of a raging river.

When hundreds of hostiles amassed in his front on August 11, he threw forward a two-company skirmish line and the regimental band blasting "Garry Owen"—which had the anticipated effect of forcing "a disorderly flight."

Custer informed Stanley that "The Indians were made up of . . . principally Uncpapas, the whole under command of Sitting-Bull,

. . . who for once has been taught a lesson he will not soon forget." Alluding to "a sentimental Gov't manipulated & directed by corrupt combinations," Custer emphasized the fact that "The arms with which they fought us (several of which were captured in the fight) were of the latest improved patterns of breech-loading repeating rifles; and their supply of metallic rifle-cartridges seemed unlimited, as they were anything but sparing in their use. So amply have they been supplied with breech-loading rifles & ammunition that neither bows nor arrows were employed against us." His conclusion is pointed: "I only regret that it was impossible for my Command to effect a crossing of the river before our presence was discovered, and while the hostile village was located near at hand, as I am confident that we could have largely reduced the necessity for appropriation for Indian supplies the coming winter."

On Friday, August 15, Custer and his command sighted Pompey's Pillar, a lone-sentinel bluff rising sheer from the Yellowstone to a craggy height of 150 feet. Here, nearly 380 miles west of Fort Rice, the Northern Pacific survey ended and the expedition prepared to return—without incident. Custer's last flurry with Indians occurred at Pompey's Pillar, where bathing big-knives were briefly fired upon by red strays, "causing a great scattering of naked men."

Custer spearheaded the return march, keeping (as usual) as much distance between himself and Stanley as he dared. He doubled back by way of the Musselshell River, penetrating unmapped virgin territory teeming with big game. In his glory now, nothing could stop him!

"The country was entirely unknown; no guides knew anything of the route before us. Gen'l S. did not think it wise to venture into the unknown & uninviting region with his Command, but I did not feel inclined to yield to obstacles. . . . At Hd.-Qrs. it was not believed that I would get thro'. So strong was this impression, that S. authorized me to burn or abandon all my waggons or other public property if (in my opinion) such steps were necessary to preserve life. I could not help but smile to myself, as I had no idea of burning or abandoning a waggon. After we had separated from the main column, Rosser (who accompanied us with the Engineers) remarked to the officers, 'How positively sanguine the Gen'l is that he will make this trip successfully!' And so I was! I assured him from the first, and from day to day, that the 7th Cav. would bring them thro' all right. What was the result? We had the good 'Custer luck' to strike across & encounter, instead of serious obstacles, the most favorable country yet met by us for marching!"

While on this dangerous lark, Custer the sharpshooter brought down an enormous elk (dubbed "King of the Forest") at 250 yards with his Remington. This and other animals he carefully prepared for preservation, having become an ardent pupil (amateur zoologist and taxidermist) of the expedition's scientific corps. As he informed Libbie, "You should see how very devoted I am to this! I can now preserve animals for all practical purposes. Often, after marching all day, a light may be seen in my tent long after the entire camp is asleep; and a looker-on might see me, with sleeves rolled above the elbow, busily engaged preparing the head of some animal killed in the chase."

The Audubon Society and Smithsonian Institution, as well as friends and family, were the recipients of Custer's rare specimens and splendid trophies. Libbie, when confronted with the visceral details of Autie's new-found joy, did not care for "a fine buffalo-head"—much less "the head & skin with claws of a big grizzly-bear."

Camp in Montana Terr.
Sept. 12th

Good-Morning, my Sunbeam!
. . . Mr. Eccleston [Rosser's assistant chief engineer] told me he has been writing the N. Pacific authorities as to whom the success of the Expedition is due: "When others saw obstacles & turned back, you went forward & led the way. As an act of justice, I want our people to know this." My Girl never saw people more "enthused" over her Bo than these R.R. representatives! . . .

←151→

Contrasting radically with Stanley's comments, Custer then proceeded to answer his wife's solicitude concerning an old scandal: "In regard to my arrest [by General Stanley] & its attendant circumstances, I am sorry it ever reached your ears. . . . Suffice it to say that I was placed in arrest for acting in strict conscientious discharge of what I knew to be my duty—a duty laid down expressly in 'Army Regulations.' Never was I more confident of the rectitude of my course, and of the official propriety of my position, knowing that I would be vindicated in the end. Gen'l Stanley was incapacitated by intoxication, so I assumed temporary command. Within 48 hrs., when sober again, Gen'l S. came to me & apologized in the most ample manner—acknowledging that he had been in the wrong, hoping I would forget it, and promising to turn over a new leaf. Twice did he repeat: 'I humbly beg your pardon, sir. I not only make this apology to you, but if you desire it, will gladly do so in the presence of all your officers.' With his subsequent faithful observance of his promise to begin anew in his official relations with me, I banished the affair from my mind. Nor do I cherish any but the kindliest sentiments towards him; for Gen'l Stanley, when not possessed by the fiend of intemperance, is one of the kindest, most agreeable & considerate officers I ever served under. Looking back I regard it, as do other officers, as a necessity; that an issue was forced on us, and that by my opposing instead of yielding, the interests of the Service were advanced. On one occasion, whiskey was destroyed by friends of Gen'l S. as the only means of getting him sober. This was publicly avowed. It had no connection with my difficulty with him, altho' the papers have coupled the two incidents together. Since my arrest, complete harmony exists between Gen'l Stanley & myself. He frequently drops in at my Hd.-Qrs., and adopts every suggestion I make."

Ft. Abe Lincoln, Dakota Terr.
Sept. 23rd

My Darling Bunkey,
    Well, here we are at last—not only "as good as new," but (if anything) heartier, healthier, more robust than ever! I have not

drawn a single sickly breath since we started on the Expedition; and if ever a lot of hale, hardy, athletic young fellows were assembled in one bunch, it is to be found in the officers of the 7th Cav. What a history & reputation this 7th Cavalry has achieved for itself! Altho' a new & young Regt., it has left all the older fellows in the lurch—until to-day it is the best & most widely known of any in the Service. . . .

The Expedition is now considered over, and I am relieved from further duty with it. . . . You may rely upon it that no grass grew under our feet on that return march! I knew that my family—consisting of One—was in advance somewhere; and, as the saying goes, I just "lit out."

Ft. Lincoln, D.T.
Sept. 28th

Darling,

. . . When you find that your dear Bo has just sent the 7th Cav. Band to serenade Gen'l Stanley on his departure for Ft. Sully, you will perhaps say to yourself, "He has been too forgiving again." Well, perhaps I have. [Libbie notes that Stanley "had been a persistent and exasperating enemy of my husband during the summer; and I could not forget or forgive, even after apologies were offered, especially as they were not offered in the presence of others."] I suppose you think I am of a very forgiving disposition. Well, perhaps I am. But I often think of the beautiful expression uttered by President Lincoln, and feel how nearly it expresses my belief: "With malice toward none, with charity for all." And I hope this will ever be mine to say.

Your devoted Boy,

Autie

Libbie packed up all her belongings and rode the rails to Toledo. Relieved at last of anxiety and suspense, but lost in a flurry of excitement and anticipation, she could hardly wait to meet her husband. Not finding him at the station, as planned, Libbie left her luggage and hurried downtown to the nearest hotel. As she went swishing along, glancing into shop windows at the latest fashions, she was suddenly swept off her feet. It was Autie, on his way to the railroad station!

Libbie almost fainted. Armstrong's sunburnt face was flushed

←153→

even redder, but she could still spot where he had shaved off a summer's growth of fiery whiskers.

"I was ribbed by some officers on the way out here. They said no man would dare shave in a railroad car going forty miles an hour unless he was getting ready to meet his mistress!"

★18★
BLACK HILLS: GOLD!

Fort Abraham Lincoln was the new home of the 7th Cavalry in Dakota Territory; and its commandant was Colonel Custer, "guardian and gatekeeper of the Northwest." Finished in the fall of '73, it stood like a lone sprawling log sentinel on barren flats along the west bank of the Missouri ("Big Muddy") River, a bowshot across from the rowdy frontier railhead of Bismarck. It was hell's waterhole, a no man's land blasted by whirlwinds of murky-yellow alkali dust, but it was all theirs: the Garryowens' own outpost.

"His sanguine temperament made it seem little short of an earthly paradise," Libbie later wrote of her husband's reactions to virtual banishment. "He did not seem to realize that the prosaic and plain Government buildings were placed on a treeless and barren plain."

"Libbie," he said, "I believe I'm the happiest man on earth!"

The Custers made their headquarters in a large frame house above Barrackroom Row. Over the door of Armstrong's sanctum sanctorum, emblazoned with trophies and mementos, hung a triply-underlined word to the wise: "*MY ROOM. Lasciate Ogni Speranza, Voi Ch'entrate* [All hope abandon, ye who enter here]. *Cave Canem* [Beware the dog]." It was in this den of dens that the "Hero of the Plains" wrote "Battling with the Sioux on the Yellowstone" and began his "War Memoirs" for *Galaxy*.

Though seemingly exiled, there was more to occupy Custer's idle hours than reading and writing. Libbie noted in her diary: "It is no light social care to be the wife of the Commanding Officer of so large a Post, and I find my time fully taken up with entertaining. . . . Autie is very busy with his official duties, for there are over 800 troops here, but he hunts a great deal & is delighted with the climate."

Spring, 1874. Gold fever struck the Northwest Frontier. It arrowed out of *Pâsâpâ*, the sacred Black Hills: the Himalayas of America, home of the gods, forbidden Abode of the Spirit of Death.

On May 15, 1874, Lieutenant General Sheridan wired Lieutenant Colonel Custer from Chicago: "Prepare at once to outfit an Expedition to the Black Hills to investigate rumors of large gold deposits & survey area for possible establishment of Military Posts."

Rich in animal, vegetable, and mineral wealth—embraced by the Belle Fourche and Cheyenne Rivers, rising from a 6000-square-mile nest of plenty amid the gaunt and scarified badlands of Wyoming and Dakota Territories—the Black Hills took their name from the rough mantle of dark pines covering their pallid heights, and from the darkness of their very mystery and grandeur.

Since the Fort Laramie Treaty of 1868, *Pâsâpâ* were respected as a Sioux-Cheyenne reserve: "set apart for the absolute and undisturbed use and occupation of the Indians." But the relentless march of industrial civilization would trample such treaties in the dust. Now, in the name of Manifest Destiny, that sanctuary of the Great Sioux Reservation was to be arbitrarily violated.

Thursday, July 2, 1874; 8 A.M. With the regimental band grinding out "Garry Owen" and "The Girl I Left Behind Me," Custer led his thousand-man expedition out of Fort Lincoln and southwestward into a wilderness of sage and cactus. On a mule behind him plodded his new orderly, kid brother Bos: an angel-faced roughneck in buckskins and porkpie hat, sporting long carroty sideburns and an impish smile. Aunt Marie, Custer's new cook, drove a chuck wagon far in the rear. Eliza had long since run off with a black mule skinner. Guiding the column was dead-eyed, rowdy-dowdy pony-express rider Martha Jane Canary: "Calamity Jane."

Sheridan's special aides, Major George A. ("Sandy") Forsyth and Captain Fred Dent Grant, complemented Custer's staff as official observers. Captain William Ludlow, chief of engineers whose duties including mapping and mining the Black Hills, was joined by such distinguished guests (the "scientific corps") as Yale paleontologist-zoologist George B. Grinnell, Minnesota geology-archeology professor Newton H. Winchell (brother of Michigan geologist Alexander Winchell), and stereoscopic photographer William H. Illingworth of St. Paul.

It promised to be "a romantic and mysterious expedition," "a regular picnic," and its fate was entirely in Custer's hands. He never felt happier, never more free. Not so Libbie. For "the black hour" had come again, "and with it the terrible parting which seemed a foreshadowing of the most intense anguish that our Heavenly Father can send to His children. When I resumed my life, and tried to portion off the day with occupations in order that the time should fly faster, I found that the one silver thread running through the dark woof of the dragging hours was the hope of the letters we were promised."

> Prospect Valley, D.T.
> 12 m. from Montana Line
> July 15th, '74

My Darling Sunbeam,

. . . Every one—officers, men & civilians—are in the best of health & spirits. We are now encamped in the most beautiful & interesting country we have seen thus far—so beautiful that I directed Capt. Ludlow, who is making a map of the country, to call it Prospect Valley. . . .

No signs of Indians till the day before yesterday, when about 20 were seen near the column. They scampered off as soon as observed. Signal-smokes were sent up all around us yesterday afternoon, but no hostile demonstrations have been made. Our Indian guides say the signals are intended to let the villages

FAVOR THE BOLD

know where we are, so that they may keep out of our way. . . .
We expect to reach the base of the Black Hills in about 3
days. . . .

Y'r devoted Boy,

Autie

P.S.—The Indians have a new name for me, but I will not
commit it to paper.

(That new name was *Wâmânûnâchâ,* "Thief-Chief" or "Prince
of Thieves" [gold-hunters]. It complemented "Squaw-Killer.")

Over 150 miles southwest to the Little Missouri, eighty miles
to the Belle Fourche, another 80 miles to Harney Peak and the
heart of the hills.

Camp near Harney's Peak
Floral Valley, D.T.
Aug. 2nd

My darling Girl,

. . . Well, little one, the Expedition has surpassed my most
sanguine expectations. We have discovered a rich & beautiful
country. We have had no Indian fights, and will have none.
We have found gold (no doubt about it!), and probably other
valuable metals. All are well, and have been the entire trip. . . .

This valley in one respect presented the most wonderful
as well as beautiful aspect. Its equal I have never seen; and
such, too, was the testimony of all who beheld it. In no public
or private park have I ever seen such a profuse display of
flowers. Every step of our march was amidst flowers of the
most exquisite colors & perfume. So luxuriant in growth are
they that men plucked them without dismounting from the
saddle! (Some belonged to new or unclassified species.) It was
a strange sight to glance back at the advancing column of
Cavalry & behold the men with beautiful bouquets in their
hands, while the head-gear of their horses was decorated with
wreathes of flowers fit to crown a queen of May. Deeming it
a most fitting appellation, I named this Floral Valley. . . .

Good-Night, my sweet Rosebud.

Y'r loving Boy,

Autie

←158→

Custer's official reports to Sheridan stated "that gold has been found at several places, and it is the belief of those who are giving their attention to this subject that it will be found in paying quantities. . . . Veins of lead & strong indications of the existence of silver have been found. . . . Veins of what the geologists term gold-bearing quartz crop out on almost every hillside. . . . Iron & plumbago have been found, and beds of gypsum of apparent inexhaustible extent. . . . On some of the water-courses, almost every panful of earth produced gold in small (yet paying) quantities. . . . The miners report that they found gold among the roots of the grass; and, from that point to the lowest point reached, gold was found in paying quantities. It has not required an expert to find gold in the Black Hills, as even men without former experience in mining have discovered it at an expense of but little time or labor."

When this news reached "civilization," the Great Sioux Reservation was doomed to extinction.

On August 27, 1874, Sheridan read on the front page of the Chicago *Inter-Ocean:*

GOLD!

The Land of Promise—Stirring
News From the Black Hills

The Glittering Treasure
Found at Last—A Belt of
Gold Territory Thirty Miles Wide

The Precious Dust
Found in the Grass Under the
Horses' Feet—Excitement
Among the Troops

The following day's headlines read:

←159→

THE GOLD FEVER

Intense Excitement in the City Yesterday
Over the News from the Black Hills

The Mining Offices and Bullion Dealers
Invaded by Anxious Inquirers

General Sheridan Warns Miners and
Prospectors to Keep Away from the Scene,
As by Treaty that Section is Exempt from
Settlement by the Whites

Some Doubts as to Whether All the
Gold Region is Within the Reservation

Sitting-Bull (*Tâtonkâyotâkâ*), spiritual chief of the Sioux Nation, was angered and saddened: "We have been deceived by the white people. The Black Hills country was set aside for us by the Government. It was ours by solemn agreement, and we made the country our home. Our homes in the Black Hills were invaded when gold was discovered there. Now, the Indian must raise his arm to protect his women, his children, his home; and if the Government lets loose an army upon us to kill without mercy, we shall fight as brave men fight. We shall meet our enemies and honorably defeat them, or we shall all of us die in disgrace."

Yellowhair's comment: "I can't say I blame the poor savages; but apparently there is no stopping progress and civilization, undesirable though they may be to the romantic spirit."

Sunday, August 30, 1874; 4:30 P.M. Colonel Custer and the Black Hills Expedition trotted triumphantly into Fort Abraham Lincoln, the "boiler-makers" again thundering "Garry Owen":

> We'll beat the bailiffs out of fun,
> We'll make the mayors and sheriffs run,
> We are the boys no man dares dun
> If he regards a whole skin!

←160→

Libbie went wild with joy when she heard that raucous, rory-tory tune. She hid behind the front door as Old Curly and his Garryowens came parading by, ashamed to be seen laughing and crying all at the same time. But when Autie dismounted in front of the stoop, Libbie lost self-control and rushed out onto the porch.

The troopers cheered and tipped their hats as they jogged past. Mrs. Custer turned as red as her bearded husband. But from "the clouds and gloom" of those long summer days, she again walked in "the broad blaze of sunshine" which her husband's happy-go-lucky spirit radiated.

"Miss Libbie," Aunt Marie remarked merrily, "you sho' has the Gin'l; and I declare, you don't mind whar you is so long as you has him!"

"Marie," Armstrong said, hugging his wife, "you're looking at the happiest twosome on earth! Our cook is the best, our horses are the best, our dogs are the best, our regiment is the best, our post is the best. Why, I declare, I wouldn't exchange places with anyone—not even the President!"

"He often said that his duties on the Plains were the happiest events of his life—not that he loved war for war's sake, but that he loved to feel that he was 'on duty.' The freedom of the Plains . . . amply replaced the allurements of civil life," wrote Lawrence Barrett.

Custer returned to Fort Lincoln—now "home" to him—to encounter official troubles that would have their shattering repercussions in days to come.

While Custer was on his "Black Hills picnic," certain citizens of Bismarck (including the Mayor) had organized a racket whereby grain and other stores en route from Fargo to Fort Lincoln were intercepted at the Missouri ferry and purloined to Bismarck warehouses. Setting spies at work, Custer learned all he needed to know in order to march his entire command into Bismarck, declare martial law, arrest the guilty parties, and confiscate the contents of their storehouses. A storm of protest burst, in which Custer was showered with such epithets as "dictator" and "tyrant," but justice in most cases was served—though the heavens fell.

An attendant aggravation was Custer's festering relationship with Robert C. Seip, civil sutler or post trader at Lincoln. When Seip (who was doubtless in league with the Bismarck gang) decided arbitrarily to raise his prices after "Custer's Bismarck Raid," and when no end of argumentation could induce him to lower them, the post commandant instructed his captains to purchase all supplies in Bismarck and resell them at cost to their troopers. Seip's violent reaction involved a letter to his patron and protector, Secretary of War William W. Belknap, who immediately ordered Custer to cease and desist from "unnecessary and illegal conduct." Custer acquiesced without choice, but accused Belknap of favoritism and jobbery in what he termed "the post-tradership racket" whereby (as of 1870) appointments of sutlers were taken out of the hands of army officers and placed in those of a spoilsmongering bureaucrat.

Custer was not alone in such accusations, for Hazen had also charged Belknap with political patronage—and suffered for it by being banished to desolate Fort Buford, on the Missouri north of the Yellowstone country.

Incidental to this dispute, in late summer of '75, Belknap stopped at Fort Lincoln on his special tour of inspection. Custer snubbed him, returned the basket of champagne sent by Seip for his reception, then savored the sweetness of revenge. Apparently he liked the taste, for he never forgave Belknap. In Barrett's words, "Custer believed the Secretary to be his enemy."

Then came another embroilment with the very man who supported him in many of his contentions about governmental corruption. Hazen had not endeared himself to Custer by his "Some Corrections to 'My Life on the Plains,'" nor were feelings more favorable with the publication of a pamphlet entitled *Our Barren Lands*. In it Hazen took Custer to task for his Yellowstone and Black Hills reports, in which "my esteemed colleague" praised the Great Northwest as "the very garden of America, only needing cultivation to develop into a Paradise." In Hazen's opinion,

←162→

this "Great Northwest" was nothing but a continuation of the "Great American Desert": "a barren waste utterly unfit for human habitation and incapable of permanent amelioration." Therefore, to encourage emigration to "Hazen's Barren Belt" would be "wicked beyond expression." The controversy raged to a mutual standstill.

★19★

WASHINGTON:
BELKNAP'S ANACONDA

"I EXPECT to be in the field
this summer with the 7th, and think there will be lively work
before us. I think the 7th Cav. may have its greatest campaign
ahead."

Wednesday, March 15, 1876. The Custers had no sooner arrived back at Fort Lincoln from a winter vacation in New York
than Armstrong was handed an urgent communiqué from Washington. He was summoned to appear at once before the House
Committee on Expenditures in the War Department, then investigating certain alleged "irregularities" and "abuses," and to give
testimony that might help turn the Tanner President's "carpetbag
government" inside out.

While in New York, the Custers had spent a good deal of time
hobnobbing with their old and influential friend—the great gun of
the *Herald* whose fiery father had glamorized "The Boy General
With the Golden Locks"—Mr. James Gordon Bennett, Jr. In
private conversation, Custer told Bennett that the Indian Bureau
was a den of thieves run by "Useless" Grant's younger brother,
Orvil. He also said that drummers, gunrunners, and carpetbaggers
were tickling Orvil's palm with thousand-dollar bills for big-paying
appointments to post traderships.

But that wasn't the worst of it. Custer also informed Bennett
that Secretary of War William W. Belknap was raking in graft
from frontier sutlers, quartermasters, and Indian agents, who were
profiteering by smuggling rifles and liquor to reservation Indians

←164→

and making soldiers pay through the nose (to cover their kick-backs to Belknap & Co.) for goods sold cheaper off limits. Custer then added jokingly: "The plea to the War Department by an honorable quartermaster, pestered by civilian grafters, is now proverbial: 'In the name of all the gods, relieve me from this position! They've almost got up to my price!' "

Custer's allegations corroborated those of Hazen, who had stirred up the hornet's nest by charging Belknap with bribery: the sale of a post tradership at Fort Sill to a sutler named Marsh. Custer could mention the same of Fort Lincoln, regarding Seip. The noose tightened around Belknap's neck.

On February 10, after the Custers had left for Fort Lincoln, a New York *Herald* editorial called for a Congressional investigation of the War Department and Indian Bureau. It branded William Belknap and Orvil Grant as boodlers and spoilsmongers, and invited the President to ask his kid brother how much of a haul he had made in the Sioux country by starving squaws and papooses whose government rations were stolen and sold at black-market prices, and whose fired-up braves were "jumping" the reservations with Army breechloaders and patent ammunition.

Fired by his conversations with Custer, Frederick Whittaker of Sheldon & Company (publishers of *Galaxy*) wrote: "The people of America will not fail to remark that Sitting-Bull's truest and most persistent allies are the Indian Department and the Indian-traders, who supply him with Winchester rifles and patent ammunition, so that his men are better armed than the troops of the War Department. . . . The corruption fund of this department is so great that public opinion has not yet succeeded in killing the abuse. Politicians of both parties are interested in the money, and nothing else holds the Indian Department together. The cost of the Indians to the Government has risen in ten years from less than a million to twenty millions annually, and Indian-agents and traders grow rich on the stealings of supplies used by Indians to kill soldiers, while the residue of the stealings goes into election funds."

In an interview with a Chicago *Times* reporter, Captain Benteen laid the blame for Indian outbreaks where he felt it belonged: "I think the Indian Bureau has been entirely responsible, and the cause has been the enormous pilfering and stealing from the Indians. . . . It is this constant robbery which goads them to outbreaks."

And Brigadier General George Crook, an old Indian fighter: "Greed and avarice on the part of the whites—in other words, the almighty dollar—is at the bottom of nine-tenths of all our Indian troubles."

"I would have more faith in the Great White Father if he had not so many bald-headed thieves working for him." These are the words of Sitting-Bull, and they explain much of what was to occur in the following months.

On December 1, 1875, Secretary of the Interior Zachariah Chandler had written War Secretary Belknap: "I have the honor to inform you that I have this day directed the Commissioner of Indian Affairs [Edward P. Smith] to notify . . . Sitting-Bull, and the others outside their reservations, that they must return to their reservations before January 31st, 1876; and that if they neglect or refuse so to move, they will be reported to the War Dep't as hostile Indians, and that a military force will be sent to compel them to obey the order of the Indian Dep't."

On the sixth, Commissioner Smith issued orders to Indian agents that all Sioux and Cheyennes found off reservations after January 31 were to be treated as hostiles (*i.e.,* to be refused shelter and supplies); that all reservation Indians were to be disarmed immediately, and that no further sale of arms and ammunition to Indians was to be enacted—under penalty of prosecution.

It is believed that many of those Indians (besides hot-blooded bucks and dog-warriors) who left reservations did so under threat or compulsion of starvation; that their defiance of the white government was a mere bid to hunt food, to provide for their victimized families. If so, then those directives from Washington were nothing less than death warrants; for without the means to hunt, the question of survival was left to chance. And that "chance" was a poor one indeed, in the dead of winter!

Having no good reason to trust the white man, Sitting-Bull determined not to suffer further degradation by surrendering himself into the deadly care of what Custer termed "a combination of rascals dedicated to enriching themselves at the Red-man's expense." In so determining, the spiritual leader of the great Sioux-Cheyenne Confederacy flung down the gauntlet before his tormentors, who contemptuously dismissed him as "Slightly Recumbent Gentleman Cow."

Grant's "Quaker Policy" was assailed unmercifully in the press, both East and West. His statement, "Our superiority of strength and advantage of civilization should make us lenient toward the Indian," was met with this rebuke in the Chicago *Tribune:* "Give us Phil Sheridan, and send Phil-anthropy to the Devil."

With Belknap's resignation on March 2, Sherman (once a figurehead) finally took control of what had been arbitrarily usurped: his full authority as General of the Army. Returning to Washington from "exile" in St. Louis, he immediately telegraphed Sheridan and Brigadier General Alfred H. Terry (commanding the Department of Dakota) that Colonel Custer had been instructed to repair at once to Fort Lincoln and prepare with equal dispatch for a spring campaign against the hostiles.

The Cheyenne *Daily Leader* rejoiced: "It is safe to say that the West now has one friend in high official position. . . . We have some confidence that the naturally perverse head of Gen. Sherman will lead him to persist that there is no peace; and after while, humanity may be beaten into the heads of the Indian-agents, ring-speculators, and pseudo-philanthropists of the East."

Custer, overjoyed by thoughts of active service and an independent command, did not welcome that inopportune communication from the House Sergeant-at-Arms, summoning him to appear before Representative Heister Clymer's investigating committee. He wired Clymer from Fort Lincoln on March 16:

"While I hold myself in readiness to obey the summons of your Committee, I telegraph to state that I am engaged upon an important Expedition intended to operate against the hostile Indians; and I expect to take the field early in April. My presence here is deemed very necessary. In view of this, would it not be satisfactory for you to forward to me such questions as may be necessary, allowing me to return my replies by mail?"

No, it was not satisfactory so to oblige an outraged Democratic Congress. Custer must testify in person.

"I am sorry to have you go," General Terry wired from St. Paul, "for I fear it will delay our movements. . . . Your services are indispensable."

Custer left Lincoln at once, alone, "and so started a train of circumstances which was to end in the untimely death of the best cavalry chief on the American continent." But he did not leave in utter reluctance; for in his pocket was a letter just received from Colonel Miles at Fort Leavenworth, containing this provocative encouragement: "You have an opportunity now of clearing Washington of your enemies & that corps of lobbyists that have controlled legislation for years."

Already charged with neglect and incompetence, Columbus Delano had resigned as Secretary of the Interior and been replaced by Zach Chandler. The Bureau of Indian Affairs, as a self-defensive gesture, then issued its fateful order to "Sitting-Bull's band and other wild & lawless Indians residing without the bounds of their reservation." Unfortunately, even if Sitting-Bull wished to obey it, this order was issued and received too late to make any difference; and it was not until spring thaw that outlying tribes heard as much as a hint of it. The die was then cast, and every "hostile" prepared for the worst.

On March 2, 1876—the very day he tendered his resignation to President Grant—the House of Representatives resolved "That William W. Belknap, late Secretary of War, be impeached of high crimes and misdemeanors while in office." The Democrats in Congress, out to "get" the Republican Administration, thus began an inquisition of "the gigantic system of fraud by which the Indian Ring played into the hands of Army contractors."

Belknap was arrested on the fifth, before he could flee the country, and later gave testimony that laid the entire blame for illegal money transactions on his former wives: two sisters who had made a consecutive killing on their husband's influence since '69. The all-male tribunal believed him, and he was subsequently acquitted, but scandal and shame continued to haunt Grant and hound his bureaucratic coterie.

Though Custer concurred with Sherman in his assertion that the Capital was "corrupt as Hell," he did not heed his warning to avoid it like "a pest-house."

Wednesday, March 29, 1876. Custer strode into the Capitol, was sworn in before the Clymer Committee, and answered questions put to him by the chairman (who, by a quirk of fate, had been Belknap's roommate at Princeton) and his associate, Mr. Robbins.

When asked (by Clymer) what effect the President's proclamation of January 11, 1875, had upon the value of post traderships along the Missouri, by its extension of the Great Sioux Reservation across the east bank of that river, Custer replied: "It greatly enhanced their value by making them a more perfect monopoly, by removing all opposition and rivalry." He then expressed his belief that the proclamation had dispossessed people who claimed (by virtue of the Homestead Act) that they had a title to such land, and that such arbitrary annexation also entailed the driving out of private (honest) traders in favor of government (dishonest) sutlers. The new law, in supporting a combination in restraint of trade, sealed the doom of free enterprise: "If any man shall introduce goods on an Indian reservation, they shall be confiscated."

In citing Seip for a profiteer, Custer stated that "the prices that were charged the officers and soldiers became so exorbitant that as many as could, purchased what they desired elsewhere. They did so until Mr. Seip made a written complaint and forwarded it to the Secretary of War, claiming that under the privilege which he held as trader, nobody—no officer even—had a right to buy anything elsewhere or bring it there, but must buy everything through him."

Custer then testified as to the alleged kickbacks involved in the Indian Ring, declaring that he had threatened Seip into a confession: that government traders "estimated their yearly profits at $15,000"; that "about one-third of it" was paid to J. M. Hedrick, Belknap's brother-in-law and inspector of internal revenue in Iowa; that another portion of it was paid to E. W. Rice, a Washington claim agent and "an intimate friend of the Secretary of War"; and that "the division of those profits was such that the trader was finally left with but about $2500 or $3000 out of the $15,000. I asked him then if he knew of any other person to whom this money was paid. He said that he knew positively only that he paid to Rice and Hedrick, but he was always under the impression that a portion of it went to the Secretary of War."

Custer's testimony now turned to Orvil L. Grant, the President's kid brother and a kingpin in the Indian Ring; that he and one A. L. Bonnafon had procured the sutlership monopoly of Standing Rock Agency and Forts Belknap, Peck (which General Stanley branded "the centre of all the villainy of the Indian Dep't"), and Berthold; and that it had come to Custer's knowledge that trader J. W. Raymond claimed to several people in Bismarck that he had paid Grant $1,000 for getting him the appointment as sutler at Fort Berthold from ex-Secretary of the Interior Columbus Delano. The absolutism of the Grant-Bonnafon combine was such, Custer later attested, that "An application came to me from the Indian agency at Standing Rock for troops to close up and remove the store kept by Mrs. Galpin, a full-blood Sioux squaw, who was engaged in trading with the Indians; and I declined to grant the request."

When asked what he believed to have been the effect (upon his troops) of Belknap's law of 1870, placing the appointments of post traders in the hands of the Secretary of War, Custer answered, "The effect has been to greatly embarrass them and add to the inconveniences of frontier life, which even under the most favorable circumstances are very great; as the troops and officers are required to pay what would be considered in the States exorbitant prices for everything, owing to the immense distances that goods have to be transported. That is the case always; but this law placing the appointment in the hands of the

Secretary of War, and then being used in the manner that he has used it—by putting these appointments at the disposal of a certain ring, and taxing the profits in this way by these exactions, all of which had to come out of the pockets of the soldiers and officers—has, as I said before, greatly increased the inconveniences and expense of living on the frontier."

After expressing his belief that Hedrick was raking in kickbacks from Fort Buford as well as Fort Lincoln, Custer made the pointed remark: "I always regarded the Secretary of War as a silent partner in all these transactions."

Samuel A. Dickey and Robert Wilson were trading partners at Fort Lincoln until the appointment of R. C. Seip; and according to Custer, Dickey and Wilson were removed "because they did not divide [their profits with Hedrick and Rice]." When a rumor reached Lincoln of their imminent removal, Dickey informed Custer: "I don't know whether you know it or not, but there isn't a post on this river that doesn't pay a tax except ours; and we don't pay simply because my brother is chairman of the Military Committee." But as soon as Dickey's brother "went out of Congress," Dickey "went out of the sutlership."

When asked if Seip was "a man of good moral character," Custer hesitated and smiled: "Well, sir, I would hate to testify to the moral character of any post trader in these times."

Returning to the controversial extension of the Great Sioux Reservation, Clymer requested Custer's opinion as to the President's "real object" in issuing that order. The rationalization was that he had issued it "out of care for the welfare of the Indians there, so as to prevent them from having unlimited supplies of rum." Custer said, "I don't believe that the Indians got one drink less by the extension of the reservation. . . . I think the profits of the traders left the morals of the Indians a long way behind. That was the general impression along the river, that the order was for the benefit of the traders."

Custer then testified that when Orvil Grant and Bonnafon attempted to remove a private trader named Thum from Fort Peck, Thum "obtained some affidavits showing that there were some frauds in the Indian Department" in which Grant and others were "mixed up"; and that when Grant saw these affidavits, he allowed Thum to continue his trade. The "alleged frauds" involved the criminal selling to army posts of corn intended for reservation Indians: one of the prime causes of discontent, and starvation, among the Northern Cheyennes and Sioux. In this manner, "that corn was paid for twice by the Government." Custer added, "Speaking of Indian supplies, I have known boats passing up the river to trade off Indian flour to citizens along the river."

When prompted, Custer got another dig at Belknap by declaring that a contractor named Smith had informed him: "There is a great deal of smuggling, particularly in the whisky trade, across the British border"; and "one of the objects of the Secretary of War's visit [to the frontier] . . . was to effect some arrangement . . . by which facilities should be provided for getting whisky across the border at some reduced rate. . . . It was some arrangement by which the traders at those posts along the frontier would have increased advantages."

Custer later cited a letter he had received from Mr. Wilson, wherein "he called attention to the sale of traderships on the Missouri River, and said that he expected to be able to prove that Belknap made these posts articles of traffic, and that he was the most corrupt official who ever occupied high position."

Clymer posed a loaded question: "Had the Secretary of War been a man of purity of character and integrity of purpose, could these frauds have continued going on?"

Answer: "They could not possibly."

"And it was because they were protected and shielded by him that they occurred?"

"They could not possibly have been carried on to anything like the extent they were without his connivance and approval; and when you ask me how the morale or character of the Army is affected, I—although belonging to the Army—think it is one of the highest commendations that could be made of the service to say that it has not been demoralized when the head has shown himself to be so unworthy."

Custer was re-examined on April 4. The investigating committee then learned how Belknap had "sealed the mouths and tied the hands" of Army officers by the issuance of an order (1873) forbidding them to "solicit, suggest, or recommend action to any member of Congress upon any military subject. . . . There has been no voice from the Army since that order was issued. . . . It is regarded by the Army as a step to place the control of all information that officers might be in possession of in the hands of the Secretary of War, so that nothing should get beyond him except that which he chose to transmit. And in connection with the recent developments, it was about the most effectual safeguard that he could have thrown around his conduct to prevent exposure."

During his jaunt in New York, Custer was foremost of those who persuaded *Herald* reporter Ralph Meeker (who had spent six months in Dakota Territory) to write an exposé of the Indian Bureau. On March 31, 1876, the *Herald* featured an extra (anonymous) article entitled "Belknap's Anaconda." Bennett allegedly sent Custer a check for $150. Seip, in his testimony, stated "that he understood General Custer had written an article for the New York *Herald* entitled 'Belknap's Anaconda'; that he cashed a draft on James Gordon Bennett for General Custer; that he knows nothing more about the matter."

Meeker, cross-examined on April 13, backed Custer's testimony by asserting that "the general opinion among the people out there [in Dakota] was that the Indian traders had to pay large sums to Orvil Grant, and that the post traders had to pay large sums to General Belknap and others in Washington; and when General Belknap came down through there, it was called a blackmailing tour on his part." He also confirmed the allegation that Belknap's "real object" in touring the Northwest was to establish a "whisky ring" on the Canadian border. "I understood that Secretary Delano and General Belknap and Commissioner Smith, I think, were going to have one grand divvy and a pool."

When questioned as to his assistance by General Custer, who had endorsed or cashed checks and telegraphically transmitted "scoops" for him in Dakota, Meeker responded: "He said that he was a Government officer, and it was his duty to see that the Government was protected, whether the officers above him were in favor of it or not. I told him I was astonished at his boldness. . . . He would generally say that he thought he was doing the right thing; that the Government, to his certain knowledge, was being defrauded; that he knew something about these Indian frauds, and that he thought they ought to be exposed. I told him I liked to hear him talk in that way, it was so different from the way many of the other officers talked. . . . I was convinced that General Belknap was a kind of a second ["Boss"] Tweed, and therefore I thought he was a man that would bear watching. . . . It was thought that the best thing I could do was to keep out of his way. So General Custer told me; and I thought that if a man like General Custer, so brave and with so good a record, would advise a newspaper correspondent to keep out of the way of the Secretary of War, he had a pretty good idea that the charges were true, and that the Secretary might lay for me. . . . It was the common talk that General Custer served him right [by snubbing him]. . . . The majority of the best people said that as the Secretary of War was the great national chief, they were glad to see there was one man who had the courage to treat him as he deserved."

Though regarding him as "one of the most splendid soldiers that ever lived," Colonel "Sandy" Forsyth (Sheridan's personal aide) thought that Custer's evidence "was all hearsay and not worth a tinker's damn"; that it was apparent "he did not know anything." The "radical [Republican] press" branded him a "retailer of gossip." However, the outcome of this explosive scandal was that many of the most flagrant abuses were abolished. Orvil Grant confessed matter-of-factly, acknowledging no regrets except that his share of the graft left much to be desired.

On March 30, 1876, the New York *World* broke a scoop, datelined Washington: "General Custer was the hero of a severe caning affair in which E. W. Rice, a claim-agent here, was the worsted party. Rice has long been an intimate friend of General Belknap's, and is believed by a good many to have been the medium through whom a large part of the post tradership money passed from the buyers to General Belknap. General Custer's testimony tended to prove this, the General testifying among other things that he had been told that in a certain instance a post-tradership was secured through the payment of $5000 to Rice. He (Rice) replied by a newspaper card, in which he said that if General Custer did say that any money was ever paid to him (Rice) for a post-tradership he was a liar. To-night Custer met Rice on G Street and gave him a very severe caning."

WHITE HOUSE:
THE UNKIND CUT

On April 1, Armstrong dashed off a note to Elizabeth, fretting back at Fort Lincoln. He had made his "Darling Sunbeam" stay put this time, because the Plains were blizzard-blown. "He took my breath away by telling me he could not endure the anxiety of having me go through such peril again. In vain I pleaded." No longer daring to press his proverbial luck where Libbie was concerned, he left her with a few comforting words: "Be sure it's all for the best, little one. You know we always find it so in the end." But "Life seemed insupportable until I received a despatch saying that my husband had again passed safely over that two hundred and fifty miles of country where every hour life is in jeopardy."

Washington, 4–8–76

My precious Darling,

I cannot tell you how overwhelmed I am with engagements, but I cannot let my little girl's birthday pass without a word from her dear Bo! . . . I have been recipient of kindest attentions from all papers except a few radical. I am surprised if a morning passes without *some* abuse of myself! But leading papers thruout the country commend my courage. . . .

"Sunset" Cox made an elaborate speech on the Indian question—citing the Battle of the Washita, "Garry-Owen," &c. After it he came up to me where I was standing & said, "Well, Custer, I guess I've taken your scalp." To which I replied, "Wait till I get you on the Plains! Then I'll turn you over to those gentle friends of yours. . . ."

Washington, 4–12–76

My Darling,

I calculate on one week more here. Should I be detained longer, I should give up all thought of a summer campaign & send for my Bunkey. . . .

The Cincinnati *Enquirer* & St. Louis *Republican* & other papers of that stamp commend me in highest degree, while the two radical papers controlled by the Belknap Clique vie with one another in abusing me. I do not let this disturb me. . . . The Belknap Clique leave no stone unturned to injure me. Mr. [Larry] Cobright, Agent for the Associated Press, said they had given him a lot of defamatory stuff about me that he had refused to use. . . . I know you are anxious, but I believe I have done nothing rashly. And all honest, straight-forward men commend my course. . . .

Washington, 4–17–76

My darling Sunbeam,

. . . To-day I appear before the Military Committee, to-morrow the Belknap Impeachment Committee, and hope to conclude my errand here. I have urged both Committees to release me; . . . for, as I have informed them, nearly all my evidence is hearsay. The Radical papers continue to serve me up regularly. Neither has said one word against Belknap. . . .

The lines you sent me are lovely. I showed them to a lady at this hotel. She said, "Your sweetheart sent them. Never your wife!" I told her "Both are one." "What? How long have you been married?" "Twelve years." "And haven't got over that?" "No. And never shall! . . ."

Your Devoted

Autie

Custer was growing desperate. Investigating committees and social engagements kept him on the run day and night. Would they never cease? Time was a-wasting. In another month, the 7th Cavalry would be marching off on its summer campaign against hostiles and renegades in the Yellowstone country. Come hell or high water, he just *had* to get back to Fort Lincoln—

←177→

before it was too late. Before General Terry perforce appointed Major Reno to take command, to leave without him, to steal his thunder and reap the glory.

The New York *Herald* editorialized: "Custer's statement that one regiment of cavalry—with pardonable pride he mentions his own Seventh—could handle the Sioux in one campaign as effec tively as ten years of treaty-making and treaty-breaking, must be seriously regarded. In any such campaign, who else has the skill, the matchless daring, to equal his leadership? The Boy General of 1864 is now the mature Indian-fighter, the darling of his troops, and in the full prime of his great powers."

Custer was at philosophical cross purposes. His romantic spirit had sided with the South, yet reason obliged him to fight for the North; and though that same spirit was in sympathy with the Indian, making his delay in Washington less dreadful than others imagined, Custer was still an instrument of Manifest Destiny.

However, in taking issue with men like Sherman and Sheridan (who advocated an assimilation-or-extermination policy), Custer wrote that a rose-colored view "is equally erroneous with that which regards the Indian as a creature possessing the human form but divested of all other attributes of humanity. . . . In him we will find the representative of a race . . . incapable of being judged by the rules or laws applicable to any other known race of men. . . . In studying the Indian character, while shocked & disgusted by many of his traits & customs, I find much to be admired and still more of deep & unvarying interest. . . . Study him, fight him, civilize him if you can, he remains still the object of your curiosity—a type of man peculiar & undefined, subjecting himself to no known law of civilization, contending determinedly against all efforts to win him from his chosen mode of life. He stands in the group of nations solitary & reserved, seeking alliance with none, mistrusting & opposing the advances of all. Civilization may & should do much for him, but it can never civilize him. . . . He cannot be himself & be civilized; he fades away & dies. Cultivation such as the white-man would give him deprives him of his identity."

←178→

Custer comes to a remarkable conclusion—remarkable in that it absolves him of the epithet of "Indian-hater," and enhances the tragic glory of his fate, at the mercy of those he most respected and admired:

"If I were an Indian, I often think I would greatly prefer to cast my lot among those of my people adhered to the free open plains rather than submit to the confined limits of a reservation —there to be the recipient of the blessed benefits of civilization, with its vices thrown in without stint or measure."

In his attempt to return to the land of his predilections, Custer fell upon the biggest stumbling block of his career: President Grant. It wasn't enough that he had arrested Grant's son Fred for drunkenness during the Black Hills Expedition of '74. It wasn't enough that the great Indian fighter had, in his *Galaxy* articles and before the Clymer Committee, attacked or questioned the Tanner President's "carpetbag-Quaker policy." Now he had helped ruin brother Orvil and Unconditional Surrender's old comrade-at-arms, General Belknap. This was the last straw!

In a vengeful fit, President Grant ordered Secretary of War Alphonso Taft not to let Colonel Custer leave Washington under any circumstances. "He'll sit here and rot, if I have my way. Let Sherman appoint Terry to command the expedition out of Fort Lincoln. I'll tame that wild man if it's the last thing I ever do."

Saturday, April 29, 1876. The Belknap Impeachment Committee told Custer he was now free to leave the Capital—so far as *they* were concerned. Relieved of this responsibility, Custer flashed telegrams to Sheridan in Chicago and Terry at St. Paul: "Am on my way!" Or so he thought. Neither Sheridan nor Terry dared "okay" any unauthorized move, so no replies came from St. Paul or Chicago. Instead, Sheridan wired Terry that unless otherwise instructed he was to lead the punitive expedition against the Sioux: official War Department orders.

George Armstrong Custer called on Alphonso Taft, who said, "My hands are tied." Then he dropped in on his last resort,

←179→

William Tecumseh Sherman, General-in-Chief of the United States Army.

"I'd be damn glad to let you go," Uncle Billy said heartily. "You're just the man to bring Sitting-Bull to his knees. Go on to Fort Lincoln. Go on to Hell! Only get Sam's 'okay' before you do so."

Custer telegraphed Terry: "I will leave Washington at earliest moment practicable. My absence from my Command is wholly against my desire."

Monday, May 1, 1876; 10 A.M. Custer sat in the White House anteroom. He was fidgeting and sweating; again and again he rose to pace the carpeted floor.

2 P.M. Still sweating it out, still no word from the President. Custer finally lost patience. He lunged out of the White House and strode up to the War Department, where he burst unbidden into General Sherman's office.

Adjutant General Edward D. Townsend informed him that Sherman was out of town, but was expected back from New York before evening. Custer then informed Townsend: "Well, I'm leaving at seven to join my command. Will you give me written authority?"

"I don't see why not!" Townsend answered, snatching paper and pen. "Sherman and Taft have both said that your getting out of here as soon as possible is the best thing you could do under the circumstances. By the way," he added with a suggestive smile, "do you have Grant's permission?"

Custer answered abstractedly: "Oh, I shall get it before I go."

Townsend nodded. "This scrap of paper won't be worth a Confederate blueback if you don't! Stop off on your way out and get Marcy's endorsement."

With Inspector General Randolph B. Marcy's written authorization tucked into his tunic pocket ("It is my understanding that Gen'l Sherman desires you to proceed directly to your station, as Gen'l Terry requested; therefore, in the absence of the Gen'l, you have my consent."), Custer hastened back to the White House.

At 3 P.M., chief Presidential aide Rufus Ingalls stepped into the anteroom and said sheepishly, "I'm sorry, Custer." He shook his bald head and shrugged. "I asked the President if he knew you were waiting outside. He said he did. I had given him your card this morning. He says he doesn't want to see you. 'Tell Colonel Custer I refuse to see him,' he says. All this time—I tell you, Custer, *all this time*—I kept urging him: 'At least spare Custer the indignity of waiting outside. Send him a message to save his time. So much is due to his past services *at least*.' So *now,* after all this time, he says: 'I don't want to see him.' Custer, I'm sorry. Truly I am."

Custer smiled weakly, laying his hand on Ingalls' shoulder. "It's all right, old fellow. You want to wait just a minute till I write a note to that man in there?"

Ingalls nodded.

Custer sat down, pulled pencil and pad out of his jacket, scribbled the following message:

5–1–76

To His Exc'y the President:—

To-day, for the third time, I have sought an interview with the President—not to solicit a favor, except to be granted a brief hearing, but to remove from his mind certain unjust impressions concerning myself which I have reason to believe are entertained against me. I desire this opportunity simply as a matter of justice; and I regret that the President has declined to give me an opportunity to submit to him a brief statement which justice to him, as well as to me, demanded.

Resp'y submitted:

G. A. Custer
Lt.-Col. 7th Cav.
Bvt. Maj.-Gen. U.S.A.

"Here. Take this in to the President."
"But aren't you going to wait for a reply?"
"It's useless. He refuses to see me!"

Poor Grant, Custer thought as he walked out of the White House. *He's dying of rum and cancer, and jackleg politics.*

Custer packed some of his duds and headed over to Sherman's hotel. It was 4 P.M. The desk clerk told him that the General wasn't back yet from New York, but was expected before dark. Custer went and wolfed down an early dinner. He popped into Sherman's hotel again at six o'clock. No; sorry, not in yet. No telling when he would show up!

Armstrong hustled back to his own hotel, finished packing, and checked out. At 7 P.M. he was off to New York aboard the evening express. *Good riddance to Washington!* Foot-loose and fancy-free at last! A wild man at large, as yet untamed by the President of the United States.

Clouds gathered on the horizon of glory, and the thunder of doom rumbled in the West.

> My race of glory run, and race of shame,
> And I shall shortly be with them that rest.

⋆21⋆

ST. PAUL:
"LAME-HIP" TERRY

"G ENERAL Custer blew into the *Herald* office like a fresh April breeze," wrote editor Joseph Clarke. "There was something so fine and broad and free in his carriage and his air, in the ruddy bronze of his face, in the laughing blue of his eyes, in the curl of his yellow hair, that one's heart went out to him. . . . Self-confidence shone in his open brow. Presently he was gone, and his absence left a painful void; the thought, 'he will risk everything rather than fail,' persisted. I do not recall another single meeting in my life that made the same impression of uplift and fatality combined."

Custer dined with Mr. and Mrs. Lawrence Barrett. "He predicted a severe campaign," the great tragedian later wrote, "but was not doubtful of the result. He was so associated with success, had escaped from so many dangers, . . . that he seemed invincible."

Charles Osborn, broker to the notorious financier and speculator Jay Gould, gave a luncheon in Custer's honor. Present was Major General Grenville M. Dodge, builder of the Union Pacific Railroad and Gould's associate in westward extension of rail travel. "Custer, in his conversation & in his assertion of what his regiment could do, said that his regiment could whip & defeat all the Indians on the Plains, and was very rash in his statements. . . . I said to him that . . . if he was going out to fight the Indians with any idea that they were to be easily whipped, he was greatly mistaken."

Dodge may have reminded Custer of Captain William J. Fetterman, who had boasted in '66: "Give me eighty men and I'll ride through the whole Sioux nation!" Fetterman was given his eighty men—was ambushed and annihilated, near Fort Phil Kearny, by a dozen Indians under Crazyhorse. He and Captain Fred Brown committed suicide, each shooting the other in preference to a slow death by torture. The so-called "Fetterman Massacre" thus became proverbial on the frontier for reckless daring and stupidity. Custer chuckled, said Fetterman was a fool; that the 7th Cavalry numbered far more than eighty men, and knew their enemy well enough not to get caught in such a ridiculous trap.

Armstrong spent only a few memorable hours in the Empire City, bidding hello and good-by to his many cultured and influential acquaintances, those who had encouraged and stood by him for the past decade. He wrote Elizabeth:

My precious Sunbeam,
. . . I have gotten more requests for articles from periodicals & dailies than 10 writers could satisfy. I am over-run with invitations! . . . Have seen hosts of friends. I hope to leave for Chicago to-night. . . . Do not be anxious. I seek to follow a moderate & prudent course, avoiding prominence. Nevertheless, everything I do (however simple & unimportant) is noticed & commented on. This only makes me more careful. And never mind about "U.S." The President is mistaken; but it will all come right at last, if I do my duty. If a consciousness of virtue establishes a claim to happiness, then I am happy! And I have no regrets. It is better to be Right than to be President!

I have heard by telegraph from Gen'l Terry. I believe a mutual good-feeling subsists between us. He is anxious for me to return. . . .
P.S.—I hope (before this reaches you) to telegraph, "I'm a-comin'!"

Fred Whittaker of *Galaxy* was one of the last in the East to bid Custer farewell. In his words: "Custer looked worn and thin, and somewhat worried, . . . a great change from the debonair cavalier.

. . . His manner conveyed the impression of a nervous man with his nerves all on edge, in a state of constant repressed impatience."

Early Tuesday morning, May 2, the following telegram from Sherman opened Sheridan's eyes: "I am this moment advised that Gen'l Custer started last night for St. Paul & Ft. Ab. Lincoln. He was not justified in starting without seeing the President or myself. Please intercept him at Chicago or St. Paul, and order him to halt & await further orders. Meantime, let the Expedition from Ft. Lincoln proceed without him."

Thursday morning, May 4, 1876. Custer stepped off the train at Chicago, where he was greeted by Colonel Forsyth of Sheridan's personal staff: "General, I'm obliged to inform you that you're under arrest by order of General Sherman." He added stiffly, "Here is my authorization," and thrust forward an official envelope.

"And here is mine, Sandy." Custer scowled, pulling out his clearance papers signed by Generals Townsend and Marcy.

"I'm sorry, Custer, but I cannot accept them. They've been countermanded by these orders."

Custer ripped open the envelope and snatched out four folded slips of paper. He skimmed over the first one, from Sheridan's adjutant: "Agreeably to instructions contained in the enclosed copy of a telegraphic despatch from the General of the Army, of the 2nd inst., the Lieut.-Gen'l Comdg. the Division directs you to remain in Chicago until the receipt of further orders from superior authority, to be furnished you thro' these Hd.-Qrs."

Custer then read Sherman's official wire. Sheridan's telegram to Terry, dated April 28, was also there for Custer to scan: "The Gen'l of the Army telegraphs me that instructions have been rec'd thro' the Sec'y of War, coming from the President, to send some one other than Custer in charge of the Expedition from Ft. Lincoln. . . . After a careful consideration of the situation, I think the best way to meet it (and that promising the most satisfaction & the greatest success) would be for you to go yourself."

Terry's reply to Sheridan, April 29: "I will go myself."

When Custer handed the slips back to their bearer, Forsyth said, "General Sheridan expressed a desire to see you at once."

"Well, I should think so!" Custer snapped, his face mantled with humiliation.

The two officers, coldly courteous to each other, hopped into a waiting hack and rode downtown to Division Headquarters.

Sheridan welcomed Custer as ardently as ever, but the boy general was in no mood for good cheer. "What's the meaning of all this, Phil?"

"Custer, I swear to Christ, I don't know any more about the cause of that order than you do. But consider yourself my honored guest while you're here."

"Thanks, but I'm not staying. Would you have any objection to my telegraphing Sherman for an explanation?"

"No. Go right ahead! And good luck!"

Moments later, a message flashed over the wires: "I have seen your despatch to Gen'l Sheridan directing me to await orders here, and am at a loss to understand that portion referring to my departure from Washington without seeing you or the President. . . . At my last interview with you, I informed you that I would leave Washington Monday night to join my Command; and you in conversation replied that it was the best thing I could do. Besides, you frequently during my stay in Washington called my attention to the necessity of my leaving as soon as possible."

Custer sweated it out all morning. When no response came, he wired another message to Sherman at 2:30 P.M.: "In leaving Washington, I had every reason to believe I was acting in strict accordance with your suggestions & wishes. I ask you, as General of the Army, to do me justice in this matter."

No answer. Custer knew why, and had hoped beyond hope. It wasn't Sherman who was putting him to the torture. Grant was working that rack from both ends, dead set on pulling his victim to pieces. Sherman had assured Custer that the President had no charges to make against him; but now, as Sherman remarked to the President's secretary (U. S. Grant, Jr.), "Custer is now subject to any measure of discipline which the President may require."

Still kicking his heels, Custer made a last-ditch effort to arouse some response out of Sherman. That evening, for the third time, he telegraphed: "After you read my despatch of to-day, I would be glad if my detention could be authorized at Ft. Lincoln, where my family is, instead of at this point."

Not a word flashed back. "Grant's Revenge" was almost complete. *Almost.* Suddenly, a legion of fighting-mad Democrats rallied round their golden-haired hero. Editorials lamented that Custer was obliged, "as it were, upon bended knees, to beg of his inferior [Grant]." Barrett defended him as "the target of political rancor," adding, "How easily could he have trimmed his sail to the popular breeze, and floated into the smooth waters of political favor. The promotion which his valor had earned—which was due to his merit, which had been bestowed upon his inferiors—lay within his grasp; but the sacrifice was one from which his proud soul revolted."

The New York *World* blasted President Grant for "the most high-handed abuse of his official power which he has perpetrated yet. . . . There has never been a President of the United States before who was capable of braving the decent opinion of the country so openly and shamefully as this, for the sake of wreaking such a miserable vengeance."

The *Herald* asserted that Custer was being persecuted "simply because he did not 'crook the pregnant hinges of the knee' to this modern Caesar." It then branded Grant as an "irresponsible despot" with "absolute power to decapitate anybody offending His Highness or his favorites."

The Los Angeles *Herald* joined its allies in proclaiming: "The honest man [Custer] will live in history; the brute [Grant] will be consigned to historic oblivion and disgrace."

However, a few "radical rags" had their say against the Cavalier of the Plains. The St. Paul *Pioneer-Press,* for one, analyzed Custer as "an extra-ordinary compound of presumptuous egotism and presumptuous mendacity which makes him the reckless and lawless being he is."

Custer recoiled at that jab: "I am not impetuous or impulsive. I resent that. Everything that I have ever done has been the result of the study I have made of imaginary military situations that might arise. When I become engaged in a campaign or battle, and a great emergency arises, everything that I ever heard or studied focuses in my mind as if the situation were under a magnifying-glass & my decision was the instantaneous result. My mind works instantaneously, but always as the result of everything I have ever studied being brought to bear on the situation. . . . I have done nothing but my duty—nothing that I have any apologies to make for doing, and nothing I would not do again under the same circumstances."

Sheridan wired a confidential message to Terry: "Custer followed Sherman's advice & one of the first things that happened was, figuratively speaking, a slap in the face when he tried to see the President. Custer seems to have taken this in his stride, as it were. But the next thing that came his way was a real 'haymaker.' Arrest & detention!"

On Friday morning, May 5, Sheridan handed Custer the following telegram from Sherman: "Have just come from the President, who orders that Gen'l Custer be allowed to rejoin his post, to remain there on duty, but not to accompany the Expedition (supposed to be on the point of starting against the hostile Indians) under Gen'l Terry."

Moments later another communiqué buzzed into General Headquarters, Military Division of the Missouri:

Washington, May 5th, 1876

Gen'l G. A. Custer, Chicago, Ill.
. . . Sent orders to Gen'l Sheridan to permit you to go to Abe Lincoln on duty, but the President adheres to his conclusion that you are not to go on the Expedition.

W. T. Sherman
General

←188→

Sheridan was in part responsible for this. In his guarded endorsement of Custer, whereby he besought Sherman's trust, Phil boasted: "I am the only officer who can control Custer. He is the only man that never failed me."

On Saturday morning, May 6, Custer arrived by rail in St. Paul, Gateway to the Northwest. He was fearful, hurt, desperate.

Swinging into Dakota Department Headquarters, Custer clasped the hand of Brigadier General Alfred H. Terry with both of his own. He smiled, but tears glimmered in his bright blue eyes. Seconds later the smile faded, became sickly, and Armstrong broke down and wept. All his iron nerve melted in convulsive sobbing.

"I beg of you, sir—you've got to help me. Damned if I'll be torn apart this way! I'd as soon a bullet in my brain. Terry, I beg of you—for God's sake, you've got to help me."

Terry stood in somber silence, his hands clasped behind him, gazing out the window. He was deeply moved, but dared not show it. He kept his back to Custer for several tense seconds, struggling to settle his mind, then turned slowly to face the man who had come to him in despair.

Alfred Howe Terry ("Hero of Fort Fisher") was full-bearded and tall, with wistful eyes and reflective bearing. The Indians called him "Lame-Hip," because he limped from a Civil War wound. Terry was soft-spoken and graceful, and he looked and acted more like a preacher than a soldier. He was an intellectual and a scholar, a Yale law graduate, and (in the estimation of his A.D.C. and brother-in-law, Captain Robert P. Hughes) "the kindest and noblest-hearted man I have ever known."

"I'll help you." He sighed, turning with a look of compassion rather than ambivalence. "I shall do whatever I can."

He later wrote: "Custer came to me, and with tears in his eyes, begged my aid. How could I resist it?"

Custer lunged forward and embraced Terry as a brother. Within a half-hour, the following dispatch flashed over the wires to the Windy City:

Hd.-Qrs., Dept. of Dakota
St. Paul, Minn.
May 6th, 1876

Adj't-Gen'l, Div. of Mo., Chicago
I forward the following:
"To His Exc'y the President (Thro' Military Channels):—
"I have seen your order, transmitted thro' the General of
the Army, directing that I be not permitted to accompany the
Expedition about to move against hostile Indians. As my entire
Regt. forms a part of the proposed Expedition, and as I am the
Senior Officer of the Regt. on duty in this Dept., I respectfully
but most earnestly request that while not allowed to go in com-
mand of the Expedition I may be permitted to serve with my
Regt. in the field. I appeal to you as a soldier to spare me the
humiliation of seeing my Regt. march to meet the enemy & I
not to share its dangers.
"G. A. Custer
Bvt. Maj.-Gen'l, U.S.A."
In forwarding the above, I wish to say expressly that I have
no desire whatever to question the orders of the President or of
my military superiors. Whether Lieut.-Col. Custer shall be permitted to accompany my column or not, I shall go in command
of it. I do not know the reasons upon which the orders already
given rest; but if those reasons do not forbid it, Lieut.-Col.
Custer's services would be very valuable with his Regt.
A. H. Terry
Comdg. Dept.

Drawing a deep breath, Custer sauntered out for a cup of
coffee. Returning to Headquarters, he overheard General Terry
and another officer bandying heated words in the telegraph office.

"Look here, Bob," Terry was saying, "this is a scandalous
shame. Custer has done nothing wrong. He has only obeyed the
law and told the truth as he sees it. I say the President is taking
a mean and cowardly advantage of his power to punish Custer
indirectly because he daresn't do it directly."

The other voice was that of Captain Robert P. Hughes, Terry's
aide-de-camp and brother-in-law. "Al, you're still a lawyer. You

make no enemies. Why even after Fort Fisher, when you jumped over the heads of all those old West Pointers, they couldn't find it in their hearts to hate you. You're too damned goodhearted, and I just hope Custer isn't playing you for a fool."

Sheridan endorsed Terry's dispatch and forwarded it to Army Headquarters, on May 7, with these comments: "I am sorry Lieut.-Col. Custer did not manifest as much interest, by staying at his post, to organize & get ready his Regt. & the Expedition as he does now to accompany it. On a previous occasion, in 1868, I asked Executive Clemency for Col. Custer to enable him to accompany his Regt. against the Indians; and I sincerely hope, if granted this time, it will have sufficient effect to prevent him from again attempting to throw discredit on his profession & his brother officers."

Articles and editorials headlined "Grant's Tyranny—Custer's Degradation" and "Grant's Revenge—Custer's Banishment," to say nothing of "Grant's Hatred" and "Custer's Humiliation," drove Old Unconditional Surrender to the wall. A buzzer flashed from East to West:

> Head-Quarters of the Army
> Washington, May 8th, 1876

Gen'l A. H. Terry, St. Paul, Minn.

Gen'l Sheridan's enclosing (yours of yesterday) touching Gen'l Custer's urgent request to go under your command with his Regt. has been submitted to the President, who sent me word that if you want Gen'l Custer along he withdraws his objections. Advise Custer to be prudent, not to take along any newspaper-men (who always make mischief), and to abstain from personalities in the future. . . .

> *W. T. Sherman*
> General

George Armstrong Custer swanked out of Department Head-quarters. It was Monday morning, May 8, and the past week now seemed like a dreadful nightmare from which he had just awakened in a joyous sweat. It was now "the boyhood of the year, the time of the singing of birds." A couple of blocks to the Metropolitan Hotel, pack his bags, then full speed ahead to Fort Lincoln—and Libbie, and a summer campaign that promised undying glory. A fighting chance for redemption, to rewin his spurs and wipe out the shame that haunted his pride.

As he neared the hotel, Custer ran into Colonel William Ludlow, Chief Engineer of the Department of Dakota.

"By God, Custer, good to see you again! How goes it, eh?"

"You needn't look so foolish, old fellow. I'm gay as a lark!"

"By God, and aren't you now!"

"I've been restored to active duty. By Executive Order, no less! Terry and I plan to light out this evening for the Wild Mizzoo."

"Oh, then he'll be in command of the expedition?"

"It's all the same! The 7th Cavalry will have the lion's share of this campaign, just as it had back in '73. And I expect I shall be in the scouting saddle, spearheading the column as usual. First chance I get, I'll cut loose from Terry and make a killing. With my Garryowens behind me, I can whip all the Indians in the Northwest!"

"Custer's Luck, eh?"

"Well, perhaps. I got away with Stanley, poor sot, so I suppose I'll be able to swing clear of Terry."

The old soldiers shook hands and patted shoulders in parting; and when Ludlow wished Custer good luck, he got this reply: "I'm going to clear my name or leave my bones on the prairie."

★22★
FORT LINCOLN:
GARRY OWEN IN GLORY

G ENERALS Custer and Terry
took a special express to Bismarck, whirling into Fort Abraham
Lincoln by Wells-Fargo stagecoach on the night of May 9, 1876.

Tuesday afternoon, May 16. Terry had lunched with the Custers, and the three of them were now alone in the parlor. Libbie
was plying a pair of horse clippers, cropping her husband's
reddish-gold ringlets as close as she dared.

"My precious scalp won't be worth a continental damn when
the Old Lady gets done!" he cackled.

Terry stirred in his seat, then said pensively, "Do you recall
that editorial in the Boston *Post?* 'The history of relations between white man and red has been an unbroken story of rapacity,
cruelty, and a complete lack of feeling on the part of the white.'
Be that as it may, it bothers me to think the editor never took
into account the history of relations between red man and red,
which is scarcely more creditable than the annals of the white
race."

Custer responded: "Those charitable busybodies back East
have satisfied themselves that we're bent on punishing the redman
solely for depredations against the white. What these angels of
mercy care to ignore is that the Sioux have been invading and
stealing land from the Crows and Shoshones for the past couple
of years. Sitting-Bull refuses to make peace with the whiteman,
and harasses every red cousin of his who does. He's an outlaw,
a bully, and the desperadoes under his influence are a far cry from

those tribes that want to live in peace with the whites. The Crows, for one, were always a peace-loving nation. They appealed to us for help, and we intend to protect them. What could be more charitable than that! Are we to defend cutthroats and criminals, whatever their race? The Sioux have long been troublemakers, proud to be called 'Scourge of the Plains,' tyrannizing their neighbors at every turn. And as a warlike nation, they enslave their victims and live off the spoils of conquest. The Sioux want war, and they shall damn soon get it: a war to the death."

Terry pursed his lips and nodded gravely.

Custer continued: "Back in '73, Chief Blackfoot of the Crow Nation told a delegation of Indian-agents 'You ought not to give the Sioux guns and ammunition. You should wipe them all out. . . .' Here's a letter I got from Jack Smith, agent upriver. He says 'About half the warriors remaining at agencies have repeating rifles—Winchesters—and all others have breechloaders. Fully half the young men have pistols—one or more. I have known Indians to have three thousand rounds of ammunition for a single gun.' Comforting facts, are they not? Especially when one considers that my troopers are obliged to limp along with single-shot Springfields, none of which are worth a damn!"

Terry nodded, sad-eyed.

"They say 'Glory, on the frontier, means being shot by an Indian from behind a rock and having your name spelled wrong in the papers.' Well, I'm damned if I'll suffer such a fate!" Custer then leaned forward and said firmly, "Terry, a man usually means what he says when he lets his wife listen to his statements. Reports are circulating that I don't want to go out on the campaign under you. Well, I want you to know I *do* want to go and serve under you—not only because I value you as a soldier, but as a friend and a man."

"God bless you, sir," Terry breathed.

That night, while reading Mrs. Alexander's three-volume *Her Dearest Foe* (the latest English novel), Armstrong marked the sentence: "I have faith in my own fortunes, and believe I shall conquer in the end."

Wednesday, May 17, 1876; 5 A.M. Chief Trumpeter Henry Voss licked his lips and sounded the "General." Its brassiness blasted across the spongy drillfield outside the stockade of Fort Lincoln.

Old Curly's Garryowens, the Fighting 7th, tumbled out of their tents and loaded the supply wagons with dew-laden white canvas. The "Assembly" blared at six o'clock, and over seven hundred crack troopers of twelve companies scuttled into rank and file for roll call. With bugles blowing "Mount," then "Forward," officers and men of the 7th U.S. Regular Cavalry swung into the saddle, wheeled away from the picket lines, and jogged by column of fours into the fort.

A raw wind was whipping out of the east, and a mist hung ominously over the "Big Muddy," but greasy weather could not dampen the spirits of alkalied cavalrymen rarin' to hit the glory trail.

With guidons streaming and horses prancing and bandsmen crashing the 7th's own battle tune, "Garry Owen," Custer's famous regiment fanned out in column of platoons and marched around the parade ground.

> Our hearts so stout have got us fame,
> For soon 'tis known from whence we came;
> Where'er we go they dread the name
> Of Garry Owen in glory!

Astride his blaze-faced, stocking-legged, snappy thoroughbred sorrel, Old Vic, Custer led the cavalcade. He was clad in fringed buckskins, bright red neckerchief, and a white broad-brimmed Western hat. He had a pearl-handled bulldog revolver on either hip, a Remington sporting rifle slung over his shoulder, and a big Indian scalping knife in his belt.

Florid-faced Custer, with his white sombrero and close-cropped golden-red hair, struck quite a contrast as he rode beside dark-bearded, fair-faced Terry with his sable campaign hat and dark-blue uniform.

On Armstrong's right trotted Elizabeth, dressed in a buckskin riding habit and scarlet hunting cap. Close behind paced Captain Tom Custer, senior officer of the five-company Custer Battalion, decked out in buckskins and a white slouch hat. He cut a dashing figure with trim sideburns and a tawny imperial that accented his bony cheeks. Beside him rode sprite-faced Boston and a new-comer to the family of personal aides, Henry Armstrong ("Harry" or "Autie") Reed: Custer's handsome, husky[5] teen-aged nephew.

Women and children lined the boardwalks of Officers' and Soapsuds Rows as the 7th Cavalry swirled slowly around the vast paradeground. With tears streaking down their cheeks, mothers held their little ones out at arm's length for a last look as proud fathers went rolling by; and toddlers, waving handkerchiefs tied to sticks and beating on old tin pans, stomped alongside the column in lusty chorus. When regiment and commander swept past the Indian quarters, a cluster of gaily colored tepees, the squaws and papooses of Yellowhair's red-skinned scouts wept and wailed while their braves thumped on tomtoms and hooted the war whoop. It was a chilling, bloodcurdling clamor; and Libbie breathed easier when it was over. "The most despairing hour seemed to have come."

The curveting hoofs of Custer's cavalry and the tramping feet of Terry's infantry chopped up the rain-soaked ground, and the slithering wheels of supply wagons and Gatling guns forged deep ruts across the gleamy flats, as the entire thousand-man expedition rolled out of Fort Abraham Lincoln to a pulsing lilt:

> The hour was sad I left the maid,
>   A ling'ring farewell taking;
> Her sighs and tears my steps delay'd—
>   I thought her heart was breaking.
>
> In hurried words her name I bless'd;
>   I breathed the vows that bind me,
> And to my heart in anguish press'd
>   The girl I left behind me.

A chilling breeze snapped at the cavalry's red-and-blue swallow-tailed headquarters pennant, emblazoned with white crossed sabers and a large gold 7. It lashed the swallow-tailed guidons with their stars and stripes, and it whipped out the gorgeous gold-fringed regimental standard with its golden eagle on a crimson field and the superscription: *7th U.S. Cavalry.* The blue-clad troopers pulled down their black campaign hats and hunched in the saddle, picturesquely slanted against the whistling wind, as they marched westward into the forbidden Yellowstone country, into a labyrinth of ravines, a land of deadly echoes.

It was 7 A.M., and cool gusts began to lighten and whisk away the heavy frost smoke hovering over the Missouri bottom lands. A warm sun slowly melted the haze, sucking veils of steam out of the sodden earth. Sunbeams burst like a shower of molten gold across the horizon, and the ribbonlike column of cavalry was mirrored in a radiant mist.

> The hope of final victory,
>   Within my bosom burning,
> Is mingling with sweet thoughts of thee
>   And of my fond returning.
> But should I ne'er return again,
>   Still worth thy love thou'lt find me;
> Dishonor's breath shall never stain
>   The name I'll leave behind me. . . .

Libbie Custer and Maggie Calhoun accompanied their husbands that first day out of Fort Lincoln. As the two-mile column snaked its way slowly through gently sloping hills, Armstrong often turned in the saddle and glanced back to admire his men. "Just look at 'em, Libbie!" he said excitedly. "Did you ever see a grander sight in all your life?"

In Libbie's words: "The soldiers, inured to many years of hardship, were the perfection of physical manhood. Their brawny limbs and lithe, well-poised bodies gave proof of the training their outdoor life had given. Their resolute faces, brave and confident, inspired one with a feeling that they were going out aware of the momentous hours awaiting them, but inwardly assured of their capability to meet them."

Captain Tom laughed and waved his hand. "Take it from us, Old Lady. A single company of Garryowens can lick the whole damn Sioux Nation!"

Libbie smiled hopefully, indulgently, but there was a gnawing fear in her heart.

The next morning, after a tearful farewell, Armstrong lifted Elizabeth onto her horse. "So long, Maggie," he said, winking at his sister. "Rest assured I shall keep Jimmy in line for you." He then nodded to the escort sergeant and lightly slapped Libbie's mount. The small party rode away to the east.

Custer stood watching for a moment, tears still in his eyes. Then he turned sharply, and his freckled face was ghostly white. Looking at his brother-in-law, he smiled shyly and cracked: "Jim, a good soldier has two mistresses. While he's loyal to one, the other must suffer." He slapped Lieutenant Calhoun on the back and swaggered off.

46 m. from Ft. Lincoln
May 20th, 9:15 P.M.

My Darling Girl,

. . . It is raining now, and has been ever since we started. Everybody is more or less disgusted—except me. The elements seem against us, but a wet season & bad roads can be looked for always in this region in the months of May & June. We have not seen any signs of Indians thus far, and hardly look for any for a few days yet. I have been extremely prudent—sufficiently so to satisfy my Little Durl. I go nowhere without taking an escort with me. I act as if Indians were near all the time! . . .

On Little Missouri, D.T.
May 30th, 10 P.M.

. . . Have had a tremendous day's work. I breakfasted at 4 o'clock, was in the saddle at 5, and between that hour & 6 P.M. I rode 50 miles over a rough country unknown to everybody—

←198→

and only myself for a guide. . . . Bloody-Knife looks on in
wonder at me because I never get tired, and says no other man
could ride all night & never sleep. I know I shall sleep soundly
when I do lie down, but actually I feel no more fatigued now
than I did before mounting my horse this morning! . . .

> Powder River (about 20 m. above
> its Mouth), Montana Terr.
> June 9th

. . . We are now in a country hitherto unvisited by white-men.
Charley Reynolds, who had been guiding the Command, lost his
way the other day; and Gen'l Terry did not know what to do.
I told him I tho't I could guide the column. He assented; so
I brought the Command to this point, over what seems to be
the only practicable route for miles on either side, thro' the
worst kind of Bad-lands. The Gen'l did not believe it possible
to find a road thro'! When, after a hard day's work, we arrived
at this river—making 32 miles in one day—he was delighted &
came to congratulate me: "Nobody but Gen'l Custer could have
brought us thro' such a country! He's the best guide I ever
saw. . . ."

> On Yellowstone (at Mouth of
> Powder River), M.T.
> June 11th, 10:30 P.M.

. . . I am again acting as guide! And thro' Unknown Bad-lands!!
Gen'l Terry came to my tent before daylight & asked me if I
would try to find a road. He seems to think I have a gift in that
way. Well, sure enough I found one, after passing thro' some
perfectly terrible country; and we arrived here safely—waggons
& all! . . . As I was up at 3 this morning & have had a hard
day's march, and as it is now going on to 12, I must hie to bed
& catch a little rest.

> Y'r devoted Boy,
> *Autie*

P.S.—We are living delightfully. I don't know what we (Tom
& I) would do without Bos to tease. *You* might just as well be
here as not!

Libbie answered:

Ft. Lincoln, June 21st

My darling Autie,

. . . I cannot but feel the greatest possible apprehension for your safety on this dangerous scout. Oh, Autie, I feel as if it was almost impossible for me to wait your return with patience. I cannot describe my feelings. I have felt so badly for the last few days, I have been perfectly unendurable to every one. Most of the time I have spent in my room, feeling myself no addition to any one's society. . . . Please look after yourself, my darling— not for me alone, but for the country we love & honor. With your bright future, and the knowledge that you are of positive use to your day & generation, do you not see that your life is precious on that account—and not only because an idolizing wife could not live without you?

And now I shall go to bed & dream of my dear Bo. God be with you, my darling. I love you always.

Your devoted Girl,
Libbie

This letter, and the ones that followed, never reached her husband. They were all returned unopened on that day of anguish yet to come.

Libbie would write: "With my husband's departure, my last happy days in garrison were ended; as a premonition of disaster that I had never known before weighed me down. I could not shake off the baleful influence of depressing thoughts. This presentiment and suspense, such as I had never known, made me selfish; and I shut into my heart the most uncontrollable anxiety, and could lighten no one else's burden. The occupations of other summers could not even give temporary interest."

★23★

YELLOWSTONE:
THE "FAR WEST"

WEDNESDAY, June 21, 1876; 3
P.M. General Terry, Colonel Custer, Colonel John Gibbon, and
Major James S. Brisbin were in council of war.

Terry spread his huge campaign map on a table in the cabin of
the supply steamer *Far West,* then moored on the Yellowstone
River at the mouth of Rosebud Creek, about 275 miles west of
Fort Lincoln. He marked out a route with his blue pencil, then
said to Custer:

"As soon as your regiment can be made ready for the march, I
want you to proceed up the Rosebud in pursuit of the Indians
whose trail was discovered by Major Reno a few days ago. Of
course, it's impossible for me to give you any definite instructions
in regard to this movement. Even if I could, I place too much
confidence in your energy and ability to wish to impose any
precise orders on you which might hamper your action when
nearly in contact with the enemy. However, these are my own
views of what your action should be. I should like you to con-
form to them unless you see sufficient reason for departing from
them."

Terry bent over the map, following the penciled line with his
finger.

"I think you should proceed up the Rosebud till you definitely
ascertain the direction in which the Indian trail leads. Should it
be found to turn towards the Littlehorn [*i.e.,* Little Bighorn], I
think you should avoid following it directly to the river. Keep

moving southward, perhaps as far as the headwaters of the Tongue, and then turn towards the Littlehorn—feeling constantly to your left—so as to prevent the Indians from escaping to the south or southeast. At the same time, Colonel Gibbon's column will proceed to the mouth of the Bighorn. As soon as it reaches that point it will cross the Yellowstone and move up at least as far as the forks of the Bighorn and Littlehorn. In this way, allowing for good timing and favorable circumstances, the Indians may be so nearly enclosed by the two columns that their escape will be impossible."

Terry eased back in his seat, eying the ceiling reflectively.

"Now I have calculated, averaging from ten to fifteen miles a day, the two columns should converge at rendezvous in approximately five days. That would set the date for concerted attack on the twenty-sixth. Now this plan of mine is founded on the belief that at some point on the Littlehorn a body of hostile Sioux will be found; and though it's impossible to make movements in perfect concert, yet by the use of guides and scouts the two columns may be brought within co-operating distance of each other. Needless to say, the success of this operation hinges on continual communication between the two columns. Now then, gentlemen. Though it's my expectation we shall arrive in the neighborhood of the Sioux village about the same time, and assist each other in the attack: if you, General Custer, arrive first, you are at liberty to attack *if* you deem prudent. Use your own good judgment, and do what you think best. It's reported that Sitting-Bull has fifteen hundred lodges, is confident, and intends making a stand."

According to the diary (6/21/76) of Lieutenant James H. Bradley, Gibbon's chief of scouts, "It is understood that if Custer arrives first, he is at liberty to attack at once if he deems prudent. We have little hope of being in at the death, as Custer will undoubtedly exert himself to the utmost to get there first & win all the laurels for himself & his Regt."

These statements, written "on the spot," refute the charge that Custer disobeyed Terry's orders by attacking the Indians on his own hook. That Terry virtually gave Custer a free hand is also confirmed by *Herald* correspondent Mark Kellogg (the newspaperman Sherman warned Custer "not to take along"), who reported: "It was announced by Gen'l Terry that Gen'l Custer's column would strike the blow."

"I wonder if we haven't already lost the element of surprise," Custer said dryly. "Reno's failure to follow up the trails has imperiled our plans by giving the Indians an intimation of our presence. Few officers have ever had such a fine opportunity to make a successful and telling strike, and few ever failed so completely to improve their opportunity. Reno made the mistake of his life in not pushing on and smashing up the village while he had the chance."

Terry shifted uneasily in his seat. "Well, General, if you find the Indians first, don't do as Reno did—run away—but if you think you can whip them, do so."

(Major Reno, detailed with a squadron to hunt up the Indian trail, searched the Tongue and Powder rivers and found nothing. His orders were not to go beyond the Tongue; but on his return march, in striking the headwaters of the Rosebud, he discovered a large Indian trail. Custer, in a *Herald* article entitled "Reno's Contempt of Orders," wrote: "Gen'l Terry, in framing the orders which were to govern Maj. Reno's movements, explicitly & positively directed that officer . . . not to move in the direction of Rosebud River; as it was feared that such a movement, if prematurely made, might 'flush the covey.'" Custer adds that Reno struck the Indian trail and followed it about twenty miles; "but faint heart never won fair lady, neither did it ever pursue & overtake an Indian village. Had Reno, after first violating his orders, pursued & overtaken the Indians, his original disobedience of orders would have been overlooked. But his determination forsook him at this point; and instead of continuing the pursuit & at least bringing the Indians to bay, he gave the order to counter-march." In referring to Reno's conduct as a "gross & inexcusable blunder," Custer boldly concludes: "A court-martial is strongly hinted at, and if one is not ordered it will not be because it is not richly deserved." Nothing came of the matter, which must have rankled Custer into a recklessness justified by Terry's complaisance. If Reno could throw caution to the winds, and get away with it, Custer apparently saw no more reason for the new self-discipline that harnessed his spirit.)

The glory hunter said to Terry, "Well, as I see it now, this maneuver of ours will result in either a fight or a footrace; and the only real question is whether Sitting-Bull will sit long enough to allow us to close the trap around him!"

Terry asked, "How long will your marches be?"

Custer replied, "At first, I reckon, about thirty miles a day. That will later allow for plenty of reconnaissance time when in the vicinity of the enemy."

A moment later, Terry said to Custer with a worried look, "In consideration of the fact that you will be taking the most dangerous route, perhaps it would be well for me to take Gibbon's squadron of horse and go with you."

Custer shook his head. "That won't be necessary, General. The 7th can handle anything it meets. Besides, an extra squadron would be of no account."

"Well, then, would you like Major Brisbin's battery of Gatling guns?"

"No. They might embarrass me. I'm strong enough without 'em."

"You're sure of that," James S. Brisbin said sardonically.

"Absolutely," Custer answered. "I don't want them. I'm afraid they'll impede my march. Besides, as I said before, the 7th Cavalry can whip every hostile in the Northwest."

The council of war broke up at sundown. As the four officers were about to leave the *Far West,* Terry turned to Custer and said earnestly, hands clasped behind his back, "Custer, I don't know what to say for the last."

"Say whatever you want to say," Custer replied offhandedly.

"Well," Terry ventured, "use your own judgment and do what you think best if you strike the trail. And whatever you do, Custer, hold onto your wounded. Rather than remain here, I shall go with Gibbon. In any event, I only hope one of the columns finds the Indians." He added, barely audible: "I'll give you written instructions tomorrow, before departure."

When Custer was out of earshot, Major Brisbin muttered hotly to General Terry, "Begging your pardon, sir, but do you think it's such a worthwhile idea turning that wild man loose to go up the Rosebud after Lord knows how many redskins?"

Terry reflected, pursing his lips. "You don't seem to have any confidence in Custer."

"None in the world," Brisbin snarled. "I have no use for him—insufferable ass."

"Don't you think Custer's regiment can handle itself?" Terry added in a troubled voice.

"No. There's enough Indians for all of us. Possibly Custer can whip 'em with the 7th; but what's the use in taking any chances?"

"Well, I've had but little experience in Indian-fighting; and Custer has had much, and is sure he can whip anything he meets."

"General," Brisbin leered, "you underrate your own ability and overrate Custer's."

Big-bodied Brisbin, known to his troops as "Old Blatherskite" and "Grasshopper Jim," was so crippled with rheumatism that he had to hop around on crutches. "Lame-Hip" Terry pitied him. White-whiskered Colonel John Gibbon, who had been Custer's artillery instructor at the Point, was in slightly better shape than his second-in-command. The Indians called him "No-Hip" because, like his superior, a Civil War wound had given him a limp. Such was the condition of army officers sent to serve on the frontier! Custer and Miles were rare exceptions.

Terry turned to Gibbon and said, "Well, John, what do *you* think?"

"My lips are sealed," Gibbon rasped. "Hear no evil, see no evil, speak no evil."

Brisbin said, "In spite of his refusal, why not put my cavalry with Custer's and go yourself in command?"

Terry frowned. "Custer is smarting under the rebuke of the

President, and wants an independent command, and I wish to give him a chance to do something."

Meeting Brother Tom, Armstrong informed him of the conference and added arrogantly, "That was very clever of Brisbin to offer to go with me. But you know, this is to be a 7th Cavalry battle; and I want all the glory for the 7th there is in it."

Eerie darkness had fallen over the Yellowstone country when "Officers' Call" brought the 7th brass hustling into a lanternlit H.Q. tent. Colonel Custer was pacing back and forth, flicking his quirt against his thigh.

"We move up the Rosebud tomorrow noon," he said sharply. "Light marching order. No wagons, no tents. And *no* sabers. Twelve packmules per company. Fifteen days' rations of hardtack, coffee, and sugar. Twelve days' rations of bacon. Twelve pounds of oats per trooper. Each man will carry one hundred rounds of carbine and twenty rounds of revolver ammunition. Two thousand rounds extra per company, to be loaded on the mules. I suggest extra forage as well. Any questions?" Custer's keen blue eyes darted to and fro.

Captain Myles Moylan spoke up: "With only twelve mules a company, General, that extra forage will break 'em down for sure."

"Well, gentlemen," Custer rasped, snapping his whip, "you may carry what supplies you damn well please. You will be held responsible for your companies. The extra forage was only a suggestion, but bear this fact in mind: we'll follow the trail no matter how far it takes us, and we may never see the supply steamer again. In that case," he added cynically, "you'd better carry along an extra supply of salt. We may have to live on horsemeat before we get through."

He was taken at his word!

24

BADLANDS: INTO THE
VALLEY OF DEATH

AT twelve noon, Thursday, June 22, 1876, bugles sounded "Boots and Saddles." Troopers of the 7th Cavalry swung into their saddles, formed column of fours, and paraded southward up the Rosebud. It was a cloud-wrapped, wind-swept day, and nerves were raw.

Custer had spared no pains to make his Fighting 7th second to none in the service. As a Garryowen expressed it, "He was one damn son-of-a-bitch; but the 7th was Custer, and Custer was the 7th." And, in Libbie's words, "His buoyant spirits at the prospect of the activity and field-life that he so loved made him like a boy."

Lieutenant Winfield Scott Edgerly (Troop D) regarded his commander as "the incarnation of energy . . . like the thoroughbred he rode, champing the bit & chafing to be off, longing for action."

Herald correspondent Mark Kellogg observed Custer "flitting to & fro in his quick eager way, . . . the keen incisive manner for which he is so well known." Here was "the most peculiar genius in the Army; a man of strong impulses, of great-hearted friendships & bitter enmities, of quick nervous temperament, undaunted courage, will & determination; a man possessing electrical mental capacity, and of iron frame & constitution; . . . the hardest rider, the greatest pusher, with the most untiring vigilance, . . . and with an ambition to succeed in all things he undertakes." Kellogg concludes: "The Gen'l is full of perfect readiness for the fray with the hostile red devils, and woe to the body of scalp-hunters that

←207→

comes within reach of himself & brave companions-in-arms! . . . I go with Custer, and will be in at the death."

"The regiment's in splendid condition, General," Terry said to Custer as they reviewed the passing cavalcade. "It's the best-looking outfit I've ever seen."

"Thank you, General," Custer responded proudly. "I've done my best to make it so—second to none. Well, I must be off." Custer shook hands with Terry, Gibbon, and Brisbin. "So long, gentlemen," he said briskly.

"Goodbye," Terry murmured. "God bless you, and Godspeed. Do what you think best if you strike the trail."

"So long," Gibbon rasped. "Remember now, there are enough Indians for all of us!"

"Good luck," Brisbin said begrudgingly.

As Custer reined his horse around, Gibbon cracked: "Now Custer, don't be greedy. Wait for us!"

Custer rose to the trot, flipping off his hat in a jaunty salute. "I won't!" he called back laughingly, then charged to the head of his command in a swirl of dust.

"Now what the hell did he mean by that?" said Brisbin.

Terry chuckled into his beard. "Custer's happy now, off with a roving command and a free hand to whip every hostile in the Northwest. I hope he finds them; for if he does, I've no doubt he'll whip them as well."

Brisbin grunted. He had his doubts. "Just hope he doesn't bite off more than he can chew."

"Well, if he should," Gibbon said, "we'll be close enough to see he doesn't choke to death."

Twilight found the 7th Cavalry bivouacked on the west bank of the Rosebud, twelve miles below the Yellowstone. With his officers gathered around him by the headquarters campfire, Colonel Custer said nervously, "It has come to my knowledge that my official actions have been criticized by certain officers of this regiment at Department Headquarters. Now I'm willing to accept recommendations from any one of you at any time, but I want them to be made in a proper manner—not over my head or behind my back. In calling your attention to that paragraph of *Army Regulations* referring to the criticism of actions of commanding officers by subordinates, let me advise you that I shall take all necessary steps to punish the offenders should there be a recurrence of the offense."

Captain Fred Benteen spoke up in his sneeringly respectful manner: "It seems to me, General, you're lashing the shoulders of *all* to get at *some*. Now as we're all present, would it not do to specify the officers you accuse?"

"Captain Benteen," Custer said dryly, "I'm not here to be catechized by you. For your own information, I want the saddle to go just where it fits. We're now starting on a scout we all hope will be successful, and I intend doing everything I can to make it both successful and pleasant for everybody. I'm certain that if any regiment in the service can do what's required of it, we can. I'll be only too glad to listen to suggestions from any officer of this command, if made in the proper manner. But I want it distinctly understood that I'll allow no grumbling, and shall exact the strictest compliance with orders from everybody—not only with mine, but with any order given by an officer to his subordinate. I don't want it said of this regiment, as one department commander said of another cavalry regiment, that 'It would be a good one if the colonel could get rid of his old captains and let the young lieutenants command the companies.' "

"Beg pardon, General," Benteen cut in, "but just who did you have in mind by that remark about grumbling?"

Custer stood with arms folded, legs firmly apart. "As I said before, I want the saddle to go just where it fits." His words were aggressive.

Benteen smirked, glancing around at his fellow officers. "Did the General ever know of any criticism or grumbling from me?"

"No, I never have." Custer smirked too. "But methinks you doth protest too much."

There had been "a lot of grumbling" since May 17, for the regiment wasn't paid till it was fourteen miles from Lincoln—and the saloons of Bismarck. Sergeant Windolph commented: "I suppose it saved many a bad head, and the trouble of rounding up some of the worst drunks, but the men resented the fact they didn't get to go on their regular spree."

Custer continued: "Until further orders, no bugle calls except in an emergency. Marches will begin at five A.M. *sharp*. Only two things will be regulated from my headquarters: when to move out and when and where to go into camp. All other details on the march will be left to your judgment and discretion. Do what's necessary for your men. This responsibility entails company commanders to keep within supporting distance of each other, not to get ahead of the scouts or very far to the rear of the column." He then said in earnest, "I want to impress upon you the extent to which I now rely on your judgment, your discretion, your loyalty. Judging from the number of lodges reported by our scouts, we'll meet at least a thousand if not fifteen hundred hostiles. But I feel proudly confident that the 7th Cavalry can whip any number of savages thrown against it. If it can't, no other regiment in the service can. But to win, we need complete harmony in our ranks; and I'm sure we have it." Custer paused, staring wistfully at the fire, and his shaggy mustachios twitched. "Nothing more, gentlemen," he muttered with a brief sigh, "except that marches will be from twenty-five to thirty miles a day. That means husband your rations, for I intend to follow the trail and hunt 'em down even if it takes us into Nebraska."

As the council was breaking up, debonair Lieutenant Winfield Scott Edgerly of Benteen's Battalion addressed Custer: "General, won't we be stepping high when we get those Injuns!"

"Won't we!" Custer said spiritedly, adding with a frown: "But we can't get 'Injuns' without hard riding, and plenty of it! That's why I'm depending on you young officers. The worst that could happen is for Sitting-Bull to slip away from us just when we've got him roped."

While strolling over to his bivouac, Edgerly heard Lieutenant George D. Wallace remark to Lieutenant Edward S. Godfrey: "Y'know, God, I think Custer's going to be killed."

"Why? What makes you think so?"

"Because. I never heard him talk that way before."

Godfrey later wrote: "This 'talk' of his, as we called it, was considered at the time as something extraordinary for General Custer; for it was not his habit to unbosom himself to his officers. In it he showed concessions and a reliance on others; there was an indefinable something that was *not* Custer. His manner and tone, usually brusque and aggressive or somewhat curt, was on this occasion conciliating and subdued. There was something akin to an appeal, as if depressed, that made a deep impression on all present."

If Custer seemed "abstracted," if he "showed a lack of self-confidence," it was simply because there was no hope for him but to burn out his official disgrace in a blaze of glory. The responsibility for his own redemption in the eyes of Grant was almost too great for him to bear. He was going to run a terrible risk, with the lives of over six hundred men at stake; and if he failed, there was no hope for him—but death. And now, for the first time since Bull Run, death frightened him. "Custer's Luck" had lost its meaning, and fear of the final summons unnerved a spirit that had scorned "the king of terrors." Afraid to live in failure, afraid to die in defeat, Custer was agonized by suicidal anxiety until he presumed to know his enemy and flattered himself with contempt therefor. By egocentric fancy, he saved himself for an immortal tragedy.

Late that night, coyotes howled in chorus with "I'll Take You Home Again, Kathleen"; and Fred Benteen, wrapped in his buffalo blanket, growled, "For Christ's sake, dry up!"

Custer drove his 7th Cavalry thirty-three miles on the second day, twenty-eight miles on the third. They were now in the heart of the Montana Badlands, where sage-tufted, cactus-studded desert was gouged with gullies and baked a powdery gray. Patches of parched brown grass rippled in a hot breeze, and the raw dews of foredawn hung in a spectral haze over the horizon.

On the twenty-fourth, scout George B. Herendeen paced alongside Custer, pointed to the right and said, "Gen'ral, that thar's

Tullock's Creek; and here's whar I'm to leave you an' go down it to the other command."

Custer glanced at Herendeen, but said nothing. When the scout realized that his mission was not to be accomplished, he fell back again.

As Brisbin put it: "Custer . . . knew Herendeen was there to go down the Tullock & communicate with us, by Terry's orders, and in this Custer disobeyed distinctly the Dept. Commander's wishes & orders. He did not wish us to know where he was or what he was doing, for fear we would get some of the credit of the campaign."

After Herendeen had dropped back, Custer remarked to scout Lieutenant Charles A. Varnum: "Here's where Reno made the mistake of his life. He had six companies, and rations enough for a week. He'd have made a name for himself if he had pushed on after 'em."

Custer's mile-long column of dusty troopers was a dark ribbon rolling over the reft and broken flats—shrouded by choking alkali clouds that burned their eyes and blistered their lips, tortured by the wavering monotony of mirages.

Captain Benteen grumbled and growled to Major Reno: "Forced-marching us, God damn him. At this rate we'll kill the mules, cripple half the horses, frazzle the men—just to beat Terry and Gibbon to the punch. That cuss is out for glory, and he doesn't give a Goddamn for any of us."

Reno nodded glumly, and said nothing.

★25★

LITTLE BIGHORN: CUSTER'S LAST STAND

Sunday, June 25, 1876; 7 a.m. It promised to be a smoldering day in the valleys of the Rosebud and the Little Bighorn. Custer gulped down a bittersweet cup of alkali-flavored coffee, then threw off his buckskin jacket to appreciate the cooling effect of perspiration. He yanked off his blood-red neckerchief, rolled up the sleeves of his blue flannel blouse, opened two buttons at the neck. He could feel the heat oozing out of the dust, simmering on the rocks. Without a shave since he left Fort Lincoln, his beard and face were streaked with dust. This hawkish redneck of the wild frontier was a far cry from that popinjay boy general of the Civil War. No bugles, no sabers, no flashy uniforms. No cinnamon-scented ringlets. Here was the new image of an old nature.

Chief scout Minton ("Mitch") Bouyer came dusting into camp with several Arikaras. He pitched off his unsaddled cayuse and ambled over to Custer. Bouyer was a beefy, bull-faced half-breed with barbed-wire whiskers. Known to the Indians as "Two-Bodies" (*Wîchânûpâ*), he was the protégé of famed frontiersman and trail blazer, Jim Bridger.

"Gin'ral," Bouyer drawled, spurting a stream of tobacco juice, "we discovered the village. Down thar on the Littlehorn. It's a big-un!"

"How big?" Custer said.

Bouyer gnawed his tobacco, spat again. "Too big fer you to

tackle," he said. "Why, they's thousands and thousands o' Sioux and Cheyenne down thar."

Custer glared at Bouyer for a few seconds, then snapped: "I'll attack 'em! If you're afraid, Bouyer . . ." he added with a leer.

Bouyer spat. "I guess I can go wharever you do."

At that moment, Charles A. ("Lonesome Charley") Reynolds came riding up and eased out of the saddle. With him were several Crows. Reynolds was a civilian scout of long standing. Frontier folk called him "Lonesome Charley" because he never said much and liked to be by himself. Short, shy-looking, white-mustached, Reynolds was "Lucky-Man" to the Indians because of his bright blue eyes and seemingly charmed life.

"Biggest bunch of Indians I ever seen over there," Reynolds said matter-of-factly.

"Didn't I tell ya?" Bouyer interjected. "That's the biggest village ever seen in the Plains, and I bin around hyar over thirty years."

"The whole valley ahead for ten, twelve miles is scratched up by their trailing lodgepoles," Reynolds said.

"Yup," Bouyer chawed. "Biggest village I ever seen."

"A heap of 'em," Reynolds sighed.

Custer frowned. "We can whip 'em."

Reynolds said, "It'll take six hours' hard fighting to whip them."

"They's too many Injuns ahead fer us to handle," Bouyer drawled.

Custer lashed out: "There aren't too many Indians on the whole North American continent for the 7th Cavalry to handle."

"Well," said Bouyer, "I can tell ya we're gonna have a God-damn big fight."

Reynolds nodded sadly. "If we go in there, we'll never come out."

Bloody-Knife, who was squatting close by, rumbled some re-mark to one of his comrades.

Custer jerked aside, glowering. "What's that he says?"

Grizzled civilian interpreter Fred F. Girard answered, "He says we'll find enough Sioux to keep us fighting two or three days."

Custer snorted. "Oh, I guess we'll get through with 'em in one day." He then crouched beside Bloody-Knife and muttered, "What do you think of these reports? They say there are large camps of the Sioux and Cheyenne."

Bloody-Knife nodded gravely, dragging on his long clay pipe. He gestured sharply as he spoke: "This gathering of enemy tribes too many for us. All nations. Heap big roundup. Them waiting for us. Sitting-Bull and Crazyhorse, them not men-without-sense. Them have eyes on us. Spirits give me warning. Bloody-Knife no see the set of tomorrow's sun."

"What do you reckon will be the outcome of it all?"

"*Death!*"

Custer turned to Stabbed, another Arikara scout. "And you?"

Stabbed responded in sign language: "I feel as my brother feels."

Custer smiled wryly. "I don't doubt you, Bloody-Knife. What you say seems reasonable. I know you people. You're tricky like the coyote. You know how to hide, to bait, to creep up and take by surprise. But Yellowhair is no jackrabbit."

Custer stood up straight and stepped over to Bouyer. "Describe the village to me. Exactly where and how far is it from here?"

Bouyer pointed. "Twelve, fifteen mile mebbe. Beyond them hills, on t'other side o' the Littlehorn. It's all o' three miles long. Made up of hundreds and hundreds o' lodges. Above it and below and west of it are thousands and thousands of cayuses bein' close-herded."

"Take me to your lookout. I want to see for myself."

Throwing a leg over his barebacked sorrel, Old Curly rode slick-heeled to the Custer Battalion bivouac. "Hey, Tom!" he said. "Move 'em out at eight o'clock sharp. I'm heading up the divide to have a look. Follow my trail at a fast walk. We'll meet yonder and cross over the ridge before noon."

Custer, Bouyer, Reynolds, Girard, and Bloody-Knife galloped westward up the "hogback" to a lookout known as the Crow's-Nest. Lieutenant Charles A. ("Knifeface") Varnum and several Indian scouts were there watching and waiting.

Morning mist veiled the valley.

"I don't see anything," Custer said.

Varnum said, "Look for worms wiggling along the ground."

Reynolds said, "There's more Indians over there, General, than you ever seen in one place before."

"How d'you know?"

"I smell 'em."

The Crow and Cree scouts nodded, mumbling ominously.

Reynolds said, "That's the biggest pony herd any man ever seen."

"Biggest village," Bouyer added. "A heap *too* big."

Custer said irritably, "I've been on the Plains a good many years, and my eyesight is as good as yours. I can't see anything that looks like Indian ponies."

Bouyer blurted, "Ef ya don't find more Injuns in that valley than ya ever seen before, you can hang me!"

"All right—all right—all right! It would do a damned lot of good to hang you, wouldn't it?"

The sun climbed, the haze lifted.

Custer adjusted his binoculars and scanned the unveiled basin far below and beyond. There were Indian ponies grazing in that sea of grass. Hundreds of them, skirting the chalky buttes that rimmed the glistening Little Bighorn and its girdle of cottonwoods.

"I don't see any village," Custer said. "And that's not much of a herd for fifteen hundred lodges."

Reynolds said, "The village is on the other side of the bluffs, across the river."

"That's whar we seen it afore daybreak," Bouyer said.

Bloody-Knife grunted.

Suddenly two bare-skinned, blanket-waving boys came sprinting across the yellow-green flat and herded the cayuses into a winding ravine, out of sight.

"D'you think they spotted us?" Custer said, lowering his field glass.

"Not likely," Bouyer replied, chewing on his tobacco. "Jest drivin' 'em down to the river fer their mornin' drink." He spat, then added, " 'Tain't half the herd. They got 'em grassin' all over."

"Take our word for it, General," Reynolds added, lighting a cigarette.

10:30 A.M. A hollow rumble in the gorge signaled the approach of the regiment. Custer scrambled down from the Crow's-Nest and called for a halt. The 7th Cavalry had marched ten twisting, rugged miles up the divide since eight o'clock.

"Jesus Christ!" Captain Tom Custer shouted, bounding out of the saddle. "We've been spotted!"

"What d'you mean?" Armstrong knit his brow.

"One of Yates's packmules dropped a box of hardtack some ways back!" Tom swallowed to catch his breath, then wiped a sleeve across his streaked face. "A trooper reported it missing, so Yates sent a detail back on the trail to find it. They found it all right, and three hungry bucks to boot! They vamoosed as soon as they saw the detail. Our men were afraid to shoot, thinking they might only be drifters or neutrals, but [Captain] Keogh says he saw Indians scouting us along the ridges since early this morning. They must've seen our dust—at least that's what Keogh thinks."

"Where's Keogh now?"

"He's been scouting the rear with some of the Crows. He ought to be up pretty soon."

"Tell him to report to me at once. Have Reno dismount the men. Bring up my flag, and order 'Officers' Call.' "

"On the bugle?"

"Yes, on the bugle. What the hell does it matter any more how much noise we make? Now get a move on!"

Custer was all nerves, stalking to and fro, snapping his cowhide lash. "My intentions were to surround the village and attack before daylight tomorrow," he told his group of edgy, seedy officers in his hair-triggered tone. "We'd have taken 'em by surprise, like we did at the Washita. But that's of no account now. Our discovery makes it imperative for us to act at once. Delay would allow the village to scatter and escape. I said this would turn out to be a fight or a footrace. If they won't make a stand, they'll have to outrun us; and we'll hunt 'em down to the last ditch. All right, gentlemen, we move at once to the attack!"

Custer flicked his whip. "The regiment will advance in three squadrons of assault. Major Reno, you will take Companies A, G, and M. Follow this trail straight down to the Littlehorn. Captain Benteen, you will take Companies D, H, and K. Follow the line of bluffs to Reno's left, scouting the ridges while he tracks the ravines. I will take Companies C, E, F, I, and L. We'll move to the right. Captain McDougall, you will take Company B to guard the packtrain. By this disposition we must cut off Sitting-Bull's escape to the south, east, or north. Gibbon and Terry will keep him from slipping away to the west. A three-mile interval between my battalion and Benteen's should be sufficient to clamp the hostiles up in a vise. If the scouts' reports are true, I have no doubt we're about to go into the fight of our lives. But I'm confident we shall be more than equal to anything we encounter. All I can say now is keep communications open and pitch into the enemy wherever you find him. Whatever you do, don't let him get away!"

"Hadn't we better keep the regiment together, General?" Benteen put in. "If this is as big a village as they say, we'll need every man we have for one massive strike."

"You have your orders," Custer muttered. Then he raised his voice again: "The respective squadrons will separate at the foot of the divide. The first company commander who notifies me that his men have paid strict obedience to my order against grumbling, that officer and company shall have the post of honor."

Captain Benteen strutted forward at once. "Your order has been strictly obeyed, General."

"Very well, then, Captain Benteen—*your* company has the advance. Lead out your entire battalion!"

As the group was breaking up, a gust of wind struck Custer's headquarters flag and knocked it down. Lieutenant Godfrey picked it up and stuck it in the ground again, but it fell a second time.

Lieutenant Wallace regarded this as "a bad omen." And Reno noticed that Custer "did not wear his usual confident & cheerful air, but seemed rather depressed, as with some premonition of coming horror."

"God damn him," Benteen growled to Reno as they trudged back to the waiting column. "Sending us off on a wild-goose chase for glory. Rendezvous with Terry and Gibbon was set for tomorrow. Has Custer sent riders through to 'em? *No!* They don't know where in the hell we are. They'll be beating about the headwaters for days trying to find us. Custer doesn't give a Goddamn for Terry."

Reno, a swarthy man with trim mustachios, answered him abruptly, "We don't know *what* Terry's orders were. There's only one man here who does, and he's the one we have to obey—live or die."

"Well, all I can say is we're going to have a big fight on our hands. A hell of a big fight!"

According to Lieutenant George D. Wallace's daybook (6/24/76), "Gen'l Custer determined to cross the divide that night [June 24–5], conceal the Command, the next day [June 25] find out the locality of the village & attack the following morning [June 26] at daylight." In so doing, he would have been acting in near-concert with Terry and Gibbon.

Lieutenant Edward S. Godfrey concurs: "The General said . . . that he had not intended to make the attack until the next morning, the 26th, but our discovery made it imperative to act at once; as delay would allow the village to scatter and escape." Now, by quirk of fate, Custer's doom was sealed.

"Move well to the left, and sweep everything before you!" Custer called to Benteen as they were about to separate. "Pitch into anything you find, and report at once!"

"I thought it was rather a senseless order," Benteen later testified. "I did not know what I was expected to find. I supposed I was to hunt up some Indians! . . . There was no plan at all."

"Let us keep together!" Reno called over to Custer as Benteen was making his left-oblique. Custer lifted his hat jauntily, as much to say, "I hear you." He and Reno were now riding parallel, Custer's squadron on the right.

At approximately two o'clock, Custer waved to Reno to bear left and cross the Little Bighorn. Varnum rode up and reported having seen a large body of Indians in the valley ahead. "Warn Reno," Custer responded; and Varnum spurred away. He passed Girard, who was dashing back from the river with the same report.

2:15 P.M. Colonel Custer and his 280-man detachment had ridden several miles across the rugged, rolling basin of the Little Bighorn. A towering dust cloud dragged over the hills ahead, slowly trailing down to the river.

Fred Girard turned in the saddle, let out a whoop, and waved his hat to Custer from the top of a bluff. "Thar goes yer Injuns, runnin' like hell!"

Custer jerked his head aside and blurted to Adjutant Cooke: "Take a message to Reno. Tell him the hostiles are a couple of miles ahead, on the jump. Tell him to go in as fast as he can, cross the river, charge the hostiles wherever he finds 'em. Tell him he'll be supported by the whole outfit. Have him send word then at once. And have him relay an immediate message to Benteen to cross the river and move up from the south, drive everything before him, and notify me at once."

Lieutenant William W. Cooke snapped a salute and bolted away. "Cookey" was a strapping Canadian with a clipped accent and Dundrearies; Custer had nicknamed him "The Queen's Own."

Custer looked back at his command, motioned to the north, shouted, "Column of twos! Right-oblique! Forward at the gallop —*ho!*"

The troopers swung northward and to the right, weaving their way swiftly along gullies that ran like deep gashes through stubbled humps and chalky hogbacks bounding the Little Bighorn.

3 P.M. Colonel Custer, Captain Tom, aide Autie Reed, Lieutenant Cooke (who had just returned from Reno's command with

a report that the Indians were amassing to meet them), and orderly-bugler Giovanni Martini rode up a ravine to the crest of a ridge overlooking the ashy bluffs that rimmed a stream known to the red man as "Greasy-Grass," to the white man as "Littlehorn."

Custer pulled out his field glass and gazed intently at the western panorama. There it lay at last, the hostile Indian encampment. Huge circles of hundreds of buffalo-hide tepees shimmered in the sunlight, while smoke from a myriad campfires veiled the horizon. And as far as the eye could see, a grazing pony herd spread across the grassy flats.

Custer strained his eyes, adjusting the binoculars to penetrate the hazy atmosphere. Dogs, old men, and squaws shuffled around the lodges. He could also spot children romping naked. But where were all the warriors?

Custer snorted. "Well, I'll be damned!" he cracked, handing the glass to Brother Tom. "*Look*—we've caught 'em napping." He slapped his thigh, rasping a dry laugh. "Custer's Luck!"

Wheeling Old Vic around, Custer whipped off his shabby gray sloucher and waved it wildly to the five companies of cavalry down in the gulch. "Come on, boys! Hey, boys, we've got 'em! We've caught 'em napping! We'll finish 'em up and head for home!"

With Vic chomping at the bit, Custer turned to Martini and said excitedly but carefully, "I want you to take a message to Captain Benteen. Ride as fast as you can, and tell him to hurry. Tell him it's a big village, and I want him to be quick, and to bring the ammunition packs."

"*Yessir!*" Martini saluted, reining away.

"Wait, orderly!" Adjutant Cooke said, spurring forward. Martini pulled up. "I'll give you a message." Cooke took out his pencil and pad, scribbled a note, then tore off the slip and handed it to the jumpy young Italian. "Now, ride as fast as you can to Captain Benteen. Take the same trail we came down. If you have time, and there's no danger, come back. But otherwise stay with your company."

Martini nodded, saluted, dashed off. The note read:

←221→

Benteen:
Come on. Big village. Be quick. Bring packs.

W. W. Cooke

P.S. Bring packs

("The Queen's Own" feared that Garibaldi's drummerboy-mascot might muddle the order with his "dago English.")

Tom Custer galloped back to his orderly, Sergeant Daniel A. Kanipe, and rattled: "Go to Cap'n McDougall. Tell him to bring packtrain straightaway. Tell him to come on quick—big Indian village. If you see Cap'n Benteen, tell him to come quick—a big Indian village."

Kanipe saluted and lurched his horse around, spanking after Martini. If one didn't get through, the other might! (They both did, but to no avail.)

Boston Custer, ambling up from the rear, passed Martini and Kanipe dusting down the trail. Armstrong yelled to his brother as he came plunging into the ravine, "Hey, Bos! You're about to go into a real fight—the greatest fight of your life! The biggest Indian camp on the North American continent is ahead, and we're going to attack it!"

Boston winced.

Armstrong was grinning like a wolf; and there was a savage sparkle in his eyes. He slapped his kid brother affectionately on the shoulder. "I reckon there'll be plenty of Indians for us all!"

Bos' voice quavered: "Mitch Bouyer says we'll find more redskins than all of us have bullets!"

Custer turned to his Crow scouts and said forcefully, by words and signs: "We're going to attack the village. We're going to have a terrible fight. You should all take heart, fight hard, make your every shot a killer. These people the Sioux are cutthroats and troublemakers. They prey upon the Crows and the palefaces. I'm going to teach them a lesson today they'll never forget. I'm going to whip every last one of them. When I finish the Sioux trouble, I'll build a fort where the Littlehorn flows into the Bighorn. Then you Crows may live in peace with us palefaces." He paused a second, then added: "I'm a great chief, but I may die in this battle. The Great Spirit look after you then! But if I live, my brother Bloody-Knife and I will take you all to Washington—to the medicine lodge of the Great White Father. Now this is the way I want it. When we attack the village, I want you to run off all the ponies you can. If any man of you isn't brave, and is afraid to take a scalp in order to stampede the herd, I'll take away his weapons and make a woman of him. If nothing happens to me, and you do as I say, I'll look after you in the future. Yellowhair is a man of his word. Help me whip the Sioux, and I'll become the Great White Father. Then we'll all live in peace and plenty."

One of the Crows gazed at the sun and moaned: "I shall not see you sink behind the Shining Mountains tonight." Then he cast his penetrating eyes on Yellowhair, saying, "You and I are going home today, by a trail we do not know."

Custer smiled wryly, pointing to Bos. "Your white brother there. His heart flutters with fear. His eyes roll in fright. When we've whipped the Sioux, he'll be a man."

Pulling off his blue fatigue blouse, Custer slipped on his fringed buckskin jacket and tied the crimson kerchief around his neck. With a flourish of his hat, he let out a whoop and led his Garry-owens at a canter up the ravine.

3:30 P.M. Colonel Custer and five companies of the 7th Cavalry swung westward to the left, jogging down Medicine-Tail Coulee toward the Little Bighorn. A vibrant crackle of carbines shattered the stillness. It burst from the cottonwood belt skirting the west bank of the river, echoing to the forward-left of Custer's command, beyond the embracing ridges.

Custer jerked his head at Cooke. "That must be Reno, giving 'em hell!"

Cooke nodded.

Custer shot a backward glance, whisked off his hat and hooted "Come on, boys!" He darted ahead at as swift a pace as the rough floor of the ravine allowed. With guidons streaming and bugles blaring, a couple of hundred cheering, bellowing horsemen thundered down the coulee behind him. Custer laughed. "Hold your horses, boys! There are plenty of 'em down there for all of us!"

The steep draw slowly opened out into a rolling river basin. Several hundred yards from the ford, a torrent of cavalrymen surged into an ambush of several Indians from Two-Moon's band of Cheyennes. Scouting Custer's advance, they determined to hold him off long enough for their fellow warriors to amass in self-defense. They fired down from the banks ahead, shot up from the mouth of the coulee, making much movement and noise. Their ruse worked.

Custer threw up his hand and drew rein in dust and gravel. The column ground to a halt behind him. He sat paralyzed for a few seconds, then realized the ruse and counterfeinted by thrusting forward with Yates' gray-horse troop, driving the snipers before him like flushed quail.

According to Gall, war chief of the Hunkpapa Sioux, "Longhair did not reach the river." Hundreds of howling Indians swept like a whirlblast down to the ford, their ponies stretching at a dead run over the shallow stream, gorging the mouth of the gully like bees aswarm in the hive. Most of Yellowhair's red scouts ran for their lives, and the last words heard from him were: "Courage, boys! We'll get 'em; and as soon as we do, we'll go home to glory!"

Custer waved and shouted. He pitched off to the right, scrambling madly up the escarpment, drawing his command over the ridge. The diversion was desperate. If his battalion were to remain effectively mounted, he needed level ground on which to maneuver. That ground lay across the river, where the villages sprawled. If he could endure broken terrain long enough to find another ford and draw the Indians onto his own ground, all would be well. If not, there was little hope but to hold a defensive position until Reno or Benteen came up.

Custer yanked the reins, dug in his heels. His leather-slapping troopers swung northward behind him, tailed by a hurricane of Indians who were dropping them out of their saddles like game on the run.

There was another ford, farther upriver, but Custer would

never reach it. Trapped between two slowly converging hordes of Sioux and Cheyennes, he was forced higher into the maze of hills that offered no escape but death. As one Teton war chief put it, "It looked like a stampede of buffalo."

4:15 P.M. Myles W. Keogh's and James Calhoun's companies, dismounted in skirmish lines, were chewed up in a matter of minutes. Tearing to the crest of a hummock topping the hogback ridge, Custer reined Old Vic around. *"Dismount your men! Dismount your men! Prepare to fight on foot!"* Bugles sounded "Dismount." Custer turned to his adjutant, ordered Captains George W. Yates and Algernon E. Smith to deploy their men at the foot of the knoll, facing the river, there to hold their ground to the last man. He and Tom would take their stand on the brow.

4:30 P.M. Inch by inch, Yates' and Smith's companies were whittled away by showers of arrows and lead. Thousands of Indians leaped from their ponies at the base of the ridge, where Keogh and Calhoun lay slaughtered in detail, and started swarming up the gullies.

4:45 P.M. Yates and Smith had stood their ground, and were wiped out to the last man.

Those fifty men on the ridge watched the hostiles coming, inch by inch, closer and closer. Fear gnawed at their stomachs; this was the end.

That ragged band of fifty troopers and civilians huddled around Custer's headquarters flag, which was firmly planted in the ashy soil. Their sweat-soaked togs were caked with alkali dust, so that they looked like a cluster of phantoms on the hilltop.

The valley of the Little Bighorn was a furnace. Smoke and dust hung in the glowing sky. Itching and burning, gagging in the stillborn atmosphere, they rubbed stinging, watery eyes and leveled their Springfields. Feathered heads popped up from gullies, then disappeared. But for every one that vanished, a dozen more appeared. Hundreds upon hundreds of feathered heads—bobbing up from arroyos that gouged the long, long slope, snaking in and out of sagebrush clumps and tall tufts of reddish-brown grass. Grass and sage the color of dry blood, soil the consistency of powdered bones.

Carbines barked, revolvers cracked. Hacking, cursing soldiers stood or knelt or lay in a tight circle, picking off the surrounding enemy as they came up the hillside. Several fear-crazed troopers lunged out of the circle and ran screaming down the slope. Death alone stopped them.

While thousands massed around the foot of the hill, launching arrows in a curved fire to the crest, a few hundred braves scrambled up the slope. Custer and his band dropped them as they came. The Indians hung back in shallow notches, fired their breechloaders, then crawled on in spurts.

Shoot the horses! Shoot 'em before they're stampeded! Pile 'em round for breastworks! Dozens of dead horses were heaped in a circle around that desperate band. The smell was sickening, but that breastwork of carcasses was their only protection.

The erratic clatter of firearms on the brow of the hill clashed weirdly with the endless drone of arrows that came showering down to a maddening chorus of shrieks and war whoops. The barricade of carcasses was no shelter against this murderous storm. When a spray of bullets from below caused troopers to duck while reloading, a spatter of shafts from above quilled their shoulders and backs. Sobbing hysterically, they sagged to the dust.

"Once I saw Yellowhair," said Left-Hand, an Arapaho mercenary. "He was dressed in buckskin. It was almost at the end of the fight. He was standing up and had pistols in his hands, shooting into the Indians."

The romantic image emerges in glory. Custer grips his pearl-handled bulldogs with stiff, aching hands. He glares into the smoldering haze, blasting at every form that springs up before him. Streaks of gunfire split through smoky drifts, and at every burst he expects to hear the cheers of Benteen's battalion. What hope was there in Reno?

Hi-yi! hi-yi! That fiendish, maniacal yell is all he hears. It falls on his ringing ears like a death knell, ripping the molten air like howls from the depths of hell.

A handful of troopers huddle around the shredded headquarters flag. They feed and fire their red-hot Springfields with numbed fingers and stiffening hands. They fumble with dirt-crusted cartridges that jam in the overheated chambers. They pry out empty shells with their penknives, because breechblock ejectors bite clean through the soft copper rims. Then they run out of carbine ammunition—a piddling hundred rounds per man—and unholster their revolvers. Twenty rounds apiece. Soon, they will be turning their rifles into clubs.

Hi-yi! hi-yi! The copper-skinned foe worms ever closer, their serpentine bodies blazed with red and yellow and blue warpaint. These are the naked bucks who have braved the trials and tortures of the medicine dance. With scalping knives clenched between their bared teeth, with tomahawks clutched in their fists, they are gathering for the kill.

5 P.M. Nearly all have bled to death. Perhaps Custer, in a daze, glares into the creeping masses of warriors. Horror and woe paralyze his senses.

"It was not more than half an hour after the long-haired chief attacked us before he and all his men were dead," said Crow-King, Chief of the Hunkpapas.

"When I reached the top of the hill I saw Yellowhair," said Waterman, an Arapaho mercenary. "He was dressed in buckskin, coat and pants, and was on his hands and knees. He had been shot through the side, and there was blood coming from his mouth. He seemed to be watching the Indians moving around him. Four soldiers were sitting up around him, but they were all badly wounded. All the other soldiers were down. Then the Indians closed in around him, and I did not see any more."

"I have talked with my people," Sitting-Bull said. "I cannot find one who saw Longhair until just before he died. He did not wear his long hair as he used to wear it. It was short, and it was of the color of the grass when the frost comes. Longhair stood like a sheaf of corn with all the ears fallen around him. He killed a man when he fell. He laughed. He had fired his last shot. He rose up on his hands and tried another shot, but his pistol would not go off. I did not see it. It was told to me. But it is true."

The romantic image begins to fade. Custer is on his knees, grasping a soggy hole in the left side of his buckskin jacket. He laughs. The charm has fled his spirit. The luck has run out at last.

Custer lifts his head, and the earth and the sky reel before his glazed eyes. Dark blood dribbles out of his mouth and ears. Tears stream down his cheeks. The spirit is fleeing.

Indians are stalking toward him. Shadows, looming all around him. They come to take his soul.

Some of the Indians shrink from him, in awe. They are certain that Yellowhair has come back from the spirit world, back from the dead, to curse them. Others are not so superstitious, and dart forward.

Did his nerveless hand point the muzzle, pull the trigger? Or was the weapon wrenched from his grasp, the *coup de grâce* delivered by a Sioux hand?

The blast blackens his face, convulsing and contorting his features.

George Armstrong Custer is gone to glory.

The blood-red sun was dipping into a sea of flame when Meyotzi and Mawissa hastened up the long, sloping knoll to view the corpse of Yellowhair. A six-year-old boy named Yellow-Bird, presumably Custer's only child, tagged after them. He frowned at his reputed father's naked white body, untouched by mutilating hands.

"He was the greatest and handsomest white chief of them all," Mawissa said. "But here he now lies, food for worms."

Meyotzi knelt beside the body, saying nothing. Mawissa took a bone sewing-awl out of her buckskin pouch. Stooping, she jabbed the point deep into each ear of the corpse. "This is so Yellowhair will hear better in the happy hunting-grounds," Mawissa murmured. "He must not have heard our chiefs when they warned him that if he ever again rode the wartrail against our people, the Great Everywhere Spirit would then cause him to be killed."

Gazing in silence, Meyotzi composed the twisted features with loving fingers. The glory and romance of an age had passed.

EPILOGUE

"THERE he is, God damn him! He'll never fight any more." Thus Frederick W. Benteen identified the livid, swollen corpse of George Armstrong Custer on Tuesday morning, June 27, 1876. He said to Reno: "You know enough of me to know I'd have gone through to him if it was possible to do so. But anyhow, I'm only too proud to say I hated him."

Custer's naked body was found in a sitting position between and leaning against the nude bodies of two of his troopers, who were lying one across the other. His upper right arm was resting on the topmost body, and his right forearm and hand supported his head in a peaceful pose. Lieutenant James H. Bradley noted: "Probably never did hero who had fallen upon the field of battle appear so much to have died a natural death. His expression was rather that of a man who had fallen asleep & enjoyed peaceful dreams, than of one who had met his death amid such fearful scenes as that field had witnessed—the features being wholly without ghastliness or any impress of fear, horror, or despair." Lieutenant Godfrey observed that "he had been shot in the left temple and the left breast. There were no powder-marks or signs of mutilation." Meyotzi had apparently cleaned and closed Yellow-hair's wounds. As Dr. Charles Kuhlman so aptly commented, "It was not the fairies who laid him here all 'clean and bright' as a mortician might have done. Only someone with some kind of sentimental interest in him would have done that."

Marcus A. Reno scratched in his journal: "As a tribute to his

←229→

bravery, the Indians had not mutilated Gen'l Custer & he lay as if asleep; but all the other men had been most brutally mangled & had been stripped of their clothing." Low-Dog, Chief of the Oglala Sioux, stated: "The wise men and chiefs of our nation gave out to our people not to mutilate the dead white chief; for he was a brave warrior and died a brave man, and his remains should be respected." As Sitting-Bull himself said, "My people did not want his scalp. He was a great chief. None of my people ever boasted to me that they had killed Custer." The passing of Yellowhair was enshrouded with that hallowed mystery worthy of a saint.

This raises the question of suicide. The code of frontiersmen advised: "When fighting Indians, save the last bullet for yourself"; a notable example of its application was Captain Fetterman, who preferred death to torture.

Many of the Crow scouts were insistent that "Son-of-Morning-star shot self," that "Longhair shoot himself at end." One of the Sioux warriors stated: "When Longhair realized he alone was alive, he put his gun against his body and pulled the trigger." And Colonel Richard I. Dodge, one of the most authoritative students of the American Indian, wrote:

"Suicide, though not common among Indians, is 'big medicine' —a high religious act. Through it the man rises superior to his gods. . . . I have never yet known a single case where the scalp of a suicide was stripped off, and in many cases the superstition is so strong as to prevent the Indians even from touching the body. If an unscalped body is found with many terrible wounds, gashed and mutilated, it was the deliberate purpose of the Indians to torment the soul; if it be found unmutilated with but one mortal wound, it is a case of suicide. . . . It is said that Custer's body was found unscalped and unmutilated. If so, my knowledge of Indians convinces me that he died by his own hand."

Many frontiersmen and Indians agreed. And as to the claim that Custer, by his very nature, could not have taken his own life, the circumstances of his fate made it most likely that he did so.

Thomas and Boston Custer, Henry Armstrong Reed, and William W. Cooke lay a few feet away from the General. According to Benteen, "There was an arc of a circle of dead horses around them." Boston and Reed were naked except for their white cotton socks. They had been butchered in the usual manner. So had Cooke, except that his magnificent Dundrearies were "scalped." Tom's body was a hideous sight. It was mangled beyond recognition. The only identification was a goddess of liberty and flag, and the initials T.W.C., tattooed above the elbow of his right arm. He had been scalped, and arrows quilled his crushed skull. His eyes and tongue had been torn out. His belly was slashed, and the entrails protruded. His heart and liver had been carved out, his thighs gashed, his genitals cut off. The Cheyennes hated him for his abuse of Meyotzi. The score was now settled.

Reno scratched in his journal: "The harrowing sight of those mutilated & decomposing bodies crowning the heights on which poor Custer fell will linger in my memory till death."

What happened to Reno, and to Benteen, on that fateful day which shocked and horrified the civilized world?

Major Reno and his battalion crossed the Little Bighorn, hung back in the cottonwoods when assailed by mounted warriors, and were soon stampeded across the river and into the hills, where Captain Benteen and his battalion came to their support. Though Benteen received Custer's urgent message, he followed Reno's trail to the river. Thus, with Reno and Benteen "holed up" in the hills—neither knowing nor, it is said, caring what had happened to Custer—hard and even desperate fighting kept up through June 26. Terry and Gibbon arrived to the rescue on the following morning, whereupon Sitting-Bull fled to suffer a later fate.

The Battle of the Little Bighorn is not ended. Controversy still rages. But the opinions of participants yet remain the last words. Captain Benteen and Lieutenant Godfrey branded Reno's retreat "a rout, a panic," and intimated that he had lost his nerve. Sitting-Bull asserted that "squaws and papooses could have dealt with Reno." Captain Moylan concluded that "Reno ought to have been shot." And so a scapegoat was found.

General Terry called Custer's action "a sad and terrible

blunder." A confidential dispatch to Sheridan comments: "For whatever errors he may have committed, he has paid the penalty; and you cannot regret his loss more than I do."

General Sheridan then made his official comment: "I do not attribute Colonel Custer's action to either recklessness or want of judgment, but to a misapprehension of the situation and to a superabundance of courage: the latter being extraordinarily developed in Custer."

General Sherman, though owning he had made "a terrible mistake," defended Custer's decision by stating flatly: "When Custer found himself in the presence of the Indians he could do nothing but attack." However, the New York *Times* quoted both Sherman and Sheridan as agreeing that Custer was "rashly imprudent to attack such a large number of Indians."

Major Reno made known the following: "Without attempting to communicate with either Terry or Gibbon, and without taking the trouble to ascertain the strength or position of the Indians, he divided his regiment into three separate battalions—an act which nothing can justify—and dashed against the Indians, thus recklessly driving his own and my commands into an ambuscade of 5000 Sioux."

Captain Benteen wrote: "Custer disobeyed orders from the fact of not wanting any other Command—or body—to have a finger in the pie, and thereby lost his life."

The Chicago *Tribune* editorialized: "He preferred to make a reckless dash and take the consequences . . . rather than . . . share the glory with others. He took the risk, and he lost." Captain Hughes added that the fiasco was caused by Custer's "foolish pride."

Sergeant Windolph philosophized: "Custer may have made a mistake to divide his command that Sunday afternoon of June 25, but the gods themselves were against him. . . . There were simply too many Indians for him." And Lieutenant Edgerly concluded: "Even if the blame for the disaster was due to General Custer, the fact remains that he and his five companies died heroic and glorious deaths."

A New York *Herald* correspondent interviewed Ulysses S. Grant: "Mr. President, was not Custer's massacre a disgraceful defeat of our troops?" Grant replied: "I regard Custer's massacre as a sacrifice of troops, brought on by Custer himself, that was wholly unnecessary—wholly unnecessary." However, the *Herald* noted, "The five massacred companies of Custer attest the inhumanity and imbecility of the Republican Administration."

"Who slew Custer?" asked James Gordon Bennett. "The celebrated peace policy of General Grant, . . . that nest of thieves, the Indian Bureau, . . . its mock humanity and pretense of piety— that is what killed Custer." The Yankton *Dakotaian* of July 7 headlined: "Custer and His Entire Command Swept Out of Existence by the Wards of the Nation and Special Pets of Eastern Orators."

In the early morning of July 6, 1876, the steamer *Far West* anchored off Fort Abraham Lincoln. On board were the wounded, and the bearers of sad tidings. A knock fell on the door of the Custer house, and Libbie and Maggie answered in their nightgowns. "At that very hour," Elizabeth later wrote, "the fears that our tortured minds had portrayed in imagination were realities. . . . The sun rose on a beautiful world, but with its earliest beams came the first knell of disaster. . . . This battle wrecked the lives of twenty-six women at Fort Lincoln, and orphaned children of officers and soldiers joined the cry to that of their bereaved mothers. From that time the life went out of the hearts of the 'women who weep,' and God asked them to walk on alone and in the shadow."

"Yellowhair has not returned," the Indians sang. "His woman is crying, crying. Looking this way, she weeps."

George Armstrong Custer, dead at the age of thirty-six, was laid in his final resting place at the United States Military Academy on Wednesday, October 10, 1877. After raising literary monuments to his memory, Elizabeth joined him on Thursday, April 6, 1933 —"into that realm where 'the war-drum throbs no longer and the battle-flags are furled.' "

SELECTED BIBLIOGRAPHY

ATHEARN, ROBERT G. *William Tecumseh Sherman and the Settlement of the West*. Norman, Okla.: University of Oklahoma Press, 1956.

BATES, CHARLES FRANCIS. *Custer's Indian Battles*. Bronxville, N.Y.: published by the author, 1936.

BRILL, CHARLES J. *Conquest of the Southern Plains*. Oklahoma City: Golden Saga Publishers, 1938.

BRININSTOOL, E. A. *Troopers with Custer*. Harrisburg, Pa.: Stackpole Co., 1952.

CHANDLER, MELBOURNE C. *Of Garry Owen in Glory*. New York: Exposition Press, 1960.

CUSTER, ELIZABETH BACON. *Boots and Saddles*. Norman, Okla.: University of Oklahoma Press, 1961.

————. *Following the Guidon*. Norman, Okla.: University of Oklahoma Press, 1966.

CUSTER, GEORGE ARMSTRONG. *My Life on the Plains*. Norman, Okla.: University of Oklahoma Press.

————. "War Memoirs," *The Galaxy: An Illustrated Magazine of Entertaining Reading*, XXI–XXII, no. 5 (January–November, 1876).

DAVIS, THEODORE R. *A Summer on the Plains*.

DELLENBAUGH, FREDERICK S. *George Armstrong Custer*. New York: Macmillan, 1917.

DODGE, COL. RICHARD I. *Thirty-Three Years among Our Wild Indians*. New York: Herman & Stevens, Inc., 1959.

DUNN, J. P. *Massacres of the Mountains.* New York: Archer House, Inc., 1958.

DUSTIN, FRED. *The Custer Fight.* Hollywood, Cal.: E. A. Brininstool, 1936.

————. *The Custer Tragedy.* Saginaw, Mich.: published privately by the author, 1939.

FOUGERA, KATHERINE GIBSON. *With Custer's Cavalry.* Caldwell, Ida.: Caxton Printers, 1940.

FROST, LAWRENCE A. *The Custer Album.* Seattle: Superior Publishing Co., 1964.

GRAHAM, COL. W. A. *The Story of the Little Big Horn.* Harrisburg, Pa.: Stackpole Co., 1952.

————. *The Custer Myth.* Harrisburg, Pa.: Stackpole Co., 1954.

———— (ed.). *The Reno Court of Inquiry.* Harrisburg, Pa.: The Stackpole Co., 1954.

GRINNELL, GEORGE BIRD. *The Fighting Cheyennes.* Norman, Okla.: University of Oklahoma Press, 1956.

HANSON, JOSEPH MILLS. *The Conquest of the Missouri.* New York: Rinehart, 1946.

HAYCOX, ERNEST. *Bugles in the Afternoon* (the best "Custer novel"). Boston: Little, Brown & Co., 1944.

HUNT, FRAZIER. *Custer, The Last of the Cavaliers.* New York: Cosmopolitan Book Corp., 1928.

KUHLMAN, DR. CHARLES. *Legend into History: The Custer Mystery.* Harrisburg, Pa.: Stackpole Co., 1951.

————. *Did Custer Disobey Orders at the Battle of the Little Big Horn?* Harrisburg, Pa.: Stackpole Co., 1957.

MERINGTON, MARGUERITE. *The Custer Story.* New York: Devin-Adair Co., 1950.

MILLER, DAVID HUMPHREYS. *Custer's Fall.* Des Moines, Ia.: Duell, Sloan & Pearce, Inc. (Meredith Press), 1957.

MONAGHAN, JAY. *Custer: The Life of George Armstrong Custer.* Boston: Little, Brown & Co., 1959.

Review of the Trial of General G. A. Custer (National Archives)

RICKEY, DON. *Forty Miles a Day on Beans and Hay.* Norman, Okla.: University of Oklahoma Press, 1963.

RISTER, CARL COKE. *Border Command.* Norman, Okla.: University of Oklahoma Press, 1944.

RONSHEIM, MILTON. *The Life of General Custer.* Cadiz, O.: printed privately, 1929.

SHERIDAN, PHILIP H. *Personal Memoirs.* 2 Vols. New York: 1888.

SPOTTS, DAVID L.: *Campaigning with Custer.* Los Angeles: Wetzel Publishing Co., 1928.

STECKMESSER, KENT LADD. *The Western Hero in History and Legend.* Norman, Okla.: University of Oklahoma Press, 1965.

STEWART, EDGAR I. *Custer's Luck.* Norman, Okla.: University of Oklahoma Press, 1955.

UTLEY, ROBERT M. *Custer and the Great Controversy.* Los Angeles: Western lore.

VAN DE WATER, FREDERIC F. *Glory-Hunter: A Life of General Custer.* New York: Bobbs-Merrill, 1934.

VESTAL, STANLEY D. *Sitting Bull, Champion of the Sioux.* Norman, Okla.: University of Oklahoma Press, 1957.

WHITTAKER, FREDERICK. *A Complete Life of Gen. George A. Custer.* New York: Sheldon & Co., 1876.

WINDOLPH, C. A., as told to Frazier and Robert Hunt. *I Fought With Custer.* New York: Charles Scribner's Sons, 1947.

INDEX